North Carolina
HIKING TRAILS

by Allen de Hart

**Appalachian
Mountain Club**

NORTH CAROLINA HIKING TRAILS
Copyright © 1982 by Allen de Hart
Printed in the United States of America.

If you find any errors in the text or maps, or can suggest improvements, you are urged to send a letter to the Appalachian Mountain Club, attention North Carolina Trails, 5 Joy Street, Boston, Massachusetts 02108.

FIRST EDITION

Edited by Arlyn Powell
Composition by Gayle Morrison, Cheryl Dunphy, and Don Spencer
Cover design by Betsey Tryon
Cartography by David Cooper
Production by Michael Cirone and Betsey Tryon
Printing by Halliday Lithograph
Cover printing by John Pow Co.

ISBN 0-910146-37-3

*To the volunteers who design, construct
and maintain the hiking trails in
North Carolina*

CONTENTS

LIST OF ILLUSTRATIONS

ACKNOWLEDGMENTS

I am specifically indebted to a number of professionals and hikers whose assistance has made this book possible. From the beginning, Kay Scott, state trails coordinator of Parks and Recreation (Raleigh), enthusiastically gave her support and found answers to hundreds of questions. Equally supportive was her supervisor, Jim Hallsey, assistant chief of the Planning and Special Studies Section of Parks and Recreation, Department of Natural Resources and Community Development (Raleigh).

On the federal level, Melinda Waldrep, trails coordinator for the U.S. Forest Service in North Carolina, gave valuable time and researched answers to my questions about Forest Service trails. Harry L. Baker, landscape architect for the Blue Ridge Parkway of the National Park Service, collected material and secured information from the park rangers that helped to determine boundary lines and trail directions (Asheville).

National Forest personnel who gave support and information are: Kim Finch, landscape architect of Croatan National Forest (New Bern); Marshall McClung, forestry technician, Tom Cooper, landscape architect, and Donnie Richardson of the Nantahala National Forest's Cheoah Ranger District (Robbinsville); Don F. Crouch, forester and acting district ranger, and Charles S. Price, forester of Nantahala's Highlands Ranger District (Highlands); Smith Nicholls, assistant ranger, and Terry Pierce of Nantahala's Tusquitee Ranger District (Murphy); and Glen Holland, forestry technician, Bill Sweet, assistant ranger, Tim Southards, forestry technician, and Bobby Marshburn, Young Adult Conservation Corps member of the Nantahala Wayah Ranger District (Franklin).

Among the Pisgah National Forest personnel are: Charles Miller, district ranger, and John Strogan, forester of Pisgah's French Broad

Ranger District (Hot Springs); George H. "Pat" Cook, district ranger, and Jim Ouzts, supervisor of forestry of the Pisgah Grandfather Ranger District (Marion); David Rhodes, recreation assistant, Bruce N. Lowe, landscape architect, and Chip Webster of the Pisgah National Forest's Pisgah Ranger District (Pisgah); and Joe Bonnette, other resources assistant, Pisgah's Toecane Ranger District (Burnsville).

From the Uwharrie National Forest are Horace Jarrett, district ranger, and James C. Brown, forester (Troy). Dr. Dan Pittillo, biology professor at Western Carolina University (Cullowhee) provided information on parts of the Bartram Trail.

Others who assisted in locating trails are: Malcolm MacLear of the Carolina Mountain Club (Asheville), and Arch Nichols, long time CMC activist and leader (Asheville); T. R. Shaw, trail supervisor (Windsor); Louise Chatfield, (Greensboro) former president of the North Carolina Trails Association; and Charles Moore, a leader in wilderness preservation (Brevard). Support for this project was also provided by Larkin Kirkman, president of the North Carolina Trails Association (Raleigh).

Fellow hikers who contributed their knowledge from the field were numerous, but four were particularly helpful. G. Forest Hargett, author and photographer (Murphy) provided information from Clay and Cherokee counties; Joel Johnson (Wilmington) assisted with the lower coastal region; Marsha Allen (Greensboro) served as a recreation intern at Greensboro College and provided Guilford County information; and Seth Washburn, professor of biology at Louisburg College (Louisburg) provided information on state flora and fauna.

A number of families provided food and shelter during the grueling field work, but two deserve generous thanks. They are Drs. Frank and Doris Hammett (Waynesville), and Dr. and Mrs. Lee Copple (Highlands). Their homes were my base headquarters while in the Pisgah and Nantahala regions.

Significant also were those hikers and backpackers who, as members of a continuous exchange of strength, were with me in snow, rain, sleet, and summer heat, and all the other discomforts common to long hikes during eight years and 2,500 mi. They are Mike Ballance, Frank Barringer, Thelma Barringer, Tom Bond, John

Borum, Richard Caviness, John Chess, Gale Clayton, Greg Frederick, Todd Gregory, Robert Hall, Rudy Hauser, Lisa Helm, David Hicks, Van Hockett, Joel Johnson, Billy Jones, Steve King, Hans Kirsch, John LeMay, Jack Lewis, Roger Moore, Lisa Myers, Billy Odom, Paul Rawls, Chuck Satterwhite, Greg Seamster, Alison Sipfle, Scott Smith, Eddie Sorie, Steve Strader, Gigi Sugg, Susan Thomas, Kenneth Tippett, Joey Ward, Mark Waters, Nancy Weaver, and Buster White.

And, the individual who requested I complete the research and write the book in the first place, Arlyn Powell, editor and publisher for the Appalachian Mountain Club (Boston); to him and all the others who believed it should and could be done, my gratitude.

Allen de Hart
Louisburg, North Carolina
September, 1981

PREFACE

A booklet written in 1584 by Phillip Amadas and published in England described North Carolina as the "goodliest land under the cope of heaven." In reporting the land's natural wealth, Amadas wrote euphoricly of "sweete, fruitfull and wholesome" soil, "sweete smelling" trees, and the "highest and reddest cedars in the world."

For North Carolina's early colonists, however, reality was much harsher than Amadas's generous hyperbole. They soon discovered, as had Hernando de Soto before them, that North Carolina's interior was an unyielding wilderness. With only the most rudimentary of maps and few if any trails, early settlers found that movement through the "goodliest land" was an arduous task fraught with unknown dangers. In fact, the first English settlement in America, established on Roanoke Island in 1585, mysteriously disappeared.

This guidebook is an invitation to explore the state that was later carved from the "goodliest land," a state that now proclaims itself "Variety Vacationland" — North Carolina. Clear directions are given to guide both the casual walker and the intrepid backpacker to a potpourri of hiking trails. Trails that range from short strolls along the brick sidewalks of a historic district to week-long journeys through remote mountain wildlands.

Many believe that we have become a society that in many respects has lost touch with the land. Our appreciation for our natural and cultural heritage has been dulled by the persistent grind of a frenetic lifestyle. We have insulated ourselves from nature and one another with a melange of "modern conveniences."

It is difficult to perceive the character of an area from the windshield of an automobile speeding along an interstate highway. And it is just as difficult to know anything about the farmer in the field we just passed in 8.3 seconds. We need to slow down. We need to look around. We need to walk!

Happily, this guidebook offers a practical, economical, and healthy way to regain our sense of perspective and appreciation — to know again, or perhaps for the first time, North Carolina and her people. In many areas of the state there remain vestiges of the environment which inspired Phillip Amadas. By seeking out the earthen paths listed herein, the hiker can recapture a sense of that pioneer spirit and can experience the exhilaration of discovering "new" places and people.

The author has performed an invaluable service for North Carolina's citizens and visitors. The broad scope of trails covered in this guidebook offers something for nearly everyone. From privately maintained trails to trails managed by local, state, and federal government. From easy walks to strenuous climbs. For some, this book will introduce them to the varied pleasures of hiking. For others with more experience, the book will identify alternative hiking opportunities on uncrowded trails closer to home.

Regardless of personal interests or physical stamina, the reader has a veritable treasure map that will enable him to discover North Carolina's natural and cultural heritage as many of our ancestors did, on foot.

James B. Hallsey
Asst. Chief of Planning
Div. of Parks and Recreation
N.C. Dept. of Natural Resources
and Community Development

INTRODUCTION

Now I see the secret of the making
of the best persons; It is to grow in
the open air and to eat and sleep
with the earth.

— Walt Whitman,
Song of the Open Road, 1856

The purpose of this book is to provide a comprehensive listing of
hiking trails in North Carolina. Their location, length, direction,
difficulty, maintenance source, and what you would likely see
during daylight are basic to the listing. A condensed description has
been necessary to allow the more than six hundred trails to be
gathered into one book.

Information on the trails represents eight years of trail research
and field work, of hiking, backpacking, and camping. A total of
1,207 trails were investigated. 218 of these were deleted because
they were used primarily by non-hikers; 163 were left out because
they were private and the owners did not wish extra traffic; and, 202
more were not listed because the U.S. Forest Service explained that
the trails were not used or were not maintained.

The combined length of the 1,207 trails runs to 3,542 miles, of
which 2,555 are included in this book. No complete record was kept
of all the extra miles walked on faint trails I should never have
explored in the first place, the miles added when I was lost, or the
accumulated distance on public roads hiking back to my vehicle.

Each mile of trail was distinctive, unique. Superlatives could have
been used to describe all the trails, but the descriptions are restrained
to invite your judgments — and so you will have plenty of surprises.

The mose distinctive in regard to length is the Appalachian Trail, at 293 miles. Other long trails are the seventy-mile Cape Hatteras Seashore Trail, the fifty-mile Bartram Trail, the 43-mile Foothills Trail, the 33-mile Uwharrie Trail, and the 28-mile Art Loeb Trail. The shortest in the book is the 75-yard Shot Pouch Trail.

Occasionally a trail would be more than a surprise; it was a jewel — uncut, untouched, unscarred, unknown, unequaled in beauty and serenity. In contrast others were eroded, neglected, mutilated by dirt bikes, or blocked with suffocating kudzu and grape vines. As word spread that a man with a funny looking unicycle was in town, questions of 'have you been on *our trail* yet' became commonplace. Every lead I followed — cow paths, wildlife paths, walkways, old slide, tote, logging, carriage, and roads and wagon, railroad beds. Hunting trails, fishermen's trails, farm trails, moonshine trails, Indian trails, surveyor's paths, and over-the-hill-to-Grandma's-house trails. Trails paved with asphalt, brick, locust tiles, pea gravel, wood chips, dirt, cement, pine straw, leaf carpets, grass, sawdust, moss, boardwalks, wet and dry creek beds, rock, and sand. It was as if I had spent a decade in a museum of natural history, a museum where someone at some time before me had walked, a courier of nature's secrets.

The research became a valuable chance to see North Carolina's people on foot from the mountains to the sea; to meet trail land-owners in their home environment — and, according to my physician, it was good for my health. Another book could be written on the personal experiences of all who became part of this adventure.

Two years ago, when it was decided that this material would be used in book form, a concerted effort was made to update information on every known trail. At press time trail research was continuing for inclusion in future revisions. Additional information for the guidebook came from reading printed material from private and public sources on North Carolina trails, recreation areas, and natural resources. I also secured county maps from the state Department of Transportation, the United States Geological Survey, and the National Forest Service. All federal and state offices involved in trails were contacted, and all county and municipal parks and recreation offices were requested to furnish lists of known trails under their supervision or in their areas. Private organizations, such as the Boy

Scouts of America, summer camps, colleges and universities, and hiking clubs, were also resources and contacts. After the state's Division of Parks and Recreation, Department of Natural Resources and Community Development, developed a state-wide trail inventory, its office became my major resource center.

How to Use the Book

At the beginning of each of the four sections on national forests there is a brief introduction followed by trail descriptions broken down by districts, sections, and specific trail areas. The major headings are alphabetized, but the individual trails are listed by number, from the lowest to the highest Forest Service trail numbers. For National Park Service lands the organization is similar. An introduction precedes each trail in the section on state parks, forests, and other sites. Under county trails, an introduction provides information on the park or group of trails; the same is true for the section on municipalities. Private trails have introductions only if they are parks or campgrounds. The section on colleges and universities has trail descriptions only.

To get maximum use from this book, become familiar with the arrangement of information, supplement it with reference maps, and acquire a guidebook on the fundamentals of hiking, backpacking, and camping. Suggested guidebooks are *Walking Softly in the Wilderness: The Sierra Club Guide to Backpacking* by John Hart and *Wilderness Handbook* by Paul Petzoldt.

Abbreviations

Abbreviations are used mainly to save space. The most frequently used are:
A.T. (Appalachian Trail); B.T. (Bartram Trail); BRP (Blue Ridge Parkway); GSMNP (Great Smoky Mountain National Park); ATC (Appalachian Trail Conference); CMC (Carolina Mountain Club); SP (State Parks); NCTA (North Carolina Trail Association); USFS (U.S. Forest Service); NPS (National Park Service); NC (state primary roads); SR (state secondary roads); FSR (National Forest Road); mp (milepost on the BRP); rt (round trip); cb (combined

trails); mi (mile/s); m (meter/s); km (kilometer/s); ft (feet); elev (elevation); jct (junction or intersection); sta (station); svc (service); rec (recreation); fac (facilities); and USGS (United States Geological Survey topographic maps).

Maps

Several maps are included with this guidebook. Because of the size of the state and the number of trails covered, it has been impossible to map each trail individually. However, a large-scale map of the state, broken up into several sections and with each trailhead marked and numbered on it, has been included. The numbers are also listed beside the trail names in the book, so the reader can refer back and forth. There are also maps available of high-use hiking areas such as the national forests. These maps, listed below, can be acquired at addresses listed in the corresponding sections of the text.

CROATAN NATIONAL FOREST MAP

NATAHALA NATIONAL FOREST MAP with Standing Indian Trail Map (Wayah Ranger District), Snowbird Area Trail Map (Cheoah Ranger District), & Joyce Kilmer-Slickrock Wilderness Map (Cheoah Ranger District)

PISGAH NATIONAL FOREST MAP of Grandfather and Toecane Ranger District with Wilson Creek Area Trail Map (Grandfather Ranger District), Linville Gorge Wilderness Map (Grandfather Ranger District), and South Toe River Trail Map (Toecane Ranger District)

PISGAH NATIONAL FOREST MAP of French Broad Ranger District

PISGAH NATIONAL FOREST MAP of Pisgah Ranger District and Shining Rock Wilderness Map (Pisgah Ranger District)

UWHARRIE NATIONAL FOREST MAP

BLUE RIDGE PARKWAY (National Park System)

GREAT SMOKY MOUNTAINS NATIONAL PARK (National Park System)

Trail Numbers and Marking

The numbers to the right of trail names identify their position on the accompanying maps, as noted above. These numbers should not be confused with trail numbers in other books or with the computerized trail numbers of the U.S. Forest Service. The USFS numbers, also included at the end of the trail writeups, are permenent numbers used by the USFS on its maps and records. Neither number will be seen on trail posts, trees, or other markers.

Trail markers or blazes can be in any color, but the Appalachian Trail is always a 2″ × 6″ vertical white blaze. Parts of the trails developed for the Mountains-to-the Sea Trail corridor have white 3″-diameter dots. The Bartram Trail has a 2″ × 6″ vertical pale yellow or cream blaze. A 2″ × 6″ vertical blue blaze is usually used on an alternate or spur route. Sometimes color-coded trail marking systems may be described on outdoor bulletin boards in campgrounds and parks near trailheads; these usually label short and long range connecting trails. Generally there are bright red marks on USFS boundary lines. The majority of trails in North Carolina are unmarked.

Trail Length and Hiking Time

Distance has been measured by the USFS, the NPS, trail organizations, or myself. I have used a Model 400 Rolatape wheel which registers each foot. Length may be stated as one-way, roundtrip, or combined with other trails for convenience or educational reasons; in rare cases it may be estimated. Trail relocations can alter the trail lengths listed in this guidebook.

Hiking time is not estimated because it varies with the purpose of the hike. The photographer-hiker taking a time sequence of a flowering plant will go much more slowly than the ridge runner, not to mention the college athletes, families on outings, and even senior citizens taking strolls. Initially I tried to use my own pace as a criterion for timing, but I discarded it after considerable experience. An average for many hikers is two miles an hour on relatively level terrain.

Degree of Difficulty

The degrees of difficulty *easy, moderate,* and *strenuous* are based on the ratings of average hikers, not professional hikers or athletes. Some hiking clubs have rated difficulty on the basis of elevation and distance; others have classified according to the walking speed of non-smoking adult males. For the purpose of this guidebook, *easy* means that, if you are in good health, you can hike the trail without fatigue or exertion. *Moderate* means you should expect some exertion and may need to take rests. *Strenuous* means that you will be climbing steep trails and experiencing-above-average exertion so numerous rest stops may be necessary.

USGS Topographical Maps

The USGS maps for the state of North Carolina are published on the scale of 1:24,000 (1 in. = 2,000 ft.); they are essential if you plan to hike or backpack with precise knowledge of where you are, not to mention of contour lines, roads, residences, lakes, forests, streams, and altitude, On a remote backcountry trail a map could be a lifesaver if you get lost. If a local blueprint company does not have topo maps, write to: Branch of Distribution, US Geological Survey, 1200 South Eads St., Arlington VA 22202. Another source for maps is the Tennessee Valley Authority, Mapping and Services Branch, 200 Haney Bldg., 311 Broad St., Chattanooga, TN 37401. If information and an index to the maps are desired, write to: National Cartographic Information Center, US Geological Survey, 507 National Center, Reston, VA 22092.

Trailheads and Directions

The *trailhead* is the beginning of the trail being described. It is near where you are likely to park your vehicle. If not, it will be near a connecting trail or some other place where you can find access. *Directions* can include a description or narrative outline of the trail. Their chief purpose is to explain how to get onto the trail and, once there, where to go. One of the most frustrating experiences I had in locating and walking trails was that directions I had received were incorrect or, in some cases, nonexistent. The USFS has an excellent and reliable system of directions using the District Ranger Station as a base point for all instruction on how to get to trailheads.

Highway intersections are frequently used here so that you will have a base point from which to orient yourself in an area. Odometer readings may vary slightly from the ones given. Elevation gain, loss, or change, listed at the end of some trails, is usually a total from the lowest to the highest points and is not cumulative for all up-and-down walking including the cols.

Three areas require hiking permits — the Smokies, Shining Rock Wilderness, and Linville Gorge Wilderness. Information on permits is described in the relevant trail sections.

What You Can See on the Trails

This book cannot attempt to include a description of the geological formations and botanical and zoological species you can see on the trails. Where botanical references are made, species are generalized and common names used. For example, there are over fifteen species of rhododendron in the state, with every county in the mountain division having *Rhododendron maximum*, rosebay or great laurel, with fluffy, light pink or whitish blossoms. The *Rhododendron catawbiense*, with large purple blossoms, is not found in all the mountain counties; its common name is purple laurel, not to be confused with mountain laurel. For the *Rhododendron calendulaceum*, I have listed the common name as flame azalea. Where the flame azalea, the *Rhododendron aborescens*, and other species grow in the same area, the listing is simply "azaleas." The same principle is applied to the trees. For example, there are thirty species of oaks in the state, and they are usually referred to generically unless there is a large concentration of one species in a particular habitat, such as chestnut oaks on a high ridge. Botanical listings in this book reflect what was representative of the flowering plants present while I was on the trail. Your hike during another season may provide a larger list.

The state has 89 species of ferns and over 3,500 species and varieties of other vascular plants. Flowering plants account for nearly 3,000, with 313 species native only to the mountains, 183 species in the piedmont, and 469 species in the coastal plains. Many others grow in two or all three areas. A recommended source book for the botany-oriented hiker is *Manual of the Vascular Flora of the Carolinas* by Radford, Ahles, and Bell.

Fewer animals than plants are seen on the trails, but the state has many species of wildlife. From among the ninety species of mammals, you will be lucky to see a dozen in a day-hike because many are nocturnal. Your chances of seeing and hearing birds — there are 415 species — are better. There are 138 species of reptiles and amphibians, 442 species of mollusks, and 418 species of fish. And, if we do not see insects, we can certainly feel them — mosquitoes, no-seeums, chiggers, mites, ticks, and spiders — all belonging to 12,000 species of *Arthropods*. A few recommended books for hikers interested in wildlife are: *Amphibians and Reptiles in the Carolinas and Virginia* by Martof, Palmer, Bailey, Harrison, and Dermid; *Birds of the Carolinas* by Potter, Parnell, and Teulings; and, *Mammals of North Carolina* by Brimley.

Health and Safety

Use care in your selection of drinking water. If you are in a national or state forest or park, use water officially designated as being uncontaminated. You may also wish to ask forest and park officials for information on water supply and purity. A listing of springs, wells, and clear streams in this book does not mean the water is safe to drink. When in doubt use Globaline or Potable-Aqua tablets, or boil the water for purification. Take a first-aid kit and a snake-bite kit. North Carolina has all four of the U.S. poisonous snakes — the rattlesnakes, copperhead, cottonmouth moccasin, and the coral.

Accidents happen on the trails, as elsewhere. A recommended book for trail health and safety is *Wilderness Survival* by Bernard Shanks. He reports that 85% of all wilderness deaths are caused by hypothermia. Hikers can suffer hypothermia in summer as well as in winter, from freezing temperatures to as high as 50° F. If you are hiking in backcountry, it is advisable to have a hiking companion.

Support Facilities and Information

Many camping areas are becoming crowded. If you choose an isolated area, remember to pack out everything you pack in. The USFS motto is 'leave no trace of your camping, minimize campfires, and then use only dead wood.' An effort has been made to mention camping facilities in the parks and forests; some areas allow camping in designated spots only. For hikers wishing to use commercial campgrounds, they will find the ones listed were chosen on the basis of proximity and full service, and not for cost or recreational facilities. If full service is indicated, it means the camp has sites for tenting and for trailers needing electricity, water, and usually sewage lines. Such camps also have hot showers, flush toilets, tables, grills, public phones, and, in some cases, food and laundry facilities. Camping information is based on my 1981 visits. Addresses and telephone numbers for further information have been included so you can get the most direct and authoritative word on the trail area and its conditions. In addition to the *Camping and Outdoor Directory* distributed by the state Department of Commerce, a recommended directory is Woodall's *Campground Directory*, published by Simon and Schuster.

Good Hiking!

With permission from the American Hiking Society, I would like to conclude with the following poem:

Imagine a trail!
Soft earth and fallen leaves.
The rich, moist scent of humus.
A face full of wind.
A sun-speckled thread of footworn
    earth unwinds ahead and behind you,
    playing hide and seek
    in the trees,

brushing past a thousand
life forms, beckoning,
leading you onward
to new sensations and
discoveries around the bend.
In that moment when you are on a trail,
your mind is free to roam,
to observe, to daydream.
All extraneous concerns drop away . . . .

Now that you have this guidebook in hand and are preparing
yourself for the open roads and the open trails, I hope you will also
become active in preserving our natural resources by joining a club
and helping to maintain our trails. And, of course, I hope you have as
much pleasure hiking the trails as I have had describing them to you.
Welcome to the hiking trails of North Carolina.

TRAILS IN THE NATIONAL FORESTS

CHAPTER I

CROATAN NATIONAL FOREST

Craven, Jones, and Carteret Counties

The Croatan National Forest is the most coastal of North Carolina's four national forests. Its 155,000 acres is almost surrounded by the Neuse, Trent, White Oak, and Newport rivers. Bogue Sound and the Atlantic Ocean flank its southern border.

Its name comes from the Algonquin Indian word for "council town," and its coastal environment provides year-round recreational opportunities. Hunting and fishing, as well as boating, swimming, skiing, camping, picnicking, and hiking, are possible here. (Naturally, timber management of the abundant softwoods is also a prime concern in the forest.)

A home for rare plants, such as the Venus fly-trap; a flyway for migratory birds and nesting area of peregrine falcons; a sanctuary for wildlife such as the black bear and alligator — the "Pocosin," meaning "swamp on a hill," is all these things. (*Pocosin* is a layer of organic topsoil which acts as a giant sponge, wet or dry. It is characteristic of this region.) Dense titi brush and bays form the gound cover beneath the tall pines.

There are at least 106 species of fish, including pickerel, perch, bass, sunfish, and bluegill, in the 4,300 acres of spring-fed freshwater lakes. The five major lakes range from 500 to 2,600 acres and generally have shallow water. At the lower end of the Neuse River are flounder and shellfish.

More than 90 species of reptile and amphibians have been discovered in this area. Among them are the loggerhead turtle, water-

3

dog, eastern tiger salamander, and alligator. Poisonous reptiles are the cottonmouth moccasin, three species of rattlesnakes, and the copperhead. The bays, swamps, marshes, and creeks provide a haven for migratory ducks and geese. Egrets, flycatchers, woodpeckers, woodcocks, hawks (including the osprey), and owls are common residents.

Large stands of pines — virgin pond, long leaf, short leaf, and loblolly — are found in the forest. Other common trees are yellow poplar, oaks (including water oak), sweet and tupelo gums, cypress, holly, and elm.

Wildflowers are profuse. Bright red pine lilies, orchids, gaillardia, butterwort, pitcher plants, sundews, and the more unusual Venus fly-trap are part of the flowering vegetation.

Maps and information are available from the District Ranger, Croatan National Forest, 435 Thurmond Rd, New Bern, NC 28560. Tel: 919-638-5628. The administrative station is 4 mi SE of New Bern on US 70 E, and L on Thurman Rd.

Neusiok Trail   1

Length: 20.4 mi (32.6 km), easy: *USGS:* Cherry Point, Core Creek, Newport; *Trailhead:* Parking lot at Pinecliff Recreation Area.

Directions and Description: From jct of US 70 and NC 101 in Havelock turn L on NC 101 and go 5.3 mi to jct of NC 101 and NC 306. Turn L on NC 306, New River Ferry Rd, and go 3.3 mi to FSR 132. Turn L on unpaved road and go 1.7 mi. to Pinecliff Recreation Area.

From the parking area follow white blazes 300 yd to Neuse River beach. If the tide is low the hike is easier on the hard sand; otherwise, follow blazes through dense beach grass and cypress knees for 1.2 mi. Turn L, climb steps, enter pine forest, and reach NC 306 at 6.5 mi. (NC 101 is 2 mi R on NC 306.) On old logging road go S to NC 101 at 9.3 mi. (Grocery store is 1 mi E at jct of NC 101 and SR 1711.) Cross NC 101 and reach jct of Bellfinger Rd (FSR 147) and FSR 169 at 12 mi. Follow Little Deep Creek Rd (FSR 169) for 4 mi, and turn L on Alligator Tram Rd (FSR 124). After 0.6 mi turn R into forest at 16.6 mi. Cross SR 1154, Mill Creek Rd, at 18.8 mi. (E 0.2

mi is E-Z Check Grocery. Owner allows hikers to park vehicles while on the trail.) The town of Newport is 7 mi W on SR 1154. Follow blazes through hard and softwoods for 1.6 mi, reaching the Newport River parking area at 20.4 mi.

The trail is recommended for late fall, winter, and early spring, but not for the summer because of the heat, poisonous snakes, and summer growth. Primitive campsites on the trail are designated by the Forest Service. USFS Trail #503.

Support Facilities: Pinecliff Recreation Area provides only day use, including picnic tables, water, and comfort stations. Newport River parking area has no facilities. Two recreation areas — Neuse River (near Croatan on US 70) and Cedar Point (near Swansboro on NC 24 and 58) — offer camping facilities. They are open from May 1 through October 31. Commercial facilities are found at the Neuse River Campground, Route 6, Box 190, New Bern, NC 28560. Tel: 919-638-2556. Full svc, rec fac. Open all year. Also, Camp Ocean Forest, Route 1, Morehead City, NC 28557. Tel: 919-326-8996. Full svc, rec fac, on Emerald Isle. Open March 1 through November 30.

Cedar Point Tideland Trail   2

Length: 1.4 mi (2.3 km), easy; *USGS:* See above; *Trailhead:* Parking lot near boat dock.

Directions and Description: From jct of NC 24 and 58 go 0.8 mi N on NC 24 to entrance of Cedar Point Campground on L (FSR 153). Go 0.4 mi, bearing L at fork on FSR 153A to parking area near White Oak River.

Enter trail from parking area W, cross first of six boardwalks at 0.1 mi, and pass first of two viewing blinds for shorebirds and other wildlife at 0.4 mi. Second viewing blind is at 0.6 mi. Cross fire road, the last boardwalk at 1.1 mi, and then return on loop trail to parking lot at 1.4 mi. The trail is well graded through pine and hardwood forest and includes 0.3 mi of cypress boardwalks in a marshland estuary. This trail is a National Recreation Trail, initially listed as the *Chautauqua Trace*. USGS Trail #502

Support Facilities: In addition to camping facilities at Cedar Point Campground, which is open May 15 through October 15, a commercial campground is Cedar Point Beach Campground. Tel: 919-326-4371. It is 0.5 mi W on NC 24 from jct of NC 24 and 58. Full svc, rec fac. Open all year.

Island Creek Trail   3

Length: 0.6 mi (0.9 km), easy; *USGS:* See above; *Trailhead:* Parking area.

Directions and Description: From Pollocksville intersection of US 17 and SR 1004 (Island Creek Rd) go E on SR 1004 for 5.5 mi to Island Creek parking area on L. Or, from business US 70 and SR 1004 jct at the Trent River bridge go W on SR 1004 for 8 mi to Island Creek parking area on R.

The picturesque loop trail is through a mature forest of large beeches, hornbeams, hickories, oaks, loblolly pines, cucumber trees, cypress, and holly along Island Creek. Large beds of Christmas fern form a ground cover. USFS Trail #166.

Neuse River Trails   4 - 5

Fishermen's trails exist along most of the Neuse River. Below are listed two Croatan National Forest recreation areas where trails have developed but are not maintained by the Forest Service.

From the Ranger Sta go 3 mi SE on US 70 to Riverdale Mini-Mart and turn L on FSR 141 to Fisher Landing Recreational Area. Picnicking, fishing, and walk-in camping are allowed. Drinking water and a comfort station are provided. (Private property exists between this area at Fisher Landing and Flanner's Beach downstream.)

A second recreational area is at Flanner's Beach. From the Ranger Sta go 6 mi SE on US 70 to Croatan and turn L on SR 1107 for 1.5 mi to Flanner's Beach Recreational Area. This area provides picnicking, camping, fishing, hiking, bathhouse, drinking water, and comfort station. Hike upstream to creek toward Fisher Landing. Both areas are open from March 1 through November 30.

CHAPTER II

NANTAHALA NATIONAL FOREST

A vast area of mountain ranges, waterfalls, lakes, and rivers in the southwest corner of the state, the Nantahala National Forest, like the Pisgah, is divided into four districts. The forest covered 420,000 acres until the Balsam-Bonas Defeat Land Purchase added another 40,000 acres in 1981.

The Cheoah Ranger District is chiefly in Graham County, with a tip projecting into Swain County. Tusquitee Ranger District covers Clay and Cherokee counties; Wayah Ranger District is mostly in Macon and Swain counties, with a bit in Jackson County too; and, Highlands Ranger District comprises a section in Macon, much of Jackson, and a southwest corner of Transylvania County.

The eight-mile long Nantahala Gorge, mostly in Swain County, has been called "The Land of the Noon Day Sun," because the precipitous gorge walls tower 2,000 feet, permitting only brief periods of sunshine on the canyon floor. But, the Nantahala Gorge is not the only deep chasm where the sunshine is limited; others include Tuckasegee, Wolf Creek, Cullasaja, Chattooga, and scores of deep north side coves.

Nantahala is also a land of hundreds of waterfalls. Whitewater Falls, south of Sapphire, is considered to be the highest cascading river (411 feet) in eastern America. Cullasaja Falls, west of Highlands, is similiar to Whitewater Falls, with cascades thundering 250 feet into the gorge. Other spectacular falls are Dry Falls, Bridal Falls, Glen Falls near Highlands, and Toxaway Falls near Sapphire.

The Joyce Kilmer Memorial Forest, a 3,800-acre sanctuary of virgin timber and pristine wilderness splendor, lies within the

Nantahala. It borders Tennessee in Graham County. No other forest in the state can compare with it for beauty.

Ten major rivers flow through the forest. The turbulent Chattooga is a national Wild and Scenic River, with headwaters in the Highland Ranger District.

The area was once the homeland of the Cherokee Indians, whose famed chief, Junaluska, saved the life of Andrew Jackson in the historical battle of Horseshoe Bend in Alabama. Later, in 1838, thousands of Cherokees marched across Tatham Gap in the Snow-bird Mountain on a "Trail of Tears" to Oklahoma under orders of U.S. Army General Winfield Scott to be resettled on a reservation.

The Nantahala region is also a land of precious stones — ruby, sapphire, garnet, and amythest. Wildlife roams its forests — deer, Russian boars, foxes, bears, mink, and raccoons. It is home for at least 38 species of birds, including grouse, turkeys, hawks, and owls. First investigated by William Bartram in 1776, its plantlife is a botanist's dream. All the hardwoods and conifers common to the southern Appalachians are found here. Rare and endangered species of flowering plants are hidden in countless vales and rock crevices, or can be found blooming on fertile slopes.

Under the supervision of the U.S. Department of Agriculture, the four districts of the Nantahala National Forest can be reached at the following addresses:

Cheoah Ranger District, USFS, Route 1, Box 16-A, Robbins-ville, NC 28711. Tel: 704-479-6431. (From Robbinsville go 1 mi W on US 129, then turn L on SR 1116.)

Highlands Ranger District, USFS, P.O. Box 749, Highlands, NC 28741. Tel: 704-526-3765. From US 64 and NC 28 jct, go into Highlands; near E Main St.

Tusquitee Ranger District, USFS, 201 Woodland Drive, Murphy, NC 28906. Tel: 704-837-5152. (Across the Hiwassee River at first traffic light L from jct of US 19-219 and US 64.)

Wayah Ranger District, USFS, P.O. Box 469, Franklin, NC 28734. Tel: 704-524-6441. (Turn at first R off US 64 from US 64 and US 441-23 S jct.)

Because the *Bartram Trail* traverses all four districts, it is des-cribed first.

Bartram Trail 6
Sections I, II, III, and IV

The Bartram Trail is named in honor of William Bartram (1739-1823), the first American-born naturalist to receive international fame for his botanical and biological research. Born in Philadelphia, Bartram's expeditions in the southeastern state traversed at least 28 counties in North Carolina, three of which were Macon, Cherokee, and Graham. The exact route of his expedition is not known, but the North Carolina Bartram Trail Society and the Nantahala National Forest staff have jointly planned the trail to run as close to the original area he explored as is feasible in the Nantahala Forest. Cut in places by private property, the trial is not continuous and hiking it requires considerable vehicle switching. Generally running E to W, it provides some remote areas where may be seen black bears, deer, wild turkeys, grouse, and a number of song birds such as tanagers, towhees, and Carolina juncos.

From Oconee State Park in South Carolina the *Bartram Trail* traverses NW over Long Mountain, turning SW as it crosses the Chattooga River into Georgia's Chattahoochee National Forest near Earl's Ford. At Warwoman Dell near Clayton it goes N to Rabun Bald. From there it is 4.2 mi to FSR 7, near the North Carolina state line and the southern entrance into the Nantahala National Forest. It is at this point that the description of the trail begins.

SECTION I

Length: 10.5 mi (16.8 km), moderate to strenuous; *USGS:* Scaly Mtn; *Trailhead:* Parking area on FSR 7.

Directions and Description: This section of the Bartram Trail is in the Highlands District of the Nantahala National Forest. From the jct of NC 106 and US 64-28 in Highlands, go S on NC 106 for 6.8 mi to Scaly Mtn jct with SR 1625 (Hale Ridge Rd). Proceed for 2.6 mi and turn L on Chattahoochee FSR 7. After 1.1 mi park near trailhead sign.

Ascend N through hardwoods, buckberry, and rosebay rhododendron, following light yellow blazes on a well graded trail built by the YCC. Cross log bridges at 0.1 mi and 0.6 mi. Skirt E of Osage

Mtn at 0.9 mi and cross ridge a 1.1 mi. Ascend and descend on graded trail between coves, with streams over which there are log bridges at 1.5 mi, 1.7 mi, 2.1 mi, and 2.4 mi; these are tributaries of Overflow Creek. (At 2.5 mi pass jct with *Hurrah Ridge Trail* R. It goes for 0.6 mi, leading to Blue Valley Rd, FSR 79.) Continue under a heavy canopy of rosebay rhododendron, large oaks, and white pines. (At 2.9 mi pass jct of *West Fork Trail* R; it travels for 1 mi, leading to Blue Valley Rd, FSR 79.) Begin ascent to NC 106 at 3.1 mi. Reach the Osage Mtn. Overlook at 3.6 mi. Cross highway, climb steps at power line, and ascend steeply through open woods of oaks and locust damaged by fire. At 4.1 mi go R on old road. There is a jct with Hickory Gap Rd (SR 1621) at 6.1 mi; turn L up this road. (SR 1621 to R leads to Broadway Gap and to SR 1620, Turtle Pond Rd, connecting with NC 106.)

Hike the road for 2.5 mi, past an open area named Lickskillet, and reach Hickory Gap at 8.6 mi. Blazes are infrequent and the road is rough in sections; a four-wheel-drive vehicle is recommended for vehicle switching. From Hickory Gap descend L on road to Forest boundary, and then climb steeply to ridge top and rock outcrop for E views of Turtle Creek area. Reach clear-cut Jones Gap at 9.6 mi; here there is a panoramic view. Continue on seeded trail and rock outcropping to Jones Knob at 10.5 mi. (The trail is under construction beyond this point. It goes over Whiterock Mtn, Fishhawk Mtn, Wolf Rock Mtn, and Cedar Cliff, descending to SR 1643 near Hickory Knoll Creek. From there the trail is on all-weather roads through Franklin to Section II.)

SECTION II

Length: 17.6 mi (28.2 km), moderate to strenuous; *USGS:* Franklin, Wayah Bald, Topton; *Trailhead:* Wallace Branch parking area.

Directions and Description: This section is in the Wayah District of the Nantahala National Forest. To approach the trailhead from the Franklin Bypass (US 64), go S of Franklin to the jct of US 441-23 and US 64. Proceed W on US 64 to the Wayah District sign at 0.9 mi, and turn R on SR 1153. Go 0.3 mi (Wayah District Office on the R) to jct with old US 64 and Pressley Rd (SR 1315). Cross old US 64 and drive 1.7 mi on Pressley Rd to end of pavement and road; park at the Wallace Branch parking area.

Cross stream and hike through young forest with scattered mature poplars and oaks. Cascades to L on Wallace Branch at 0.3 mi. Enter white pine stand at 0.4 mi and cross old road at 0.5 mi. (Trail may be overgrown and blazes difficult to see. The former *Bartram Trail* turned R and followed through a white pine forest for 0.7 mi to the *Trimont-Bartram Trail #7* on the ridge. Motorcyclists now use this trail extensively and the yellow blazes have been painted black. Nevertheless, it is a more open and scenic trail than the current well graded trail built by the YCC and YACC.) Cross small stream and begin ascent on NE side of ridge. Reach ridge crest at 0.8 mi, and continue on slope to jct with old *Trimont-Bartram Trail* at 1.3 mi. Turn L and follow ridge W. (This jct can be confusing for E-bound hikers; yellow blazes are painted on both trails at the fork. Also, yellow blazes extend to E for 0.4 mi to jct of the former *Bartram Trail* on the R, and on old *Trimont Trail #8* leading to residential area in Franklin to the E at 4.1 mi.) Motorcyclists and horseback riders use the trail in this area.

At 1.6 mi, passing S of Bruce Knob, turn sharply to R and reach gap at 1.8 mi. Begin long ascent, steep in spots, along the ridge spine. Reach crest at 2.3 mi, then descend to Locust Tree Gap at 2.5 mi. Traverse large black cohosh garden. Ascend and skirt S of Wilkes Knob (3,800 ft) at 3.2 mi. Descend and ascend over knobs for 2.1 mi, and reach gravel road to 5.3 mi. Continue on ridge, skirting N side of knob, descending and ascending over knobs for another 2.2 mi; reach a grazing road at 7.5 mi. Follow grazing road for 0.1 mi, then turn L and leave old road at 7.7 mi, ascending at sharp R. Along ascent are trillium, doll's eyes, maiden hair fern, wild orchids, and bee balm. Hardwoods include hickory and locust. At 8 mi skirt S side of knob in horseshoe shape and ascend from plateau at 8.6 mi. A deep rock fissure is found at 9.2 mi, near a sharp R. Reach old lodge and grassy field at 9.6 mi. Follow old road to jct with the *Appalachian Trail* at 10 mi. Turn L, following the *A.T.* through chestnut oaks, mountain laurel, and azaleas to Wayah (Indian word for "wolf") Bald monument (5,342 ft) at 10.2 mi. Outstanding views, particularly E.

Follow yellow and white blazes into forest on R and descend

through yellow birch, spruce, and rhododendron, with Canadian violets and other wildflowers. At 11.9 mi pass old jct of *A.T.* and *Bartram Trail*. Spring is on R at 12 mi. Turn R off the *A.T.* at 12.1 mi onto McDonald Ridge W of Wine Spring Bald. Enter open grazing field of orchard grass and clover at 12.4 mi. Blazes are infrequent. Follow seeded road through two more grazing fields for 1.7 mi, and then reach Sawmill Gap and FSR 711 at 14.1 mi. Turn L from gate, go thirty yd, turn R on seeded road, and ascend. At 14.6 mi turn L on bank and follow to crest of rocky ridge. Follow ridge up and down from cols for 1.8 mi. There are partial views of Nantahala Lake. Reach SR 1310 at 17.6 mi, near stream on R. It is 0.5 mi R on SR 1310 to Lake's End Camp Store, and 7.1 mi L to Wayah Gap.

(For hikers who wish to hike the old *Trimont-Bartram Trail*, request permission on an individual basis from Henry Walls, tel: 704-524-5568 or 704-524-2314, in Franklin. His property adjoins the old trail route off the Trimont Trail street in W. Franklin. The trail runs 13.1 mi from the Amoco Station on Harrison St to Wayah Bald. It includes 4.1 mi on old roads, where it is marked with faded blue and yellow blazes. It joins the current *Bartam Trail* on the Trimont Ridge.)

The remainder of Section II to Tutula Gap is under construction. A temporary route is found by turning R on SR 1310 and then L on SR 1400. At the bridge over the Nantahala River, follow FSR 308 R before crossing the bridge. (Apple Tree Group Camp is across the river.) Follow the road to FSR 35 and Beechertown. The present *Bartram Trail* sign at the Junaluska Gap on SR 1400 is confusing because neither the blue-blazed *London Bald Trail* nor the blue-blazed *Junaluska Trail* make connections at Tulula Gap. Both trails connect with other trails to form loops in the camp area.

SECTION III

Length: 11.5 mi (18.4 km), moderate to strenuous; *USGS:* Topton, Hewitt, Robbinsville, Andrews; *Trailhead:* Tulula Gap, jct of US 129 and SR 1200.

Directions and Description: This section is in the Cheoah District of the Nantahala National Forest. From Topton jct of US 19-129 proceed W on US 129 for 2.1 mi to jct of US 129 and SR 1200. Park on L side of SR 1200. (It is 11 mi W on US 129 and then 1.1 mi on SR 1116 to the Cheoah Ranger District headquarters.)

Trail sign is to the S of US 129 highway bank; begin on graded trail with cream-colored blazes on W side of Snowbird Mtn ridge. At 0.3 mi enter burned-over open slope with new growth, berries, and flowers. Cross log bridge at 0.4 mi, re-enter the young forest, and bear R on the ridge crest at 0.7 mi. Curve around a knoll at 1.3 mi, and return to the ridge at 1.6 mi. At 2 mi follow the Graham-Cherokee county line; reach Jutts Gap (3,700 ft) at 5.1 mi, ascend on switchbacks S of knob, and skirt S side of Little Bald (4,300 ft) at 6.3 mi. At 8.5 mi reach Teyahalee Bald (Joanna Bald) lookout tower (4,716 ft), with TV transmitting station. From Joanna Bald hike of FSR 423-B, rough and rocky in places, for 3 mi to Tatham Gap (3,645 ft) at 11.5 mi.

To the L is Andrews and to the R is Robbinsville. Descending to Robbinsville it is 3.3 mi to pavement on FSR 423. After leaving Forest boundary on SR 1110, it is another 2.5 mi to jct of SR 1127 near the large lumber company in Robbinsville. Turn R through the town on SR 1127 and go an additional 1.5 mi to US 129.

Some of the vegetation in this section includes oaks, birch, red maples, hemlock, wild cherry, sourwood, dogwood, azaleas, rhododendron, chestnut sprouts, scrub pine, prickly ash, hickory, striped maple, locust, and a wide variety of wildflowers. Elev gain is 2,116 ft.

SECTION IV

This section is in the Tusquitee Ranger District of the Nantahala National Forest. Construction has progressed on approximately 10 mi of the trail, to Porterfield Gap (3,462 ft). Hikers on this section should prepare for a twenty-mile or more round-trip unless an exit can be arranged up from Little Snowbird Creek using a four-wheel-drive vehicle.

The trail, however, crosses a number of significant points along the rim of the Snowbird Mountains, one of which is Walker Field (4,015 ft), reached 2 mi after ascending from Tatham Gap. Others are Old Billy Top (4,120 ft) at 3.6 mi and Old Mattie Top (3,736 ft). Rocky Spring Top (3,791 ft) is approximately 0.5 mi from Porterfield Gap. In an isolated area, few hikers walk this section. Summer vegetation can turn it quickly into a manway or even make it too overgrown to traverse. For more information on the *Bartram Trail* contact the North Carolina Bartram Trail Society, Route 3, Box 406 Sylva, NC 28723. Tel: 704-293-9661.

Directions and Description: USGS maps are Marble, Andrews, Robbinsville quadrangles, and the trailhead is at Tatham Gap, FSR 423. Traveling from Topton on US 219, turn in to Robbinsville at sign of Court House. Pass the Court House (R), cross the street, and go two blocks, turning L on SR 1127. Continue for 1 mi to SR 1110 on L at Tatham Gap sign. Take L and go 2.5 mi on paved road to Forest boundary. Enter the forest on FSR 423, and ascend for 3.3 mi on a gravel road to Tatham Gap. Park and enter on R, following cream-colored blazes.

SECTION I
CHEOAH RANGER DISTRICT

Tsali Area, Graham and Swain Counties

Tsali Recreation Area

The Tsali Campground and Fishing Access Area provides a ramp for boating, fishing in Fontana Lake, water skiing, camping (without showers or flush toilets), horseback riding, picnicking, nature study, and hiking. From Bryson City go 9 mi SW on US 19 to its jct with NC 28. Go W on NC 28 for 3.6 mi, turn R at the Tsali campground sign, and reach the parking area after 1.6 mi, on a gravel road, FSR 521.

Tsali Trail **9**

Length: 17.4 mi (28.7 km), easy to moderate; *USGS:* Noland Creek; *Trailhead:* Parking area.

Directions and Description: The *Tsali Trail* has also been designated the *Tsali Horse Trail*; it consists of 17.4 mi of excellently constructed trail with campground, hitching racks, and an observation point halfway along the trail at the Graham and Swain county line. Hiking and backpacking are permitted on the trail.

From the parking area take either the R or L loop; they circle the peninsula with dips or curves at more than forty coves. Vegetation is that of the lower slope (less than 2,000 ft elev) Appalachian hardwood forest. Most of the forest is open, with light understory, but often there are small patches of berries, summac, sourwood, and mountain laurel. There is scattered spruce, scrub and white pine, and poplar. Wildflowers include sunflower, cone flower, loosestrife, pinxter, false fox glove, horsemint, phlox, gentian, orchids, henbit, and violets. USFS Trail #38.

Support Facilities: One of the nearest commercial campgrounds is Lost Mine Campground, 8 mi SW on US 19 from jct of US 19 and NC 28. Turn off at sign and proceed for 1 mi L up Silver Creek. Full svc, rec fac. Open March 10 through November 1. Tel: 704-488-6445.

Snowbird Area, Graham County

Snowbird Loop Nature Trail   10

Length: 0.5 mi (0.8 km), easy; *USGS:* Robbinsville; *Trailhead:* Snowbird picnic area on SR 1127.

Directions and Description: From Cheoah Ranger Sta go SW on SR 1116 for 2.3 mi to jct with SR 1127 and turn R sharply on SR 1127. Go 1.3 mi to Snowbird picnic area before crossing Snowbird Creek bridge; park.

Well graded nature trail follows Snowbird Creek upstream across the road. Circle up slope for a return of 0.5 mi. Vegetation is chiefly hemlock, holly, rhododendron, cucumber tree, oak, maple, and there are extra large sassafras trees. Understory is light. USFS Trail #39.

Hooper Bald Trail   11

Length: 10 mi (16 km), moderate to strenuous; *USGS:* Santeetlah Creek, Big Junction; *Trailhead:* Parking area on FSR 81C.

Directions and Description: From Cheoah Ranger Sta go SW on SR 1116 for 2.3 mi to jct with SR 1127 and turn R sharply on SR 1127. Drive 6.9 mi to jct with FSR 81 (Big Santeetlah Rd) at Santeetlah Gap. Turn L and follow FSR 81 for 8 mi; turn L on FSR 81C, cross Johns Creek, and drive another 1.2 mi to parking area.

Hike from this point across Whigg Branch and Santeetlah Creek on unmarked and unblazed trail following old road (passable for 4WD vehicle) to jct of old road on L at 0.5 mi. (Trail on L is overgrown to Huckleberry Knob.) Continue up L side of cascading Santeetlah Creek under canopy of young yellow birch, hemlock, and beech nut with borders and patches of blackberry, sunflower, spice bush, Joe-pye weed, phlox, and crimson beebalm. Cross stream at 0.9 mi and another stream at 2 mi. Continue ascending on old road, which gradually becomes steeper, to jct of old trails at 3.4 mi. Turn R (S) to Hooper Bald (5429 ft), clearing at 3.9 mi. At 4.1 mi reach jct with *King Meadows Road Trail* (USFS Trail #63) on L, but continue straight over Warm Springs Bald to old sled road. Follow road through hardwoods — mostly yellow birch and beech nut — to Big Junction (5,400 ft) at 4.7 mi, the North Carolina-Tennessee state line, and instersect with *Big Snowbird Trail* Turn R and follow NW on state line to Haw Knob (5,472 ft) at 6.4 mi. A number of open views of the Cherokee National Forest in Tennessee are on the L. Descend to jct with old road at 7 mi, and turn R. Follow old road W of Little Haw Knob to Mud Gap (4,500 ft) at 8.5 mi; travel is through haw, buckeye, oaks, and maple with understory of mountian laurel. Continue descent on old road E of Johns Knob to Stratton Gap (4,280 ft) and FSR 81 at 10 mi. Vehicle switching necessary, or hike R (E) on FSR 81 to FSR 81C at 2.8 mi, and turn R for another 1.2 mi to origin of hike. USFS Trail #60.

Cedar Top Trail   12

Length: 5.4 mi rt (8.6 km), moderate to strenuous; *USGS:* Santeetlah Creek; *Trailhead:* Santeetlah Gap.

Directions and Description: From Cheoah Ranger Sta drive SW on SR 1116 for 2.3 mi to jct with SR 1127 and turn R sharply on SR 1127. Drive 6.9 mi to jct with FSR 81 (Big Santeetlah Rd) at Santeetlah Gap; park.

The unmarked and unblazed trail begins on SR 1127 bank with steps to forest edge, across from private house. Proceed to ridge crest at 0.2 mi; turn R and follow ridge up and down knobs for 2.4 mi to fork. Turn L and ascend; former trail R is overgrown following lumbering. Reach Cedar Top (4,008 ft) at 2.7 mi.

Forest vegetation consists of mature oaks, black birch, poplar, white pine, hickory, locust, hemlock, and sourwood, among patches of Carolina lily and New England tea. Return by the same route. (The trail may be passable to continue SW on ridge to Seven Springs Gap at 4.2 mi, and to Patrick Meadows (4,701 ft) at 6.2 mi. At 7.6 mi reach jct with *Hooper Bald Trail*, where a turn R will provide an exit at FSR 81C for a total hike of 11 mi. *Hooper Bald Trail* is an old road, descending R.) Elev change 1,408 ft. USFS Trail #61.

Big Snowbird Trail, Middle Falls Trail, and Sassafras Creek Trail   13-15

Length: 12.7 mi (20.3 km), strenuous; *USGS:* Santeetlah Creek, Big Junction; *Trailhead:* End of FSR 81.

Directions and Description: This trail is 25.4 mi long if one returns by same route; it is a minimum of 17.2 mi if another trail is used. *Middle Falls Trail* is a one-mile loop spur off *Big Snowbird Trail,* and *Sassafrass Creek Trail* is a loop spur of 2.5 mi off *Big Snowbird Trail.*

From the jct of US 219 and SR 1127 in Robbinsville, go 3.3 mi to jct with SR 1116 (from which it is 2.3 mi R to Cheoah Ranger Sta) and bear L at fork on US 1127 for 2.2 mi to jct with SR 1115. Turn L on SR 1115 and go another 2.2 mi to jct with SR 1121. Turn sharp L at jct and continue for 1 mi to bridge over Snowbird Creek. Look for "Dead End" sign and "One Way" sign on R at bridge over Little Snowbird Creek. This is SR 1120, which becomes FSR 75. Proceed on this gravel road for 6 mi to the Junction parking area — a total of 13.7 mi from Robbinsville and 12.7 mi from Cheoah Ranger Sta.

Begin trail on old railroad grade that crosses a number of earthen hummocks and goes under large poplars and maples. At 0.2 mi *Snowbird Mountain Trail* begins on the L. Continue on road L of cascading Snowbird Creek. The understory is composed of rhododendron, wild hydrangea, sweet pepper bush, and forest trees of hemlock, birch, basswood, and cucumber tree. At 2.9 mi reach jct of *Sassafras Creek Trail* on L, 250 yd beyond the creek. (This trail is an alternate to the *Big Snowbird Trail*. If hiker chooses this trail, ascend on old railroad grade for 0.7 mi to Sassafras Falls; beyond falls leave road and bear R, climbing steeply to Burnt-Rock Ridge at 2 mi. Descend to mouth of Little Flat Branch and rejoin *Big Snowbird Trail* at 2.5 mi.) Continue on old railroad grade and reach an alternate trail, *Middle Falls Trail,* at 4.1 mi. (This trail, R, near Mouse Knob Branch, ascends steeply for 0.2 mi, and then descends gradually to the *Big Snowbird Trail* after 1 mi. It is an alternate that avoids eleven fordings of Snowbird Creek, which may be impossible to cross at high water.)

Follow upstream to Middle Falls and large pool at 5.1 mi. At 5.2 mi *Sassafrass Creek Trail* jct is on L. Trail follows old railroad bed with debris from timber operations, passing Flat Branch, Upper Falls, Meadow Branch, Rockbar Branch, and Bearpen Branch to jct of *Mitchell Lick Trail* at 11.1 mi. Turn L and reach Mitchell Lick at 11.2 mi. Ascend to Laurel Top (5,317 ft) with scenic views, then reach Big Junction at 12.7 mi, and jct with *Hooper Bald Trail*. Backtrack, or take an alternate trail such as *Hooper Bald Trail* NW for 4.5 mi to Stratton Gap and FSR 81. This plan requires vehicle switching. Elev change, 2,600 ft. Big Snowbird Trail — USFS Trail #64; Middle Falls Trail — USFS Trail #64-A; Sassafras Creek Trail — USFS Trail #65.

Mitchell Lick Trail   16

Length: 1.7 mi (2.7 km), moderate; *USGS:* Big Junction, Santeetlah Creek; *Trailhead:* Snowbird Trail near Mitchell Lick.

Directions and Description: The trail is a connection between *Big Snowbird Trail* and *King Meadows Trail,* with optional linkage to *Hooper Bald Trail*. From jct of *Big Snowbird Trail* near Mitchell Lick (11.1 mi from Junction parking area) ascend NE on old jeep road for 0.7 mi, gradually at first, then steeply over rough terrain. Descend steeply to Snowbird Creek and Snowbird Creek divide near Squally Valley. Reach *King Meadows Trail* at 1.7 mi. Forest vegetation is mainly young hardwoods and spruce. Turn L for 0.4 mi to

Hooper Bald Trail and R on *King Meadows Trail* for 5.7 mi to Junction and FSR 75. USFS Trail #154.

Snowbird Mountain Trail   18

Length: 10.4 mi (16.8 km), strenuous; *USGS:* Santeetlah Creek, Marble, Big Junction, McDaniel Bald; *Trailhead:* End of FSR 75.

Directions and Description: This trail is 20.8 mi long if backtracking, or a minimum of 16.5 mi long if additional trails are used for exit. From Junction parking area at end of FSR 75 (see description of *Big Snowbird Trail*), follow *Big Snowbird Trail* over earthen hummocks for 0.2 mi, then turn sharply L at large poplar tree with red markings. On graded trail cross two streams lined with vegetation including birch, poplar, ferns, sassafras, spice bush, hemlock, rhododendron, and violets. Reach Wildcat, or Deep, Gap (3,340 ft) at 1.3 mi. Turn R, ascending to Wildcat Knob on Sassafras Ridge. Continue to descend and ascend over and around knolls along the Sassafras Ridge to the North Carolina-Tennessee state line. At 5 mi reach Bee Gap (4,040 ft), where a faint trail bears R, descending along Falls Branch to Sassafras Falls and *Sassafras Trail*. Continue traversing on gradual and sometimes steep grades through scattered grassy fields and young hardwoods. Reach Pantherflat Top (4,680 ft) at 8.4 mi and Dillard Top at 8.9 mi. The jct with *Big Snowbird Trail* comes at 10.4 mi. Return options include backtracking, or descending SE on *Big Snowbird Trail* for 11.2 mi farther, or taking *Mitchell Lick Trail* NE to *Hooper Bald Trail* and FSR 81C for additional 6.1 mi. Another route follows *Big Snowbird Trail* for 6.2 mi more to *Hooper Bald Trail*, going along the state line to Stratton Gap and FSR 81. USFS Trail #415.

Support Facilities: Two USFS campgrounds are in this area. To reach Horse Cove campground, take SR 1116 from the Ranger Sta. Go 2.3 mi NW to SR 1127 and turn R. Go 9.4 mi to Horse Cove. To reach Cheoah Campground take SR 1116 from the Ranger Sta, traveling 1.1 mi R to US 129, and then L on US 129 for 6.4 mi to Cheoah campground. Both have tables and grills and offer sites for tenting and picnicking. Comfort stations consist of pit toilets. Boating, water skiing, and fishing are allowed. One of the nearest commercial campgrounds in Tuskeegee Campground, Route 2, Box

160, Robbinsville, NC 28771. Tel: 704-479-8464. Full svc, rec fac. Open May 1 through October 31. Its location is 7 mi S of Fontana Dam on NC 28.

Fontana Village Area, Graham County

Look Rock Trail   **19**

Length: 2 mi rt (3.2 km), moderate; *USGS:* Fontana Dam; *Trailhead:* SW end of Fontana Village.

Directions and Description: From the SW end of Fontana Village on SR 1246, near last cottages, look for Look Rock sign across a T intersection. Ascend gradually up a slope on the R side of a stream. Cross the stream at 0.5 mi and reach by switchbacks the former *Appalachian Trail* at 1 mi. The trail is now the *Yellow Creek Mtn Trail* from Tapoco W to Walker Gap E. USFS Trail #40.

Lewellyn Cove Nature Trail   **20**

Length: 0.7 mi (1.1 km), easy; *USGS:* Fontana Dam; *Trailhead:* Parking at USFS sign.

Directions and Description: From Fontana Village entrance road and Fontana Texaco station, drive 1.4 mi E on NC 28 to parking area. Well graded and heavily used loop trail is across the highway. Fifty indigenous trees and shrubs are labeled with botanical and common names. A visitor usage trail connecting with Fontana Village, the *Fontana Village Trail* (USFS Trail #157), runs from the stream in Lewellyn Cove for 0.9 mi. (Other planned connections will run to the golf course and swimming pool area.) USFS Trail #50.

Support Facilities: In addition to camping facilities in the Fontana Village area, a commercial campground, Tuskeegee Campground, is found 7 mi SE of Fontana Dam on NC 28. Full svc, no rec. Open May 1-October 31. Address: Route 2, Box 160, Robbinsville, NC 28771. Tel: 704-479-8464.

Deep Creek Area, Graham County

Deep Creek Trail   22

Length: 4.6 mi rt (7.4 km), strenuous; *USGS:* Tapoco; *Trailhead:* End of FSR 445.

Directions and Description: From the bridge on US 219 over the Little Tennessee River in Tapoco, go 1.6 mi SE on US 129 and turn R onto FSR 445 across the Cheoah River bridge. (Robbinsville is 13 mi SE on US 129). After 0.2 mi bear L at fork. Farther along the road may be rough and passable only to jeep traffic. Go 5.3 mi to parking area.

Trail continues ahead ascending steadily on the R of the cascading Deep Creek. The trail ascends 1.2 mi through an impressive wilderness area to the Hudson Deaden Branch. At 2 mi the climb is steeper, with switchbacks and continues to be so to jct with *Hangover Lead Trail* (USFS Trail #43) at Saddle Tree Gap (5,120 ft) on the Joyce Kilmer Wilderness Area boundary. To reach Hangover Lookout (5,249 ft), turn L for 0.2 mi. Here there are magnificent views of the Joyce Kilmer-Slick Rock Wilderness and the Smokies. Return by the same route or use trails in the Kilmer area. Elev gain, 2,449 ft. USFS Trail #46.

Yellow Creek Mountains Area, Graham County

Yellow Creek Mountain Trail   23

Length: 9 mi (14.4 km), strenuous; *USGS:* Tapoco, Fontana Dam; *Trailhead:* Tapoco Village at SR 1247.

Directions and Description: In Tapoco (14.5 mi from Robbinsville on US 129) at jct of US 129 and SR 1247 — which leads to NC 28 and Fontana Village — park in a small area on US 129.

Walk 30 yd on SR 1247 and cross Yellow Creek R on blue-blazed trail. (Until 1947 this was the circuitous route followed by the *Appalachian Trail* between the Smokies and the Cheoah Mountains. It was reopened in 1971 by the Boy Scouts of Tapoco, Troop #415.) Climb steeply up switchbacks through rhododendron, scrub pine, white pine, oak, dogwood, maple, mountain laurel, and bearberry. Reach Bearpen Gap at 1.2 mi, and then Oldfield Gap Rd (SR 1249) at 1.5 mi. Lumbering in the area has left overgrowth and a number of side roads. Water is found infrequently on the trail. Continue on the ridge, ascending and descending over knolls, then climbing steeply at 2.9 mi. Reach Kirkland Gap (2,800 ft at 5.3 mi), then Green Gap (3,455 ft) at 7.5 mi. *Look Rock Trail* is L of the Gap. It descends 1 mi to the SW corner of Fontana Village, connecting with SR 1246. Arrive at Walker Gap (3,450 ft) at 9 mi, joining the current route of the *Appalachian Trail*. Backtrack or take the *A.T.* N to NC 28 and then go L for 2.7 mi. Another route would be to take the *A.T.* S to Yellow Creek Gap (SR 1242) at 3.7 mi. Vehicle switching would be necessary. Elev change, 2,350 ft. USFS Trail #48.

Grassy Gap Trail   24

Length: 5 mi rt (8 km), strenuous; *USGS:* Hewitt, Wesser; *Trailhead:* End of SR 1232.

Directions and Description: From jct of NC 28 and SR 1232 at Panther Creek bridge and backwater of Fontana Lake (2 mi W of Tasli Campground on NC 28), drive up SR 1232 beside Panther Creek for 2.3 mi to parking area.

Panther Creek Trail forks R and *Grassy Gap Trail* forks L. Follow up Rock Creek, bearing L of *Cook Branch Trail*. Continue to follow Rock Creek, bearing L at 1 mi at the confluence of Rock Creek and an unnamed stream. Follow the unnamed stream past a number of cascading streams and at 2 mi begin steep half-mile climb to the *Appalachian Trail* at Grassy Gap (3,050 ft). Backtrack or follow L on the *A.T.* for 2.9 mi to the Nantahala River and Wesser. Or, follow R (W) for 4 mi to Sassafras Gap on the *A.T.* and make a connection with *Bear Creek-Ledbetter Trail*. USFS Trail #66.

Panther Creek Trail   26

Length: 7.2 mi rt (11.5 km), easy to moderate; *USGS:* Hewitt; *Trailhead:* End of SR 1232.

Directions and Description: From jct of NC 28 and SR 1232 at

Panther Creek bridge and backwater of Fontana Lake, drive up SR 1232 beside Panther Creek for 2.3 mi to parking area.

Panther Creek Trail forks R and *Grassy Gap Trail* forks L. Follow *Panther Creek Trail* up Shell Stand Creek, crossing White-oak Branch at 1.4 mi and approaching Reid Branch at 1.8 mi. Jct with *Reid Branch Trail* (USFS #155) is on R. (*Reid Branch Trail* #27 ascends N for 0.5 mi to FSR 410 and exits to SR 1232, which goes back to NC 28.) Continue on *Panther Creek Trail* L of fork, passing through stands of rhododendron, birch, oak, maple, and scattered spruce. Reach terminus of trail at 3.6 mi near confluence of Deep Creek and Whiteoak Creek. Backtrack. USFS Trail #68.

JOYCE KILMER MEMORIAL FOREST
AND
SLICKROCK WILDERNESS AREA

The Joyce Kilmer Memorial Forest, of which 3,800 acres are in the Little Santeetlah Creek watershed, and the Slickrock Creek watershed, with 10,700 acres, together form two basins separated by the ridge between Stratton Bald and Haoe Lookout. The Smokies are north across the Little Tennessee River, and the Cherokee National Forest in Tennessee is to the west.

Filled with virgin timber, the Kilmer Memorial was established by Congress in 1936 to honor the famous author of "Trees," Joyce Kilmer, a soldier who was killed in World War I at the battle of Ovreq. In 1936 the U.S. Forest Service also purchased the Slickrock Creek basin from the Babcock Lumber Company of Pennsylvania, which had cut more than 70% of the timber in the watershed.

This wilderness is rich in both flora and fauna. Hundreds of species of shrubs, wilflowers, vines, ferns, mosses, lichens, and herbaceous plants form the understory. Rhododendron, mountain laurel, and azaleas are also abundant. Trees include poplar, hemlock, sycamore, basswood, oak, maple, birch, and beech. Animal life includes boar, fox, bear, deer, raccoon, mink, and other smaller mammals. Two species of poisonous snakes — the copperhead and the timber rattler — are in the area. In addition to the song birds, the wilderness has grouse, wild turkey, owls, and ravens. Hunting and fishing are allowed in the wilderness under specific state laws. The closest campground near the Kilmer entrance is at Horse Cove on SR 1127 in the Nantahala Forest. Signs are easily followed on US 129 from Robbinsville or Tapoco. There are more than sixty miles of hiking trails in the wilderness.

Listed below are brief descriptions of the hiking trails as currently maintained by the Cheoah Ranger District of the Nantahala National Forest. The *Hiker's Guide to the Smokies* gives complete details on fifteen trails. Hikers should refer to that guidebook, plus maps and information from the Ranger's headquarters in Robbinsville.

Kilmer Trails

Entrance Directions: If entrance is via the Santeetlah Gap, turn L on SR 1116 at the Kilmer sign 1 mi W of Robbinsville on US 129. Follow signs and take SR 1127 at intersection. Follow SR 1127 to the parking lot. There is also access following the signs N of Santeetlah Lake from Robbinsville on US 129 to SR 1145 and SR 1134, crossing the Cheoah River below the Santeetlah Lake Dam. *USGS* quad maps for Kilmer are Santeetlah Creek, Tapoco, and Big Junction.

Haoe Lead Trail   28

Length: 6.5 mi (10.4 km), moderate to strenuous.
Directions and Description: Start at Joyce Kilmer Memorial Forest parking lot at the end of SR 1127, pass Haoe Lookout (5,249 ft) at 5.1 mi, and connect with *Stratton Bald Trail* (USFS Trail #54) at 6.5 mi. USFS Trail #53.

Jenkins Meadow Trail   29

Length: 2 mi (3.2 km), strenuous.
Directions and Description: This is a spur connecting trail from *Naked Ground Trail* (USFS Trail #55), at the crossroads of FSP 416

and SR 1127 near Horse Cove Campground, to *Haoe Lead Trail*. USFS Trail #53-A.

Stratton Bald Trail   30

Length: 10 mi (16 km), moderate to strenuous.

Directions and Description: This trail runs from near Rattler Ford Group Campground bridge near jct of FSR 317 and SR 1127 to jct with *Fodderstack Trail* (USFS Trail #95) at Tennessee-North Carolina state line. (This trail requires backtracking 10 mi or taking other trails for exit at a minimum of 6 mi.) USFS Trail #54.

Naked Ground Trail   31

Length: 6 mi (9.6 km), easy to strenuous.

Directions and Description: This trail goes from crossroads of FSR 416 and SR 1127 near Horse Cove to Naked Ground (4,840 ft) and Stratton Bald, connecting with *Haoe Lead Trail*. USFS Trial #55.

Joyce Kilmer Memorial Trail   32

Length: 1.2 mi (1.9 km), easy.

Directions and Description: From Joyce Kilmer picnic area at the cul de sac of FSR 416, this trail runs from SR 1127 to *Poplar Cove Loop Trail* (USFS Trail #58), and then returns. This trail has virgin timber and is one of the most popular trails in the Kilmer Forest. USFS Trail #56.

Wolf Laurel Trail   33

Length: 0.6 mi (1 km), easy.

Directions and Description: From Santeetlah Gap take FSR 81 to Fork Ridge Rd (FSR 81F) and go 3 mi to trailhead. A 4WD may be necessary on part of FSR 81F. USFS Trail #57.

Poplar Cove Loop Trail   34

Length: 0.7 mi (1.1 km), easy.

Directions and Description: A loop trail connecting with the *Joyce Kilmer Memorial Trail* (USFS Trail #56), this trail has extraordinarily large poplars in a stand of virgin timber. A trail guide for the Joyce Kilmer Memorial Forest has been published in *Brown's Guide to Georgia* by G. Forest Hargett in November, 1980. USFS Trail #58.

Slickrock Creek Trails

Entrance Directions: Take US 219 North of Robbinsville, pass first Kilmer sign, and continue for 12 mi, turning L on the Slickrock Rd across the Cheoah River bridge. Take either the Deep Creek Rd L or FSR 62 R to Grassy Branch Trail at 3.6 mi. Go on to Big Fat Gap parking area. USGS quad maps for Slickrock are Big Junction, Whiteoak Flats, and Tapoco.

Big Fat Branch Trail   35

Length: 1.4 mi (2.2 km), easy to strenuous.
Directions and Description: From the cul de sac of FSR 62 at Big Fat Gap, go 1.4 mi to jct of *Nichols Cove Trail* (USFS Trail #44), near *Slickrock Creek Trail* (USFS #42). USFS Trail #41.

Slickrock Creek Trail   36

Length: 12.2 mi (19.5 km), easy to strenuous.
Directions and Description: From Naked Ground (S) connection at *Haoe Lead Trail*, this trail runs partly along North Carolina-Tennessee state line to connect with *Nichols Cove Trial* and then go on to Calderwood Lake. From there *Ike Branch Trail* connects and provides an exit (or entrance if this is hiked in reverse) at US 129 bridge below Lake Cheoah.

Hangover Lead Trail   37

Length: 5.5 mi (8.8 km), moderate to strenuous.

Directions and Description: From Haoe Lookout (5,249 ft) this trail runs to jct with *Yellowhammer Gap Trail* (USFS Trail #49) at Yellowhammer Gap. USFS Trail #43.

Nichols Cove Trail 38

Length: 2.8 mi (4.5 km), moderate.
Directions and Description: From jct of *Slickrock Trail* and *Slickrock Creek Trail* (S) this trail runs to jct with *Slickrock Creek Trail* (N) near Slickrock Creek. USFS Trail #44.

Ike Branch Trail 39

Length: 2.5 mi (4 km), moderate.
Directions and Description: From corner of bridge at Little Tennessee River near Calderwood Lake, follow trail downstream on L to jct with *Slickrock Creek Trail* at 0.7 mi and then another with *Slickrock Creek Trail* USFS Trail #45. at 2.5 mi.

Yellowhammer Gap Trail 40

Length: 1.7 mi (2.7 km), moderate.
Directions and Description: From Yellowhammer Gap (which connects with *Ike Branch Trail*) go to *Nichols Cove Trail* (USFS Trail #44) for a connection after 1.7 mi. USFS Trail #49.

Nolton Ridge Area, Graham and Swain Counties

Bear Creek-Ledbetter Trail 41

Length: 8 mi (12.8 km), moderate to strenuous; *USGS:* Hewitt; *Trailhead:* End of SR 1201.
Directions and Description: This is a 16 mi round trip trail or a minimum of 13.4 mi using alternate trails. From jct of US 129 and 19 in Topton, take US 129 W for 4.1 mi to sign of Bear Creek Scenic Railroad; turn R. (It is 7.6 mi on US 129 W to Robbinsville.) Cross

over railroad, pass log cottage and mobile home on L, enter edge of forest, and park.

Follow road through young forest of mixed hardwoods, spruce, poplar, rhododendron, tag alder, mountain laurel, yellow root, and a wide variety of ferns and flowers along the creek. At 0.3 mi cross old bridge onto seeded road. At 0.7 mi cross Dee Branch, and cross Bear Creek at 0.9 mi. From this point on, the trail is on the R side of Bear Creek, but it crosses Cherry Branch at 1.7 mi. Ruins of a few old houses are near the trail. Cross from Graham into Swain County at 3.5 mi and reach the *Ledbetter Trail* #42 on the R at 3.7 mi. Skirt Little Bald on an even contour at 4 mi, curving R at the headwaters of Ledbetter Creek. Continue skirting around ridges and coves, crossing Mudcut Branch at 6.2 mi and then a number of unnamed brooks flowing SE from Cheoah Bald mountain range. At 8 mi a service road leads L up to the Sassafras Gap Lean-to, 120 yd SE of the *Appalachian Trail*. (On the *A.T.* it is 5.4 mi NW to Stekoah Gap, SR 1211, and then L to Robbinsville or R to Fontana Village. On the *A.T.* R (SE), it is 7 mi to the Nantahala River and Wesser. The route is scenic for viewing the Nantahala Gorge. A relocation of the *A.T.* around the Jump-up affords an optional route.) Cheoah Bald (5,062 ft) is on the *A.T.* 1.1 mi L from Sassafras Gap. Elev gain, 1,820 ft. USFS Trail #62.

Cheoah Mountains Area, Graham County

Old Roughy Trail   **43**

Length: 7.8 mi (12.5 km), strenuous; *USGS:* Robbinsville, Fontana Dam; *Trailhead:* Cheoah Point Campground.

Directions and Description: This trail is a segment of the 50-mi *Santeetlah Loop Trail*. For information on the complete *Santeetlah Loop Trail* write the Wenoca Group, Joseph Leconte Chapter, Sierra Club, Route 6, Box 123, Hendersonville, NC 28739.

From Robbinsville jct of US 129 and SR 1277, Sweetwater Road, go W on US 129 for 7 mi and turn L on SR 1146 at Cheoah Point Campground. Follow sign for 0.7 mi to campground and park.

From blue-blazed sign on telephone pole near campground entrance go up the ridge covered with white pines to US 129 at 0.2 mi. Cross highway, climb steeply under power line, and reach Cheoah Mtn ridge at 0.7 mi. Leave the ridge at 1.8 mi, cross stream at 2.2 mi, and return to ridge at 2.7 mi. Cross old road at 2.8 mi. Vegetation is mixed hardwoods, rhododendron, hemlock, and mountian laurel. Descend slightly from ridge and cross Hazelnut Spring at 4.2. Continue to ascend, following S slope of ridge at points. Reach Locust Lick Log Gap at 5.2 mi, and How Gap at 6.2 mi. At 6.9 mi there is a jct with a partially used FS road, go L for 4 mi to Yellow Creek Gap on SR 1242. Continue ahead to Wauchecha Bald, where firetower is no longer in use, at 7.1 mi. Here there is a jct with *Wauchecha Bald Trail #45* (USFS Trail #47); follow *Wauchecha Bald Trail* for 0.7 mi to fork. Wauchecha bears R for 0.6 mi to the *Appalachian Trail* S, and *Cody Gap Trail #46* (USFS Trail #156) bears L for 0.5 mi to the *Appalachian Trail* N. (It is 2.4 mi N on the *A.T.* from Cody Gap to Yellow Creek Gap and SR1242.) USFS Trail #69.

Cheoah Ranger Station Area, Graham County

Massey Branch Fitness Trail   **47**

Length: 0.7 mi (1.1 km), easy to moderate; *USGS:* Robbinsville; *Trailhead:* Parking area on SR 1116.

Directions and Description: From jct of US 129 and SR 1116 at Cheoah Ranger District sign NW of Robbinsville, go SW on SR 1116 for 0.6 mi. (Ranger office is 0.5 mi farther.) Park on space by the road bank opposite Massey Branch Fitness Trail sign.

Climb up 120 yd to begin trail on even contour. There are 14 stations on a wood chip-covered loop trail under white pines, oaks, and maples. Excellent view of part of Santeetlah Lake.

SECTION II

HIGHLANDS RANGER DISTRICT

Cliffside and Vanhook Area, Macon County

Cliffside Lake and Vanhook Glade Recreation Areas

Cliffside Lake and Vanhook Glade Recreation Areas provide camping, picnicking, fishing, swimming, boating, nature study, and hiking on interconnecting trails. Service facilities do not include hook-up sites for campers.

Directions and Description: In Highlands at jct of US 64 and NC 28, proceed N on US 64 and NC 28 for 4.4 mi to Cliffside entrance. Go for 1.4 mi on FSR 57. The Vanhook Glade campground is on US 64 and NC 28 0.2 mi before the Cliffside entrance. Vegetation in the area is mature forest of spruce, white pine, oak, maple, rhododendron, buckberry, and includes numerous species of wildflowers. Fish are chiefly rainbow and brook trout.

Clifftop Vista Trail and Potts Memorial Trail   48-49

Length: 2.5 mi rt cb (4 km), easy to moderate; *USGS:* Highlands; *Trailhead:* Parking area.

Directions and Description: From parking area go W on the road across Skitty Creek for a few yd, where the trail begins at a sign. Take either R or L to summit of ridge. If R, pass or take as a side trail *Pott Memorial Trail* to a white pine plantation. Continue in a circular direction and reach a gazebo at 1.8 mi, where scenic views are provided of Flat Mountain and the Cullasaja River basin. (The *Clifftop Nature Trail* continues R.) Turn L, following switchbacks down to origin. USFS Trails #2A-2B.

Clifftop Nature Trail   50

Length: 1.1 mi (1.8 km), moderate; *USGS:* See above; *Trailhead:* Parking area.

Directions and Description: From entrance at US 64 and NC 28 go 0.7 mi on FSR 57 to small parking area on R and follow sign up switchbacks on L. The graded interpretive trail provides descriptions of the trees and shrubs in a mixed hardwood forest of buckberry, sourwood, sweet pepper bush, and dead chestnut.

Vanhook Trail   51

Length: 1.8 mi (2.9 km), easy; *USGS:* See above; *Trailhead:* Vanhook campground.

Directions and Description: From Vanhook Glade Campground go 0.3 mi through forest to FSR 57 and hike 0.6 mi to Cliffside Lake area on a connecting trail between camping areas. Return by the same route. USFS Trail #2C.

Homesite Road Trail and Skitty Creek Trail   52-53

Length: 2.8 mi rt (4.5 km), easy, *USGS:* See above; *Trailhead:* Parking area near Cliffside Lake.

Directions and Description: This trail can be hiked from the Cliffside Lake Dam, following Skitty Creek for a few yd before turning E through hardwood forest. At old road on which there are private homes, turn R and reach a gate at 1.4 mi at US 64. Dry Falls is to R 0.4 mi on US 64 and Bridal Veil Falls is to L 0.4 mi on US 64. Return by the same route or follow US 64 N for 0.2 mi to Skitty Creek Trail; alternatively, provide a vehicle shuttle. USFS Trail #2E.

Cliffside Loop Trail   54

Length: 0.8 mi (1.3 km), easy; *USGS:* See above; *Trailhead:* Parking area near Cliffside Lake.

Directions and Description: From the parking area at Cliffside Lake walk to the loop on the road and circle the lake, or join the *Homesite Road Trail* for a longer hike. USFS Trail #2.

Dry Falls Trail   55

Length: 0.1 mi (0.2 km), easy: *USGS:* See above; *Trailhead:* Parking area on US 64-NC 28.

Directions and Description: From parking area follow signs and descend to 70-ft waterfall with trail running underneath. Rare plants are in the area, watered by a constant mist from the updraft in the Cullasaja Gorge. The surrounding stone is shist and gneiss, between 500 and 800 million years old. It is shaped by the Cullasaja River, "Cullasaja" meaning honey or sugar water in Cherokee. USFS Trail #2D.

Chinquapin Mountain and Glen Falls Area, Macon County

Chinquapin Mountain Trail   56

Length: 3.2 mi rt (5.1 km), moderate; *USGS:* Highlands; *Trailhead:* Glen Falls parking area.

Directions and Description: From jct of US 64 and NC 28 and 106 in Highlands, go SW on NC 106 for 1.7 mi to sign for Glen Falls Scenic Area. Turn L and proceed on gravel road for 1 mi to parking area.

Follow trail sign, bearing R at fork with *Glen Falls Trail.* Descend, crossing East Fork a number of times and passing through hardwoods, conifers, and rhododendron. Rock-hopping is necessary in spots. At 0.5 mi there is a jct with other access point from NC 106. Gradually ascend on switchbacks, passing spur trail to views of Blue Valley, to summit of Chinquapin Mtn. (4,160 ft). Return by same route. Elev change, 680 ft. USFS Trail #3.

Glen Falls Trail   57

Length: 2.8 mi rt (4.5 km), moderate to strenuous; *USGS:* Highlands; *Trailhead:* Glen Falls parking area.

Directions and Description: Follow same directions as above to the parking area. Enter the trail by following gray blazes, bearing L. (Trail to R is the *Chinquapin Mtn Trail.*) Trail descends steeply through mixed hardwoods and by the three major cascades. Spur trails lead to impressive views from the main trail. Descend to FSR

79C, Blue Valley Rd, at 1.4 mi. Return by same route, or use vehicle shuttle placed on the Blue Valley Rd. Off NC 28, near Georgia state line. (It is SR 1618 before it becomes FSR 79C.) Elev change, 840 ft. USFS Trail #8.

Chattooga River Area, Jackson and Macon Counties

Bad Creek Trail   58

Length: 7 mi rt (12.2 km), moderate; *USGS:* Highlands, Cashier; *Trailhead:* Bullpen Rd.

Directions and Description: From jct of US 64 and NC 28 in Highlands go SE on Main St, which then becomes Horse Cove Rd, for 4.6 mi to end of pavement and jct with Bullpen Rd, SR 1178. Bear R and go 3 mi to the Chattooga River, cross bridge, and continue for another 3 mi to a parking area and sign for *Bad Creek Trail*.

Descend steeply to river corridor and follow downstream to Ellicott's Rock. Return by the same route or hike out on *Ellicott's Rock Trail* to FSR 441F, where vehicle shuttle from FSR 441 (SR 1178) would be necessary. USFS Trail #6.

Slick Rock Trail   59

Length: 0.2 mi (0.3 km), easy; *USGS:* Highlands; *Trailhead:* Parking on roadside.

Directions and Description: Follow directions given above from Highlands, turning off R at SR 1178 and going for 0.7 mi; park in narrow area on R.

Unmarked trail ascends for 0.1 mi to large rock formation with scenic views W into the Chattooga River basin. A wide variety of lichens and mosses grow in the crevices and apertures. This scenic spot is the site for the filming of *The Mating Game*. USFS Trail #15.

Ellicott's Rock Trail   60

Length: 7 mi rt (11.2 km), moderate; *USGS:* Highlands; *Trail-head:* Parking area on FSR 441F.

Directions and Descripton: From Highlands follow the directions given above, turning R at SR 1178 and going 1.7 mi. (Pass primitive Ammons campsite on R at 1.1 mi.) Turn R on FSR 441F. Go 0.3 mi farther to parking area for *Ellicott's Rock Trail.*

Hike on old road on even grade or gradually descending to Ellicott's Rock Wilderness Area boundary at 2 mi. At 3 mi bear L off the old road, descending steeply to the Chattooga River at 3.5 mi. To locate Ellicott's Rock, a survey marker for the North Carolina-South Carolina-Georgia state boundaries, cross the river and go down-stream for approximately 0.1 mi. Exploratory trails in the area can be confusing, and another rock, the Commissioner's Rock, is some-times claimed to be the true boundary jct of the three states. It is a few feet downstream from Ellicott's Rock. It bears the inscription "LAT 35 AD 1813 NC-SC." Both of these rocks were named for early surveyors of the state lines. The vegetation in this area is mixed hardwoods with scattered pine and spruce. Return by the same route or hike out for 3.5 mi on the *Bad Creek Trail* to the Bullpen Rd. USFS Trail #820.

Chattooga River Trail   61

Length: 2.2 mi (3.5 km), easy; *USGS:* Highlands; *Trailhead:* Near Chattooga River Bridge on Bullpen Rd.

Directions and Description: Follow the directions given above from Highlands and turn R at Bull Pen Rd, SR 1178. Go 3 mi to the Chattooga River bridge; park. (If hiking the loop section of the trail, the old road L of the parking area could be used for parking, since the trail will exit there.)

The trail is blazed gray and green. Follow the well-graded trail through a forest of large oak, maple, white pine, and beech, with an understory growth of large holly and rhododendron. The Chattooga cascades nearby on the R through huge boulders, large potholes, sandbars, and pools. At 0.8 mi turn L on the *Loop Trail,* ascending on switchbacks to old road, and return to parking area. (The *Chattooga River Trail,* often used by fishermen, continues upstream and is being developed through a stand of hemlock and white pine near large rock formations.) USFS Trail #825.

Whitewater River Area, Transylvania County

Whitewater Falls Trail   62

Length: 2 mi rt (3.2 km), easy; *USGS:* Cashiers; *Trailhead:* Parking area.

Directions and Description: From jct of US 64 and NC 281 in Sapphire, take NC 281 (formerly SR 1171) for 8.6 mi to sign for Whitewater Falls Scenic Area. Turn L for 0.3 mi to parking area with views of Lake Jocassee.

Hike for 0.2 mi on paved trail to overlook for view of the resplendent 411-foot stairstep falls. (Trail to R of overlook descends steeply on steps and is under construction by the YCC as a connector trail to the *Cherokee Foothills Trail*.) Turn L at overlook and progress over earth mounds to the Tongue Rock at 100 yd. Follow old road to the river, which is reached at 0.6 mi, ford it unless water is too high, and go upstream for another 0.4 mi. Return by the same route. Picnicking and primitive camping are allowed in the area. Use extreme care in exploring downstream, since lives have been lost by people going over the falls. Vegetation in the area includes white pine, hemlock, oaks, maple, thimbleberry, rhododendron, and woodland sunflowers. USFS Trail #7.

West Blue Valley Area, Macon County

West Fork Trail and Hurrah Ridge Trail   63-64

Length: 1.9 mi rt cb (3 km), moderate; *USGS:* Highlands, Scaly Mtn; *Trailhead:* End of FSR 79.

Directions and Description: These two spur trails form a loop with the *Bartram Trail*. From US 64 and NC 28 jct in Highlands, take NC 28 S for 6 mi to SR 1618, Blue Valley Rd, which becomes FSR 79. Turn R on it and go 6 mi to West Fork of Overflow Creek; park.

Begin on R before crossing Overflow Creek; ascend on rocky and frequently wet trail for 0.9 mi to the *Bartram Trail*. (On *Bartram*

Trail R it is 0.7 mi to Osage Mtn Vista at NC 106.) Turn L on *Bartram Trail* and go for 0.4 mi. Turn L again on *Hurrah Ridge Trail*. (*Bartram Trail* continues on for 2.9 mi to Hale Ridge Rd, FSR 7.) Descend on *Hurrah Ridge Trail* to parking area through dry area with mixed hardwoods and hemlock. Hike can be reversed to follow the *Bartram Trail* farther. Other vegetation on the trail is rhododendron, mountain laurel, white pine, and wildflowers common to the area. USFS Trails #14 and 808.

Yellow Mtn Area, Macon and Jackson Counties

Yellow Mountain Trail   65

Length: 9.4 mi rt (15 km), strenuous; *USGS:* Highlands, Glenville; *Trailhead:* Parking area at Cole Gap.

Directions and Description: From jct of US 64 and NC 28 in Highlands, proceed E on US 64 for 2.6 mi to SR 1538, Buck Creek Rd, on the L at Shortoff Baptist Church sign. (From Cashiers W on US 64 it is 7.4 mi. to the same spot.) Go 2.2 mi to Cole Gap (4,200 ft) and park on the L of the road; trail sign is on R.

Gray-blazed trail ascends gradually on old woods road through hardwoods and abundant wildflowers. Orchids, trillium, false fox glove, Solomon's seal, hellebore, starry campion, sunflowers, and a number of rare species such as wolfsbane and grass of Parnassus line the trail. There is a small spring at 0.6 mi on R. Reach Cole Mtn (4,600 ft) at 0.9 mi, descend gradually, and then begin steep climb on switchbacks to Shortoff Mtn at 1.4 mi. Skirt S of summit for scenic views; descend and ascend along Shortoff Mtn range (5,000 ft). At 2 mi bear L (N) along the Jackson-Macon County line. Descend to gap at 2.5 mi, and ascend to Goat Knob (4,640 ft) at 2.7 mi. Descend steeply, join an old road, turn R, and reach Yellow Mtn Gap at 3.2 mi. Continue on graded trail up switchbacks bordered by laurel, rhododendron, berries, and hardwoods to the summit of Yellow Mtn (5,127 ft) at 4.7 mi. Spectacular views from Yellow and Cole Mtns of Standing Indian, Whiterock Mtn, and Albert Mtn. The old firetower, no longer used, has been vandalized but part of it is locked up and used for TV transmission. The rock formations, composed mainly of gneiss, have a wide variety of mosses and lichens on them. Backtrack, or arrange for a shuttle 1 mi from the summit by driving 6.8 mi E on US 64 from Highlands to Norton Rd and turning L. Go 2 mi to Yellow Mtn Rd, and park at jct with jeep trail to summit. USFS Trail #31.

East Fork Area, Jackson County

Whiteside Mountain Trail   66

Length: 2 mi (3.2 km), moderate; *USGS:* Highlands; *Trailhead:* Parking area.

Directions and Description: This trail in the Nantahala National Forest has been designated a National Recreation Trail; it was completed in 1974. From Cashiers go W on US 64 to the Jackson and Macon County line, and turn L on SR 1600, Wildcat Ridge Rd. Go 1 mi to Whiteside Mtn sign and turn L into the parking area. (From Highlands jct of US 64-NC 28, go E on US 64 for 5.4 mi and turn R on SR 1600.)

Begin hike up steps. Ascend following gray blazes R to ridge and turn L at 0.2 mi. At 0.7 mi reach Devils Point, the summit (4,930 ft), for magnificent views of the Chattooga River Valley, Timber Ridge, Blackrock Mtn, Yellow Mtn, and Terrapin Mtn. Follow precipitous edge of sheer cliffs, 400 to 600 ft high, to overlook at 1.1 mi. Begin descent on old road to parking area to complete the loop. The granite landmark is composed of feldspar, quartz, and mica. Vegetation consists of oaks, birches, maple, rosebay rhododendron, mountain laurel, flame azalea, sweet pepper bush, scattered conifers, and abundant wildflowers common to rock outcroppings.

Silver Run Trail   67

Length: 1 mi rt (1.6 km), easy; *USGS:* Cashiers; *Trailhead:* Parking on NC 107.

Directions and Description: From Cashiers at jct of US 64 and NC 107, take NC 107 S for 4 mi and park on L side of highway. Descend into damp forest of rhododendron, hemlock, and poplar with dense understory to stream near Silver Run Creek, part of the headwaters of the famous Upper Falls of the Whitewater River. Backtrack.

Bonas Defeat Area, Jackson County

Tuskasegee Gorge Trail   **68**

This trail is in part of the Bonas Defeat acquisition made by the USFS in 1981. Surveying is in progress to ascertain the boundary lines of the area, and it is unclear at this point as to whether this is an official trail. Hikers exploring the gorge have created a number of footpaths, confusing other hikers who follow about the nearest or safest route. Following a straight forward line, the hike is approximately 4 mi round trip, and is completed by either backtracking or following the gravel road up from the powerhouse. USGS topo maps covering the area are Lake Toxaway and Big Ridge. The descent into the gorge is considered strenuous and dangerous.

At the Tuckasegee jct of NC 107 and NC 281 (SE of Cullowhee on NC 107), turn E on NC 281 and go 8.3 mi on paved road and another 5.8 mi on all-weather gravel road to Phillips Store. Park on R near fence. From the E take NC 281 at jct with US 64, 8 mi W of Rosman. Go 3.3 mi on paved road and another 7.9 mi on all-weather gravel road to Phillips Store. Park on L near fence. Request permission from the store owner to enter the gate and hike over the bald hill. (Some hikers have been entering the gorge from a private driveway 0.2 mi W of Phillips Store. Permission there should be requested from the landowner, whose house is off the curve.)

From the hilltop descend SW to corner of pasture, cross barbed wire fence at 0.2 mi, and descend to road. Pass gaging station, follow pathway through forest by the lake, and reach another road. Follow road and take a sharp L to Tanasee Lake at 0.5 mi. Cross dam with care. Descend into the gorge by twisting around huge boulders, rock-hopping, and avoiding a fall into any of the hundreds of water-carved potholes. After passing Doe Branch on the L, the Bonas Defeat Cliffs loom upward. (The legend of "Bonas Defeat" is that a hunting dog named Boney chased a deer on the cliff edge;

the deer jumped sideways, missing the cliff, but Boney dived over it, meeting his defeat.) Continue descent to powerhouse. Backtrack, or follow gravel road back, ascending to first fork; take R. At return to the next fork near the dam, bear L and follow original entrance route. (See *Wolf Creek Trail* below.)

Wolf Creek Gorge Trail 69

Another unofficial trail in the Bonas Defeat area is this one. Less known than the Tuckasegee, it is more tranquil, pristine, and wild. Like the Tuckasegee, soft spots in the rock have been carved by the rapids. Exploring at the waterfalls can be hazardous.

Follow the directions as given above for the Tuckasegee Gorge, except that the trailhead is W 1.5 mi from Phillips Store and 0.5 mi from the Wolf Creek Dam on NC 281. Park at the Wolf Creek Baptist Church. Descend on clear footpath behind the church and bear slightly L and down across the old road at 0.2 mi. At 0.4 mi reach Wolf Creek, whose fury has sculpted potholes, pools, waterfalls, and whitewater slides. An exploratory path descends into the chasm on the L of the waterfall. Huge hemlock and birch, white pines, oaks, rhododendron, mountain laurel, willow, mosses, ferns, and wildflowers, provide the area with natural beauty. Return on the same route. (Wolf Creek flows SW for 1.4 mi to confluence with the Tuckasegee River at the powerhouse. Descent can also be made on SR 1139 by going 0.3 mi W on NC 281 from the church.)

SECTION III

TUSQUITEE RANGER DISTRICT

Fires Creek Area, Clay County

Fires Creek Wildlife Management Sanctuary

The 16,000-acre Fires Creek Wildlife Management Area has three recreational sites listed for primitive camping; they are at

Huskins Branch Hunter Camp near the entrance, Bristol Camp deeper into the forest, and a picnic section at Leatherwood Falls. Other sites for camping are along the creeks and roads. No camping is allowed in designated wildlife openings. Fishing for rainbow, brook, and brown trout is allowed according to North Carolina Game Lands regulations. Bear hunting and use of ORV's are prohibited. Hunting for wild turkey, Russian boar, deer, and grouse is permitted in season. Both copperheads and timber rattlers are in the sanctuary. Among the birds are woodpeckers, warblers, owls, hawks, towhees, and doves. The area is considered to be ideal for backpacking; the longest trail, traversing the boundary on a high and elongated rim, runs for over 25 miles.

Rim Trail   70

Length: 24.9 mi (39.4 km), strenuous; *USGS:* Andrews, Topton, Hayesville; *Trailhead:* Leatherwood Falls parking area.

Directions and Description: From Hayesville jct with NC 69, go W 4.9 mi to Hill's Grocery on R at jct with SR 1302. (Or, from Murphy go E 9.2 mi from US 129-19.) Follow SR 1302 for 3.7 mi and turn L on gravel road, SR 1344. After 1.7 mi enter gate, reaching Leatherwood Falls parking area and picnic ground at 2 mi.

Water is infrequent on this trail. Begin on R of parking area, following blue blaze across the arched bridge into a white pine stand. Turn L of the chemical comfort station at 0.1 mi, and curve L to Leatherwood Falls, over an elevated bridge, and to the top of the falls and the *Loop Trail* at 0.3 mi. Turn R, reach FSR at 0.4 mi, take a sharp turn R up the bank at 0.6 mi, and follow switchbacks. Join and rejoin old logging roads. At 1.6 mi there is a jct with old trail on ridge; bear R. Pass through an experimental forest section of hardwoods and begin steep, rocky ascent at 1.8 mi. Reach a plateau at 2 mi, and an intermittent spring at 2.2 mi. Ascend on switchbacks constructed by the YACC in 1980 to another ridge crest on the Cherokee-Clay County line at 3.2 mi. Follow old road W of Shortoff Knob to spring on L at 3.3 mi and cross Big Peachtree Bald (4,186 ft), with Peachtree Valley to L at 4.4 mi. Follow rim with Valley River on SE and precipitous edge on NW to Will King Gap at 5.4 mi and N, toward Chestnut Flats. Follow contour grade until ascent to

Big Stamp Lookout (4,437 ft) is reached at 7.9 mi. As the trail skirts the summit, an access route of 0.2 mi is on the S side. (This access route is also a road descending into the heart of Fires Creek.) Views from the lookout are impressive, with Snowbird Mtns and Kilmer Forest N, the Smokies NE, and Lake Chatuge S.

Continue along rim, with exceptionally steep drops on N side; pass at 9.1 mi a faint trail descending N, the *McClellan Creek Trail #71*. Ascend and descend over knobs — Whiteoak Knob, Defeat Knob, Beal Knob — and reach Sassafras Knob at 12.3 mi. Skirt S of Weatherman Bald (4,960 ft) at 12.9 mi and reach the boundary of Cherokee, Macon, and Clay counties at County Corner at 13.6 mi. (*Old Road Gap Trail #72* L descends N for 1.5 mi to FSR, and L 1.1 mi to Junaluska Gap Rd, SR 1505. L on SR 1505 it is 3.5 mi to Andrews.) At this jct *Shinbone Ridge Trail* descends R (SW) for 1.5 mi to trailhead on Fires Creek, near confluence of Fires Creek and Potrock Branch.

Follow *Rim Trail* SE on crest to fork at 14.9 mi. Choose L fork to views from Signal Bald, named for Cherokee Indian use of smoke signals here, at 14.8 mi. Between Signal Bald and Tusquitee Bald (5,240 ft) is jct L with *Chunky Gal Trail*. (*Chunky Gal Trail* runs for 21.6 mi, descending E and SE to Glade Gap and then ascending to White Oak Stamp and the *Appalachian Trail*.) Tusquitee is the Cherokee word for "where the water dogs laughed;" the name is based on a legend of thirsty — and talking — water dogs. Descend from Tusquitee Bald, bearing S and SW toward Potrock Bald (5,215 ft) at 16.1 mi. Potrock gets its name from small and large "bowls" appearing to have been caused by Indian carvings or the weather. Spring is on R at 17 mi.

On a gentle grade reach Matlock Bald (4,949 ft) at 17.1 mi. Edge of rim on S becomes steep down to Snake Branch as trail continues SW on the rim to Chestnut Stomp Knob (4,400 ft) at 18.3 mi. From there continue descent to Shearer Gap, Cold Sprig Gap, Pigpen Gap, Deep Gap, Phone Line Gap, Squirrel Spring Gap, and finally to Carver Gap (2,996 ft) at 22.8 mi. *Bristol Cabin Trail* jct is here; it goes R for 1.2 mi, descending to Bristol Camp on Fires Creek Rd. After 0.3 mi farther along rim *Omphus Ridge Trail* intersects and descends R for 1.3 mi to Fires Creek Rd. From this jct the trail descends W on a wide rim, reaching Fires Creek Rd at 24.8 mi. It is another 0.1 mi L to the parking area, for a total of 24.9 mi.

Forest vegetation includes larger and denser groves of rhododendron at lower elevations, but common to both lowland and
upland are black birch, locust, sassafras, hickory, oak, sourwood,
beech, maple, poplar, white and Virginia pine, mountain laurel,
chestnut sprouts, and witch hazel. Among the flowers are azaleas,
trillium, may apple, Turk's cap lily, starry campion, columbine,
orchids, jewel weed, fetterbush, galax, asters, and trailing arbutus.
USFS Trail #70.

Leatherwood Falls Loop Trail   73

Length: 0.7 mi (1.1 km), easy; *USGS:* Hayesville; *Trailhead:*
Parking area.

Directions and Description: Cross arched bridge and follow *Rim
Trail* as described above for 0.3 mi to the top of Leatherwood Falls.
Turn L and skirt the mountainside through rhododendron and hard-
woods with occasional views of the falls. Descend to FSR at 0.6 mi.
Turn L, cross bridge, and return to the parking area.

Omphus Ridge Trail and Bristol Cabin Trail   74-75

Length: 4.9 mi rt cb (7.8 km), moderate to strenuous; *USGS:*
Hayesville; *Trailhead:* Bristol Camp.

Directions and Description: Both of these trails leave Fires Creek
Rd, 2 mi apart, and connect with the *Rim Trail* 0.3 mi apart. They
provide an excellent loop trail combination from Bristol Camp.
From Bristol Camp's open fields cross footbridge and follow signs
marked *Bristol Trail*, beginning steep climb at 0.7 mi. Reach Carver
Gap (2,996 ft) on the *Rim Trail* at 1.2 mi. Turn R to jct with *Omphus
Ridge Trail* at 1.5 mi, and R again for descent on *Omphus Ridge
Trail*. Reach FSR at 2.9 mi. Turn R and follow FSR in and out of
coves for 2 mi to Bristol Camp.

Trail Ridge Trail   76

Length: 5.4 mi rt (8.6 km), strenuous; *USGS:* Highlands,
Andrews; *Trailhead:* Bristol Camp.

Directions and Description: This is an exceptionally steep, blue-blazed trail from Bristol Camp to Big Stamp Lookout. Follow sign a few yards beyond Bristol Camp, where trail ascends L of road up steep incline. At 0.5 mi are Indian bowls and surveyor's bench marks. Reach gravel FSR at 2.2 mi, and follow road to Big Stamp at 2.7 mi. Backtrack. (Trail is an easier descent for *Rim Trail* backpackers than it is an access route with a backpack.)

Shinbone Trail   77

Length: 3 mi rt (4.8 km), moderate to strenuous; *USGS:* Andrews, Topton; *Trailhead:* Fires Creek Rd.

Directions and Description: From the Leatherwood parking area go 9 mi on the gravel road, taking the second road sharply R; go to the Shinbone Ridge parking area up Fires Creek. Ascend through mixed hardwood, scattered conifers, and rhododendron to County Corner on the *Rim Trail* at 1.5 mi. Backtrack, or plan for longer hike on the *Rim Trail*. Elev gain, 1,649 ft.

Chunky Gal Mountains Area, Clay County

Chunky Gal Trail   78

Length: 20.2 mi (32.3 km), strenuous; *USGS:* Rainbow Springs, Shooting Creek, Topton; *Trailhead:* Appalachian Trail.

Directions and Description: This trail has exceptional potential for an extended backpacking trip. It is a connector trail between the *Applachian Trail* on the Tennessee Valley Divide and the *Rim Trail* on the eastern rim of the Fires Creek Basin. Access to either end is by foot trail — 3.1 mi SE on the *A.T.* or 3.4 mi W from Tuni Gap. Another access is from Fires Creek, for 3.4 mi on the *Shinbone Trail*. Whatever way you choose, the minimum hiking distance, avoiding backtracking, is 26.7 mi. To extend the excursion, more than 10 mi of the *Rim Trail* could be used, as could long distances on the *A.T.*

On US 64, 2 mi W of Rainbow Springs, or 0.5 mi W of the Macon-Clay County line, turn L on unmarked gravel FSR 71.

Follow the narrow, winding road for 6 mi over Penland Gap to its jct at Deep Gap with the *A.T.* At Deep Gap there is a picnic area and parking lot.

From there begin the hike on the graded *A.T.* section, ascending steeply S to a footbridge at 1.2 mi. Reach the Yellow Mtn crest and descend to Wateroak Gap at 2.3 mi. Ascend to ridge, skirt NW of Big Laurel Mtn. (5,100 ft), descend, and reach jct with blue-blazed *Chunky Gal Trail* R at 3.1 mi (4,700 ft).

The legend of *Chunky Gal Trail* is that a plump Indian maiden fell in love with an Indian youth of another tribe near here. To break up the romance her parents banished the boy, but she deserted her family and followed him over the mountain.

Follow *Chunky Gal Trail* along Chunky Gal Mtn ridge and over knobs, skirting to the R toward Buck Creek Valley and the Pitch Pine Barrens. Among the scraggly pines grows western prairie grass, uncommon to the Appalachian region. The geological formations contain quartz, garnets, and olivine. Dip into Bear Gap and Grassy Gap and reach the jct with *Riley Cove Trail* at 3.9 mi. Continue L to Riley Knob and descend to Glade Gap at 5.5 mi, and then to US 64. (It is 6.8 mi W to Shooting Creek and 16 mi to Hayesville.)

Following the signs, cross US 64 and then old US 64 to trail entrance by Glade Branch. At 5.7 mi cross footbridge, ascending by switchbacks W and paralleling a power line to summit of Bruce Ridge. Continue ascent on even ground or gradual grade, surrounded by rhododendron and large boulders, to Chunky Gal Mtn (4,840 ft). Skirt R of Shooting Creek Bald (5,010 ft), also known as Boteler Peak, and intersect unmaintained trail at 8.7 mi. Proceed on ridge and descend to Perry Gap at 9.3 mi. Logging road is on R. Follow gated road N to Tate Gap at 10.4 mi; leave road and continue on footpath with slight ascent and then descent for 2 mi. Turn L and descend to Tusquitee Gap and road at 13 mi. (Dirt bikes have cut trails in this area.)

Cross road from Tusquitee Gap and hike NW, skirting Little Niggerhead peak, descending, and walking on level ground for about 2 mi. At 15.9 mi watch for trail relocation sharply W onto logging road and turn L (S) on road for 100 yd. Bear R in recently lumbered area. Ford small stream and the Big Tuni Creek to Bob Allison Camp at 16.8 mi. (The Bob Allison Camp can be reached from Hayesville Square by following Tusquitee Rd on SR 1307 for 10 mi to end of pavement. Continue L (N) for 4.5 mi, following SR 1311, which becomes FSR 440 to Bob Allison Camp, 0.8 mi S of Tuni Gap.)

From FSR 440 continue from concrete bridge at Big Tuni Creek on relocated trail — steep, rough, and rocky. Parts of this trail are not well graded and go on jeep roads, up wet creek bed, and through forest sections marked for lumbering. After 1.3 mi turn L on steep switchbacks to Dead Line Ridge and reach the *Rim Trail* at 20.2 mi, between Signal Bald R and Tusquitee Bald L. Both peaks have outstanding scenery and Tusquitee provides views of Shooting Creek Bald SE, Wine Spring Bald E, Chatuge Lake S, and Nantahala Lake NE.

Forest vegetation on the trail includes mature oak, birch, poplar, maple, hickory, locust, pine, spruce, and beech. Some of the understory plants are rhododendron, azaleas, mountain laurel, buckberry, dogwood, and sassafras. Among the wildflowers are Indian pipe, rattlesnake plantain, asters, vetch, galax, fire pink, cohosh, Carolina lily, orchids, bee balm, trillium, goldenrod, and a number of rare or endangered species near the Buck Creek area.

Backtrack to FSR 440 at Bob Allison Camp, or hike the *Rim Trail* to exit at Fires Creek (see Fires Creek Area description). Either way, vehicle shuttle will be necessary. USFS Trail #77.

Chatuge Lake Area, Clay County

Jackrabbit Mountain Recreation Area

Jackrabbit Mountain Recreation Area has a hundred camping sites, picnicking facilities, boating, swimming, skiing, lake fishing, nature study, and hiking. Comfort stations and cold water showers are available. Open May 23-October 31. (Nearest commercial campground is Ho Hum Campground on NC 175 near the entrance to Jackrabbit Mtn campground. Open April 1-November 15. Full svc, rec fac. Tel: 704-386-6740.) Entry to Jackrabbit is from US 64 jct with NC 175 (4.7 mi E of NC 67 jct in Hayesville). Go S on NC 175 for 3.4 mi, turn R at Jackrabbit on SR 1155, and proceed 1.2 mi to the campground.

Jackrabbit Mtn Scenic Trail   80

Length: 2.4 mi (3.8 km), easy; *USGS:* Shooting Creek; *Trailhead:* Parking area in campground or at boat ramp parking lot.

Directions and Description: Follow trail sign on R of entry to a blue-blazed trail through generally open forest of white oaks, sourwood, and pines. Cleared spots provide views of the Chatuge Lake. Reach crest of ridge at 0.6 mi, cross wooden bridge near spring at 1.3 mi, pass edge of Chatuge Lake at 1.6 mi, and reach the boat ramp parking area at 2.1 mi. Return to camping area parking lot at 2.4 mi.

Hiwassee Lake Area, Cherokee County

Hanging Dog Recreation Area

Located on Lake Hiwassee, Hanging Dog Recreation Area has 69 campsites, a picnic area with tables and grills, and boat launching facilities for fishing, boating, and skiing. Flush toilets are available but there are no showers. Open April 1-October 31. One of the nearest commercial campgrounds is Pied Piper Camp Resorts, Route 6, Box 100, Murphy, NC 28906. Tel: 704-644-5771. Full svc, exceptional rec fac. Open all year. From downtown Murphy at jct of Tennessee St and Valley River Ave (Business Route 19) take Tennessee St W — it becomes SR 1326 — and drive 4.4 mi to Campground sign and road to L. Go 1.1 mi to campground entrance.

Shore Trail   81

Length: 2.1 mi rt (3.4 km), easy; *USGS:* Murphy; *Trailhead:* Campground.

Directions and Description: The trail connects from Section B, spaces 25-26, to Lake Hiwassee and from B to Section C, spaces 42-43. On an even grade hike through oaks, pines, sourwood, dogwood, maple, and birch.

SECTION IV

WAYAH RANGER DISTRICT

Nantahala Lake Area, Macon County

Apple Tree Group Camp

Apple Tree Group Camp is designed for group tent camping at four campsites, each of which can serve up to 40; they are labelled A through D. Water, sanitary facilities, and cold showers are provided. The area has more than 35 miles of hiking trails. Reservations are necessary; contact the District Ranger, Nantahala National Forest, Route 2, Box 194-B, Franklin, NC 28734. Tel: 704-524-6441.

Access from Bryson City is on US 19 SW to Beechertown Power Sta. Turn L on SR 1310, following up the river for 4.4 mi to FSR 308 at a horseshoe curve. Go 3.1 mi farther on gravel road to jct with SR 1401. Turn R, cross bridge, and turn R to camp entrance. From Franklin on US 64 W, turn R at Wayah Gap sign and follow SR 1310 W for 9.3 mi to Wayah Gap; go past Lake Side Camp Store to SR 1400, Andrews Rd (which becomes SR 1401), and turn L. Go 2.4 mi, cross bridge, and turn R to camp entrance. Enter gate and go 0.5 mi to campground.

Apple Tree Trail   **82**

Length: 4.4 mi rt (7 km), moderate to strenuous; *USGS:* Topton; *Trailhead:* Apple Tree Branch.

Directions and Description: Park across road from Apple Tree Branch and follow yellow blazes R side of the branch on old road. Cross branch and pass jct with blue-blazed *Junaluska Trail* on L at 0.3 mi. Cross stream again at 0.7 mi, and then pass faint road jct. Continue on gradual grade through forest of oaks, elm, white pine, beech, sassafras, silver bell, mountain laurel, rhododendron, and numerous wildflowers, including orchids. At 1.1 mi pass jct with green-blazed *Laurel Creek Trail* on R. Continue ahead to white-blazed *Diamond Valley Trail* jct at 1.4 mi on L. (*Diamond Valley Trail* is 0.9-mi connector with *Junaluska Trail* at Dicks Creek and an exit to SR 1401, FSR 327.) Continue R with yellow blazes and reach summit of knob at 1.7 mi. Climb steeply up a second knob and reach the summit of a third peak SE of London Ball at 2.2 mi, and then reach jct with blue-blazed *London Bald Trail*. Elev gain, 1,180 ft. Backtrack, or turn L to follow *London Bald Trail* for 6.5 mi out to Junaluska Gap and SR 1401. Or, turn R and follow *London Bald Trail* for 2.2 mi to its NE terminus at Southerland Gap, and proceed for 6.8 mi to the *Nantahala Trail* and back to camp. It is another 0.3 mi from the campground to *Apple Tree Trail* parking area; a loop of 11.5 mi can be completed in this way. USFS Trail #190.

Junaluska Trail   83

Length: 4.3 mi (6.9 km), moderate; *USGS:* Topton; *Trailhead:* Apple Tree parking area.

Directions and Description: Follow directions as given above for 0.3 mi to jct, L, with blue-blazed trail off *Apple Tree Trail.* Skirt E of mountain, curving SW with SR 1401 on L to jct with white-blazed *Diamond Valley Trail* at 1.6 mi. Continue on an even grade through mixed hardwoods, spruce, and rhododendron; occasionally go in and out of small coves to jct with *Hickory Branch Trail* at 3 mi. (*Hickory Branch Trail* is a 1.3-mi connector trail between this point and the *London Bald Trail.*) Cross Matherson Branch at 3.5 mi, and jct with *London Bald Trail* at 4.2 mi. Turn L to the highway, SR 1401, in Junaluska Gap at 4.3 mi. Backtrack or use vehicle switching.

(The *Bartram Trail* sign at the Gap does not indicate where the *Bartram Trail* is currently located. Across the highway at Junaluska Gap the *Choga Trail* to Big Choga Creek and the *Tusquitee Loop*

Trail are unmaintained and severely overgrown in sections.) USFS Trail #19.

Diamond Valley Trail   87

Length: 0.9 mi (1.4 km), easy; *USGS:* Topton; *Trailhead:* Apple Tree Trail parking area.

Directions and Description: Follow directions above for *Apple Tree Trail* for 1.4 mi to *Diamond Valley Trail* jct on L. Descend for 0.9 mi, following Diamond Valley Creek to jct with *Junaluska Trail* in clearing at SR 1401 and Dicks Creek. Backtrack, or return L on the *Junaluska Trail* for a loop total of 4.2 mi. USFS Trail #19B.

Laurel Creek Trail   88

Length: 1.5 mi (2.4 km), moderate; *USGS:* Topton; *Trailhead:* Apple Tree Trail parking area.

Directions and Description: This trail is similar to *Diamond Valley Trail*, in that access and exit are dependent on other trails. The total loop, in this example, is 5.2 mi. Follow directions as given above for the *Apple Tree Trail* for 1.1 mi, and then turn R. Descend on a green-blazed trail, first on a slight ridge in hardwoods and then in dense and damp groves of rhododendron, along Piercy Creek to Laurel Branch at 1.5 mi. A loop trail at jct with *Nantahala Trail* R requires another 5.5 mi of more strenuous hiking. USFS Trail #19F.

Nantahala Trail   89

Length: 6.8 mi (10.8 km), strenuous; *USGS:* Topton; *Trailhead:* Apple Tree Trail parking area or camping site C.

Directions and Description: This trail requires either backtracking for a total hike of 13.6 mi, or connecting with other trails such as *Apple Tree Trail* and *London Bald* or *Laurel Creek Trails*. If *Apple Tree Trail* is used, follow directions as given above and turn R on blue-blazed *London Bald Trail*. Follow for 2.2 mi to Southerland Gap — the beginning or end of the *Nantahala Trail*. Descend on old road to *Laurel Creek Trail* at 5.7 mi. Continue through large stand of white pine, turn R, cross Pierce Creek and follow old FS roads, most of which have been seeded. Care must be used in turning at double blazes, since summer overgrowth can be dense. At 8.9 mi turn R, go up ravine, and cross ridge at 9.2 mi. At 9.5 mi take sharp L downstream on road near the Nantahala River. At 11 mi reach another road and turn sharp L. Gate is at 11.1 mi; exit between campsite B and C at 11.2 mi. (*Laurel Creek Trail* reduces the distance, but part of the Nantahala has to be backtracked.) USFS Trail #19G.

London Bald Trail   90

Length: 6.6 mi (10.6 km), strenuous; *USGS:* Topton; *Trailhead:* Junaluska Gap parking area.

Directions and Description: This trail requires either backtracking for a total hike of 13.2 mi, connecting with other trails for longer loop, or using longer trail connections with vehicle switching. Begin at Junaluska Gap sign and follow blue-blazed trail L from *Junaluska Trail,* ascending along ridge before bearing L and up Pine Branch. After crossing Pine Branch continue to ascend and skirt E boundary of Cherokee-Macon County line. Reach jct with *Apple Tree Trail* at 4.4 mi. (*Apple Tree Trail* descends R for 2.2 mi to campground.) Continue on blue-blazed trail, descending and skirting E side of ridges to Southerland Gap at 6.6 mi. Backtrack or take the *Nantahala Trail* R for another 6.8 mi to campground. USFS Trail #19C.

Standing Indian Area, Macon County

Standing Indian Campground

Standing Indian Campground, a Forest Service facility, has camping and picnic sites which are open all year. Reservations are not required and space is provided on a first come, first served basis. Permits are required for cutting dead firewood, and licenses are necessary for fishing and hunting. Water and sanitary facilities are provided, but there are no showers. A special parking area — Backcountry Information Center — for hikers and backpackers has been constructed on the L fork from the entrance gate. If campground is filled, and it often is, one of the nearest campgrounds is the Kountry Kampground, Route 2, Box 355, Franklin, NC 28734. Tel: 704-524-4339. At jct of US 64-441 S of Franklin, go S on US 441 for 2 mi. Open April 15-October 31. Full svc, no rec.

The Cherokee Indian legend of Standing Indian Mountain says that a Cherokee warrior was posted on the mountaintop to warn the tribe of impending danger from an evil winged monster which had carried off a village child. Beseeching the Great Spirit to destroy the monster, the tribe was rewarded with a thunderstorm of awesome fury that destroyed the beast, shattered the mountain top to bald rubble, and turned the warrior into a stone effigy, the "standing Indian," in the process.

Forest vegetation in the area includes oaks, maple, pines, hemlock, poplar, birch, beech, rhododendron, locust, hickory, basswood, wild cherry, mountain laurel, sassafras, azaleas, berries, and an abundant list of wildflowers, ferns, and mosses. Wildlife includes deer, bear, turkey, grouse, fox, raccoon, and a wide range of songbirds.

Bearpen Gap Trail   91

Length: 4 mi rt (6.4 km), strenuous; *USGS:* Rainbow Springs, Prentiss; *Trailhead:* Parking area at Bearpen Creek.

Directions and Description: From the Backcountry Information parking area on FSR 67-2 go 3.5 mi to the Bearpen Creek parking area. Ascend and curve R around the ridge to cascading Bearpen Creek, leaving it after 1 mi, but returning for a number of crossings before reaching FSR 83 (Ball Creek Rd) W of Bearpen Gap. (A 0.4-mi spur trail L leads steeply to Albert Mtn firetower [5,250 ft], with sweeping views.) Elev gain, 1,690 ft. Backtrack, or follow the *Appalachian Trail* L for 2.7 mi to *Hurricane Creek Trail,* and to the L; or, go R on the *Appalachian Trail* for 6.3 mi to *Timber Ridge Trail,* and turn R. USFS Trail #22.

Kimsey Creek Trail   92

Length: 7.4 mi rt (11.8 km), moderate; *USGS:* Rainbow Springs; *Trailhead:* Backcountry Information Center.

Directions and Description: From the Backcountry Information parking area follow the blue-blazed trail to the campground, cross bridge, follow *Park Creek Trail* N for 0.1 mi, and turn L at *Kimsey Creek Trail* sign. Skirt E of mtn and follow gradually ascending grade up Kimsey Creek. Three wildlife grazing fields are on this trail. At 2.6 mi pass confluence with Little Kimsey Creek; reach Deep Gap and the *Appalachian Trail* at 3.7 mi. Backtrack, or go L on the *A.T.* for 2.5 mi to return on the *Lower Ridge Trail* to the campground, for a total circuit of 9.7 mi. USFS Trail #23.

Lower Ridge Trail   93

Length: 7 mi rt (11.2 km), strenuous; *USGS:* Rainbow Springs; *Trailhead:* Backcountry Information Center.

Directions and Description: This is a frequently used and exceptionally steep trail. It also has outstanding views of the Nantahala Valley. Begin at the Backcountry Information parking area, follow the blue-blazed trail to the campground, cross bridge, and follow trail sign L between campground and Nantahala River. At 0.6 mi trail ascends steeply on switchbacks and reaches John Gap at 1.6 mi. From John Gap continue ascent on Lower Ridge to W of Frog Mtn, and then on to Frank Gap. Reach Standing Indian (5,499 ft) at 3.5 mi; here there are spectacular views of the Blue Ridge Mtns and the Tallulah River Gorge running into Georgia. Elev gain, 2,099 ft. Backtrack, or loop back to camp on the *Kimsey Creek Trail,* going R on the *A.T.* for 2.5 mi at Deep Gap; or, go L on the *A.T.* for 3.5 mi to *Beech Gap Trail.* Vehicle switching to a parking area on FSR 67-2 would be necessary to accomplish the latter option. USFS Trail #28.

Big Laurel Falls Trail   94

Length: 1 mi rt (1.6 km), easy; *USGS:* Rainbow Springs; *Trailhead:* Mooney Creek parking area.

Directions and Description: From the Backcountry Information parking area, drive up E of the Nantahala River for 5.5 mi to parking area at the confluence of Mooney Creek and Mountainside Branch. (*Timber Ridge Trail* begins here also.) Take the trail to the R on old railroad grade covered with dense rhododendron. Curve L around Scream Ridge and follow to the base of Big Laurel Falls at the confluence of Kilby Creek, Gulf Fork, and Big Laurel Branch at 0.5 mi. Backtrack. USFS Trail #29.

Park Ridge Trail   95

Length: 6.4 mi rt (9.9 km), strenuous; *USGS:* Rainbow Springs; *Trailhead:* Backcountry Information Center.

Directions and Description: From Backcountry Information parking area follow blue blazes across the bridge to *Kimsey Creek Trail* and *Park Creek Trail*. At 0.5 mi turn L and ascend E of Bee Tree Knob at 1 mi. Continue ascent to Park Gap on FSR 71-1 and parking area at 3.2 mi. Backtrack, return on *Park Creek Trail* for 5.1 mi loop, or use vehicle switching. USFS Trail #32.

Park Creek Trail   96

Length: 10.2 mi rt (16.3 km), moderate; *USGS:* Rainbow Springs; *Trailhead:* Backcountry Information Center.

Directions and Description: From Backcountry Information parking area follow the blue blazes across the bridge past *Kimsey Creek Trail* and *Park Ridge Trail* at 0.5 mi. Continue straight downriver to confluence with Park Creek at 1.6 mi. The small dam on the Nantahala River is constructed to permit upstream migration for spawning trout. Follow up cascading Park Creek, with trail flanked by mixed hardwoods and dense rhododendron, ferns, mossy rocks, and profuse wildflowers. At 4.5 mi begin switchbacks on FSR 71-1; reach fork Gap at 5.1 mi. Backtrack, return on *Park Ridge Trail* for a total loop of 8.3 mi, or, return by vehicle switching. USFS Trail #33.

Big Indian Trail and Beech Gap Trail   97-98

Length: 7 mi rt cb (11.2 km), easy to strenuous; *USGS:* Rainbow Springs; *Trailhead:* FSR 67-2.

Directions and Description: From Backcountry Information parking area go 3 mi on FSR 67-2 to parking area, sign for *Big Indian Trail,* and Big Indian Road, FSR 67-A. (This is designated a horse trail, but use by hikers, fishermen, and hunters is allowed.) Begin at the footbridge crossing the Nantahala River and follow Big Indian Creek for 1.5 mi to jct with *Beech Gap Trail.* Reach Kilby Gap at 2.1 mi. Continue ascending steeply through dense rhododendron, mountain laurel, and birch to Beech Gap on the *Appalachian Trail* at 3.5 mi. Backtrack, turning R at the jct of the two trails and hiking out for 0.5 mi to FSR 67-2 for a loop. Or, hike L 2.5 mi on the *A.T.* and turn L on the *Timber Ridge Trail* for 1.8 mi to parking area at Money Creek. (ORV's are allowed on FSR 67-A and it is not recommended that hikers use it for a return loop). USFS Trails #34 and 34-A.

Hurricane Creek Trail   99

Length: 4 mi rt (6.4 km), strenuous; *USGS:* Rainbow Springs, Prentiss; *Trailhead:* Parking area on FSR 67-2.

Directions and Description: From Backcountry Information parking area go 2 mi ahead to blue-blazed sign for trail on L. Trail ascends, on old logging roads, steeply in places. Forest management providing for lumbering, young forest growth, and wildlife grazing is evident on this trail. Reach the *A.T.* at 2 mi. Backtrack; turn L for 2.3-mi loop descent by Long Branch, with another 2.3 mi to Backcountry Information Center; or, go R on the *A.T.* for 1.5 mi for connection with *Bearpen Trail* and turn R. USFS Trail #36.

Long Branch Trail   100

Length: 4.6 mi rt (7.4 km), moderate; *USGS:* Rainbow Springs; *Trailhead:* Backcountry Information Center.

Directions and Description: From the parking area at the Backcountry Information Center go E across the road and climb gradually, R of Long Branch, partly on Blackwell Ridge. Along the ridge are scenic views of the Standing Indian Basin. After 2.3 mi reach the *Appalachian Trail* near Glassmine Gap. Parts of the trail are in open areas set aside for wildlife grazing. Return by the same route, or hike

R on the *A.T.* for 2.3 mi to jct with *Hurricane Creek Trail* and turn R for a loop of 8.6 mi. USFS Trail #86.

Timber Ridge Trail 101

Length: 3.6 mi rt (5.8 km), moderate; *USGS:* Rainbow Springs, Prentiss; *Trailhead:* Mooney Creek parking area.

Directions and Description: From Backcountry Information parking area go up the road, FSR 67-2, for 5.5 mi to Mooney Creek parking area. Begin ascent opposite the *Big Laurel Falls Trail*, passing through stands of birch and rhododendron. On higher elevations of Timber Ridge the vegetation is more open, with a canopy of oaks over fern beds. Reach the *A.T.* at 1.8 mi, 0.5 mi W of Carter Gap. Backtrack; or, make a loop by turning R on the *A.T.* for 2.5 mi and descending R on the *Beech Gap Trail* for 2.5 mi to FSR 67-2 and then proceeding up the road for 0.5 mi to the parking area — a total of 7.4 mi. Another route would be to turn L on the *A.T.* and hike 5.2 mi to Mooney Gap, then turn L on FSR 83, going 0.5 mi to jct of FSR 67-2, turning L and hiking road 1.8 mi down to Mooney Falls, and continuing on 0.7 mi to the parking area for a round trip total of 10 mi. USFS Trail #1314.

Mooney Falls Trail 102

Length: 0.2 mi rt (0.3 km), easy; *USGS:* Prentiss; *Trailhead:* Mooney Falls.

Directions and Description: From Backcountry Information Center go up the road, FSR 67-2, for 5.5 mi to curve at Mooney Creek, turning L up Mooney Creek for 0.7 mi to roadside parking for Mooney Falls. Hike 0.1 mi through a tunnel of rhododendron and mountain laurel under hardwoods to cascading falls. Remains of the American chestnut may be found at the falls, and on the ground wildflowers are prominent. Backtrack.

John Wasilik Memorial Poplar Trail 103

Length: 1.4 mi rt (2.2 km), easy; *USGS:* Rainbow Springs; *Trailhead:* Rock Gap parking area.

Directions and Description: From Wallace Gap on old US 64 go 0.4 mi on the Standing Indian Campground road, FSR 67, to Rock Gap. Follow the trail sign to graded trail through an impressive and significant stand of yellow poplar and cherry. The second largest yellow poplar in the U.S. (25 ft in circumference and 8 ft in diameter) is on this trail. An early Wayah District ranger, John Wasilik, has been remembered by naming the poplar in his honor. Return by the same route to the parking area.

Savannah Ridge Area, Jackson County

Cullowhee Trail   **104**

Length: 5.1 mi (8.2 km), moderate to strenuous; *USGS:* Corbin Knob, Greens Creek, Glenville, Sylva (S); *Trailhead:* Cullowhee Gap.

Directions and Description: Northern access to *Cullowhee Trail* is from jct of NC 107 and SR 1001, Speedwell Road, 1.3 mi SE on NC 107 from main entrance of Western Carolina University. Turn R on SR 1001 and go 6.4 mi to Cullowhee Gap (3,720 ft). Park in small area on L of highway. (Southern access to *Cullowhee Trail* is from jct of US 64-NC 28 and SR 1001, 3.3 mi E on US 64-NC 28 from jct of US 441-23 in Franklin. Turn L on SR 1001 and go 9.7 mi to Cullowhee Gap and park in small area to R of Gap.)

Hike across the highway and climb steps through a white pine stand. Follow graded trail with gradual incline on SE side of Kirby Knob for 0.7 mi to steep switchbacks and vista of Cowee Mtns. Reach ridge crest of Savannah Ridge at 0.9 mi bearing N through hardwoods on even grade except for knobs. Reach Kirby Knob at 1.5 mi, and Sheep Knob at 2.8 mi. Descend through hardwoods to white pine stand near Tatham Creek at 3.9 mi. Bear R and follow seeded FS road downstream; reach the FS gate at 5 mi. Continue on woods road past Buchanan house on L to terminus of trail and end of SR 1309 at 5.1 mi. Backtrack or use vehicle switching.

If vehicle switching, the entrance is on SR 1309 from US 441-23. At jct of US 441-23 and SR 1309 at Tatham Creek Campground (5.2

mi S from jct of US 441-23 and Business 23 Bypass in Sylva, and 11.4 mi N from jct of US 441-23 and US 64-NC 28 in Franklin) go 0.9 mi on SR 1309 to end of road. This is the *Cullowhee Trail* ingress or egress. Do not park at private gated road on R. Instead, request permission from the landowner to the L, Roy Buchanan, for permission to park on the edge of his property.

Support Facilities: Fort Tatham Campground (see above). Full svc, excellent rec fac. Open March 1 through November 10. Address: Route 2, Box 206, Sylva, NC 28779. Tel: 704-586-6662.

Wayah Gap Area, Macon County

A. Rufus Morgan Trail   105

Length: 1 mi rt (1.6 km), moderate; *USGS:* Wayah Bald; *Trailhead:* FSR 388 parking area.

Directions and Description: From US 64 and US 441-23 jct S of Franklin, go W on US 64 for 3.8 mi. Turn R at sign for Wayah Bald, and go 0.2 mi to sign for Lyndon B. Johnson Conservation Center at jct of old US 64 and SR 1310. Turn L and go 4.1 mi to Broadtree Rd, FSR 388, and turn L. Proceed for 2 mi on gravel FSR 388 and park at trail sign on R.

Ascend on switchbacks through open woods of tall poplar, cucumber tree, maple, oak, and birch, with ferns and wildflowers banking the trail. Wildlife, particularly deer, may be seen on this trail. Cross stream at 0.2 mi and reach lower cascades of Left Prong of Rough Fork at 0.4 mi. Continue on trail to base of upper falls at 0.5 mi. Return on the same route.

Shot Pouch Trail   106

This trail is unique in that it runs only 75 yd from the parking area to the *Appalachian Trail* and another 25 yd to a grazing field for wildlife. An excellent connector point for the *A.T.*, the parking area is 0.9 mi from Wayah Gap on the Wayah Bald Rd. Wayah Gap is 9.7 mi from US 64 and US 441-23 jct in S Franklin. It is on US 64 W and SR 1310.

CHAPTER III

PISGAH NATIONAL FOREST

Pisgah National Forest, with 487,000 acres, is the largest of the state's four national forests. Its scattered boundaries encircle four districts — Pisgah Ranger District in Buncombe, Haywood, Henderson, and Transylvania counties; Grandfather Ranger District in Avery, Burke, Caldwell, McDowell, and Watauga counties; Toecane Ranger District in Avery, Buncombe, Madison, Mitchell, and Yancey counties; and, the French Broad Ranger District in Haywood and Madison counties.

The Pisgah is a natural world unto itself, with the Blue Ridge Parkway dividing it, the Appalachian Trail on its border with Tennessee, and such extraordinary natural wonders as the Shining Rock and Linville Gorge Wilderness Areas, Looking Glass Rock, Mt Pisgah, Mt Mitchell, Linville Falls, Bald Mountain, and Roan Mountain.

It is also the site of a number of historic firsts. Gifford Pinchot, hired by George Vanderbilt to manage his vast Biltmore Estate, initiated the first forest management program here in 1892, and six years later, Dr. Carl A. Schenck opened here the first school of forestry, the Biltmore Forest School, in America. The Cradle of Forestry is located in the Pisgah Ranger District, on US 276.

The wilderness areas, watersheds, and streams provide protection for the many species of wildlife common to the Appalachian region. More than two hundred species of plants have been found in the Roan Mountain area alone, and, 39 of 55 species of wild orchids in the state are found in the Pisgah. Dominant trees are the oak, birch, maple, and poplar. Conifers range from the fragrant balsam and red

61

spruce to short leaf pines. Primary among the fish is the brook trout, often stocked in the cascading tributaries.

Pisgah has 21 recreational areas for fishing, picnicking, nature study, hiking, and camping. Some of the areas are designed for primitive camping and have limited facilities to protect the ecology. A directory of these facilities may be requested from one of the addresses below.

For hikers, the Forest Service provides hundreds of miles of trails interconnecting throughout the districts. The design, planning, maintenance, and relocation of the trail system requires considerable manpower, a resource becoming rare and valuable. Outdoor sports authorities estimate that 48,000,000 Americans will be hiking or backpacking this year (1981) in recreational areas and forests. With Forest Service programs already understaffed and recreation budget cuts planned on the federal level, the future of the trail system should concern every hiker. More volunteer trail workers will continue to be essential.

If some hikers' favorite trails are omitted from this book, it is because the USFS is closing some and relocating and combining others; some are lumbering or sportsmen's trails that have become overgrown.

Functioning under the supervision of the U.S. Department of Agriculture, the Forest Service maintains the following district offices in the Pisgah National Forest:

Pisgah Ranger District, USFS, P.O. Box 8, Pisgah Forest, NC 28768. Tel: 704-877-3265. Two miles N of Brevard on US 276 W.

Grandfather Ranger District, USFS, P.O. Box 519, Marion, NC 28752. Tel: 704-652-4841. Downtown in the Library Building, corner of West Court and Logan Streets.

Toecane Ranger District, USFS, P.O. Box 128, Burnsville, NC 28714. Tel: 704-682-6146. On US 19 Bypass in Burnsville.

French Broad Ranger District, USFS, P.O. Box 128, Hot Springs, NC 28743. Tel: 704-622-3202. One-half mi W of Hot Springs on US 26.

The USFS Supervisor's Office for North Carolina is located at P.O. Box 2750, Asheville, NC 28802. Tel: 704-258-2850. Fifty South French Broad Ave in Asheville.

SECTION I

FRENCH BROAD RANGER DISTRICT

Hot Springs Area, Marshall County

Rocky Bluff Recreation Area

The Rocky Bluff Recreation Area provides camping, picnicking, hiking, nature study, and fishing in Spring Creek. On a high ridge under tall white pines and oaks, the campground is 3.3 mi S from Hot Springs on NC 209. Visitors from the Waynesville area should take NC 209 N from I-40 through the communities of Trust and Luck. Campground has flush toilets and lavatories, but no showers.

Spring Creek Nature Trail   107

Length: 1.6 mi (2.6 km), easy; *USGS:* Spring Creek; *Trailhead:* Center of Rocky Bluff campground.

Directions and Description: From the S edge of the center of the campground descend gradually, following the trail R at all forks for 0.5 mi until the second vista at Spring Creek near large rock formation is reached. Turn L for 65 yd and then turn R to follow well graded and scenic trail around the mtn on the L side of the cascading creek. At 1.2 mi turn L and begin ascent on old road to the campground. Some of the vegetation on the trail is white pine, oak, sycamore, spruce, fetterbush, moose wood, basswood, maple, partridgeberry, liverwort, and abundant wildflowers.

Van Cliff Trail   108

Length: 2.7 mi (4.3 km), strenuous; *USGS:* Spring Creek; *Trailhead:* Center of Rocky Bluff campground.

Directions and Description: From the S edge of the center of the campground follow old seeded road on blue-blazed trail to fork at 0.1 mi. Turn R over rocky treadway of poison ivy and climb to NC

209 at 0.3 mi. Turn L on highway for 50 yd and go R on old road. Ascend, sometimes steeply, on R of cascading Long Mtn Branch. At 0.7 mi turn sharply over L over the branch and follow another old road, hiking N side of ridge. Forest trees consist of white pine, spruce, basswood, oak, and hickory. Parts of the trail have running cedar, cancer root, Indian pipe, sunflowers, and nettles. Make sharp L over stream in a cove at 0.9 mi. Reach the top of a ridge at 1.3 mi, and begin descent into rocky ravine at 1.6 mi. Follow old road and switchbacks to NC 209 at 2.2 mi. Cross highway and descend steeply, turn sharp R among boulders at 2.4 mi, cross Long Mtn Branch at 2.5 mi, and return to campground at 2.7 mi. (This trail is also known as the *Long Mtn Branch Trail*.)

Big Laurel Creek Trail   109

Length: 6 mi rt (9.6 km), easy; *USGS:* Hot Springs; *Trailhead:* Parking area at jct of US 25-70 and NC 208.

Directions and Description: Park in the parking area on E side of Big Laurel (1,600 ft). Enter on private gravel road, descending slightly, bearing R to fork for 0.1 mi. Arrive at private dwelling and gate at 0.2 mi. Follow old railroad grade with vertical cliffs on L and whitewater rapids on R. Pass spring at 0.4 mi on L and a burley tobacco barn on L at 0.7 mi; cross the Pisgah National Forest boundary at 0.9 mi. On a trail of unsurpassed beauty, pass rapids at 1.2 mi. Turn L at 2.9 mi to Runion, an old logging and mining settlement. Reach the railroad and French Broad River at 3 mi. Backtrack.

In the spring and summer of 1977 and 1978, the North Carolina Natural Heritage Program of the Department of Natural Resources and Community Development, Division of Parks and Recreation, made a botanical study of this 3-mi trail. The discovery of over 250 species of vascular plants was an overwhelming surprise. Five species listed as threatened or endangered were found. A few of the trees and flowering plants are silverbell, hemlock, birch, oak, elm, alder, poplar, sweet shrub, Dutchman's pipe, bluebells, orchids, ferns, spring beauty, trillium, soapwort, and chicory.

Bringham Hollow Trail   110

Length: 2.4 mi rt (3.9 km), strenuous; *USGS:* Hot Spring (NC-TN); *Trailhead:* Gosnell residence on SR 1306.

Directions and Description: From US 25-70 and NC 208, go 5 mi on NC 208 to SR 1306. Turn L on cement bridge over Little Laurel Creek, with Bringman chapel on R after crossing. Go 0.7 mi to end of the road at the Gosnell residence. Request permission to park. Hike up road by barn, grain, and hay fields to NW corner of pasture. Enter forest at 0.4 mi on faint road, cross fence, and begin a difficult climb on a primitive, unmarked, and unmaintained road bed of hummocks, loose rocks, and nettles. At 0.7 mi climb up embankment on R near Deep Creek. For the next 0.3 mi the old road has been washed out under dense rhododendron and considerable gymnastic ability is required to rock-hop through. Stay with the main stream all the way up the ravine. At 1 mi, and out of the rhododendron thicket, begin to climb L slope up ridge away from the creek bed, which may be dry in places. Reach Deep Gap, also called Little Paint Gap, at 1.2 mi; here is the jct with the *Appalachian Trail* and *Little Paint Creek Trail*. Return by the same route, or take the *A.T.* for 2 mi N to Allen Gap where vehicle switching will be necessary. USFS Trail #298.

Jack Branch Trail   112

Length: 5 mi rt (8 km), moderate; *USGS:* Hot Springs; *Trailhead:* Parking area on the French Broad River at Jack Branch.

Directions and Description: From US 25-70 at the N end of the French Broad River bridge in Hot Springs, turn on Paint Rock Road. Follow downriver for 4.1 mi to end of pavement, and then continue for another 0.3 mi. Park on L by the river, across from Bartley Island.

Enter trail near sign, following unmarked trail on old road in deep ravine up E slope and away from Jack Branch at 0.1 mi. Forest contains poplar, spruce, sycamore, birch, maple, and oak, with rhododendron, fetterbush, and buffalo nut in lower areas, and pines, chestnut oak, and mountain laurel in upper areas. At 0.4 mi leave the rhododendron patches and enter open woods of hickory and poplar. Reach crest of ridge at 0.5 mi, following the crest through large patches of wintergreen and trailing arbutus. In a generally dry area blueberries and azaleas grow. At 0.9 mi turn NW, following slight upgrade in and out of coves to 1.9 mi. Begin ascent NE to Tennessee boundary line, reaching a gentle gap at 2.5 mi. Backtrack. (Primitive trails lead L for 1.9 mi to Bearpen Gap and *Ricker Branch Trail*, and R for 3.5 mi to Rich Mtn Lookout Tower) Elev change, 1,400 ft. USFS Trail #299.

Pump Gap Trail   114

Length: 3 mi rt (4.8 km), moderate; *USGS:* Hot Springs; *Trailhead:* Parking area on Silver Mine Creek.

Directions and Description: From N side of French Broad River bridge on US 25-70 in Hot Springs, curl under the bridge on Lover's Leap Rd for 0.3 mi to USFS boundary gate and parking area on Silver Mine Creek.

Begin hike on old road, crossing Silver Mine Creek a number of times, passing two USFS explosive storage bunkers, and entering narrow blue-blazed trail at 0.4 mi. Vegetation includes poplar, maple, spruce, locust, ironwood, gum, and rhododendron. Stream has moss-covered rocks, cascades, and pools. At 1.1 mi take R fork, cross stream, and begin steep ascent in a vale. Reach *Appalachian Trail* in Pump Gap at 1.5 mi. Backtrack, or make a loop by following the *A.T.* to the R for 2.5 mi to point of origin at USFS gate.

This section of the *A.T.* has astonishing views of the French Broad River from craggy overlooks 500 to 1,000 ft high. Lover's Leap Rock is 0.6 mi from trailhead. *Pump Gap Trail* extends beyond the *A.T.* jct, descending by faint blue blazes for 0.6 mi to fork. L fork curls up for another 0.6 mi to peak and a USFS road. If R fork, an unmarked and overgrown trail, is taken, the hiker can follow an old roadbed to the confluence of the Big Laurel River and the French Broad River at 1.3 mi from Pump Gap. Options here are to return on the same route, follow railroad down the river for 3 mi to Hot Springs, or go up the French Broad River on the railroad for 0.5 mi to the *Big Laurel River Trail*. The latter route runs 3 mi up a gentle grade to Hurricane at US 25-70. Vehicle switching necessary. USFS Trail #309.

Support Facilities: The commercial campground nearest to the Hot Springs area is Stone Mountain Campground, Del Rio, TN 37727. Tel: 615-623-3509. Full svc.

Camp Creek Bald Area, Marshall County

Fork Ridge Trail   115

Length: 4 mi rt (6.4 km), strenuous; *USGS:* Greystone; *Trail-head:* Parking area by Big Creek on FSR 111.

Directions and Description: This trail is also known as *Big Creek Trail.* From jct of US 25-70 and NC 208, follow NC 208 up Big Laurel Creek for 3.5 mi to jct with NC 212 at Belva. Turn R on NC 212 and proceed for 10.7 mi to SR 1312, which forks L at Carmen. Follow SR 1312 for 0.7 mi to where pavement ends at a fire warden station. Continue for another 0.6 mi on a gravel road and enter Pisgah National Forest; road is now FSR 111. After 1 mi more reach parking area on L at Wildcat Hollow Creek and Big Creek.

Trail begins by sign on R side of parking area, ascending gradu-ally on well graded slope, running E of Fork Ridge. Reach ridge crest at 0.7 mi. Forest flora consists of hickory, oak, maple, poplar, basswood, and birch. The lower elevation understory has rosebay rhododendron and buckeye, while at higher elevations there are laurel, flame azalea, and copious patches of large, sweet, high bush blueberries. Spots of wintergreen, dwarf iris, and galax furnish groundcover. Wildlife consists chiefly of bear, deer, turkey, and grouse. After reaching a sag at 0.9 mi, ascend steadily, sometimes steeply, on switchbacks to jct with the *Appalachian Trail* at 2 mi. Return. (For another route, follow the *A.T.* for 8.6 mi R to Devil Fork Gap on NC 212, where vehicle switching would be necessary. Two shelters, Jerry Cabin near the Fork Ridge Trail jct, and Locust Ridge Lean-to to the N at 6.9 mi are on the *A.T.* The S route on the *A.T.* runs 11.4 mi to Allen Gap, NC 208.) Elev change 1,400 ft. USFS Trail #285.

Green Ridge Trail   116

Length: 3.9 mi (6.2 km), strenuous; *USGS:* Greystone, Flag Pond (NC-TN); *Trailhead:* USFS boundary at Dry Creek on SR 1312.

Directions and Description: From jct of NC 208 and 212 at Belva, turn on NC 212 and proceed 10.7 mi to Carmen Church of God at fork of NC 212 and SR 1312. Turn L at fork and go 1.3 mi to Shelton Sawmill on R. Park on R in small area on old road beside Dry Creek.

Follow old road up R side of creek, crossing creek repeatedly. At 0.5 mi bear R at fork of old roads. Forest vegetation is ironwood, poplar, white pine, spruce, oak, and birch. Both spring and summer wildflowers are exceptionally profuse and include starry campion, beebalm, trillium, orchids, twisted-stalk, hellebore, meadow rue, Indian-physic, and phlox. Forest animals include bear, bobcat, game fowl such as wild turkey and grouse, and among the reptiles, the deadly timber rattler. Creek goes underground in places, appearing dry; thus its name. At 1.4 mi old road ends and trail begins across the creek. Cross small cove streams in curve of switchbacks at 1.7 and 1.8 mi. Waterfalls is at 1.9 mi on R. Continue to ascend on well graded trail, often overgrown in summer with nettles, to Green Ridge and the *A.T.* at 3.9 mi. It is 2.8 mi R to Locust Ridge Lean-to on the *A.T.* and 4.2 mi to Devil Fork Gap on NC 212. Elev change, 2,420 ft. USFS Trail #287.

Golden Ridge Trail   117

Length: 2.4 mi (3.8 km), strenuous; *USGS:* Hot Springs; *Trailhead:* At Spaulding house on NC 208.

Directions and Description: From jct of US 25-70 and NC 208, turn on NC 208 and go 4.4 mi to private driveway on L. Cross wooden bridge over Little Laurel Creek, pass first house on R, and stop at second house, the Spaulding residence. Request permission to park.

Follow logging road R of old barn and chickenhouse up to another barn at 0.2 mi. Since original trail is overgrown, cross field toward logging road. Pass through summer vegetation with berries, cone flower, and rampant love vine. Ascend steeply, extreme grade in one spot. Reach crest of ridge at 0.4 mi and turn L to red marker indicating NF boundary. Forest vegetation includes oak, holly, white pine, maple, Virginia pine, and hickory. Ground covers include wintergreen, partridgeberry, and galax. Continue along center of ridge, gradually climbing to 1.4 mi. Cross a shallow gap, ascend to peak, and descend to wide gap at 2 mi. Ascend to Spring Mtn and jct with *A.T.* at 2.4 mi. Return by the same route or take the *A.T.* (*A.T.* R runs 3.4 mi to Allen Gap and NC 208. L it is 0.2 mi to Spring Mtn Lean-to, and 1.9 mi to Rich Mtn FS road.) Elev change, 1,960 ft. USFS Trail #291.

White Oak Trail   118

Length: 2.4 mi rt (3.8 km), moderate; *USGS:* Greystone (NC-TN); *Trailhead:* Big Rocky Branch picnic area.

Directions and Description: This trail is easily confused with *White Oak Flats Trail* on Whiteoak Flats, a few miles NE. At jct of NC 212 and NC 208, go 6.8 mi NE on NC 212 to Hickey Fork Rd, SR 1310, and turn L. Go on gravel road for 0.7 mi, pass commerical trout farm, enter NF at 1.1 mi, cross bridge of East Prong Creek at 1.4 mi, and arrive at Big Rocky Branch parking and picnic area at 2.5 mi.

Trail begins on old road in parking area, following up L side of Hickey Fork stream for 0.8 mi to horseshoe curve. At beginning of the curve the trail ascends L on slope opposite a large stand of poplar in the cove. (Road R forks, with the first fork ending at 0.4 mi and the other one to the R ending at 0.4 mi.) Follow upslope to switchbacks on E of ridge. Ascend to crest of ridge at 1.2 mi. Beyond this point trail is overgrown and passage to *Pounding Mill Trail* on Seng Ridge will be difficult. Backtrack. Trail area shows evidence of motorcycle use near Hickey Fork. USFS Trail #293.

Pounding Mill Trail   119

Length: 9.6 mi rt (15.4 km), strenuous; *USGS:* Hot Springs, Greystone, White Rock; *Trailhead:* Confluence of Pounding Mill Branch and Little Laurel Creek.

Directions and Description: From jct of US 25-70 and NC 208, take NC 208 for 7.2 mi to bridge over Little Laurel Creek. Sixty yd beyond is USFS gated and seeded road on R. The space for parking is small. If space is passed, turn around at the Gulf Svc Sta on the R around the curve. Hike back across the bridge to a numbered electricity pole (3/41), descend from highway bank, cross creek at 0.1 mi, and cross the Pounding Mill Branch at 0.2 mi. Area is filled with trees and rhododendron, hiding the stream confluence. Wild-flowers, including buttercups, blood root, trillium, and water leaf, are prominent near the stream head. Follow upstream for 2.6 mi to Pounding Mill Gap. (*Angelico Knob Trail* leads R, to old road which connects with Duckmill Creek.) Continue ahead to Seng Gap at 3.3 mi, where faint trail, *Hickey Fork Trail* (USFS Trail #292), leads R. Ascend and descend two knobs, reaching faint sign of *White Oak Trail* at 4.1 mi on R. Continue straight on Seng Ridge and at 4.8 mi reach jct with the *Appalachian Trail* SW of the Camp Creek Bald Lookout Tower (4,844 ft). (Spur to R leads 0.2 mi to firetower for impressive views of Smokies.) Backtrack or use the *A.T.* for loop possibilities. On the *A.T.* it is 5.9 mi S to Allen Gap and NC 208; and, it is 13.1 mi N to Devil Fork Gap and NC 212. Parts of the *Pounding Mill Trail* may have heavy overgrowth. Elev change, 2,764 ft. USFS Trail #297.

Harmon Den Area, Haywood County

Groundhog Creek Trail and Rube Rock Trail   121-122

Length: 5 mi rt (8 km), moderate; *USGS:* Waterville; *Trailhead:* Parking area on N side of I-40 in Big Bend.

Directions and Description: On I-40, 5.9 mi W from Welcome Center and Rest Area (0.5 mi before I-40 tunnel and 4.7 mi from Tennessee-North Carolina state line), park at parking space by locked gate on R.

Hike 0.2 mi up USFS road loop and look for blue-blazed trail on R. Follow through poplar, spruce, hickory, pine, maple, and birch in a ravine. Reach ridge crest at 0.4 mi, and jct with *Rube Rock Trail* on R at 0.5 mi. (*Rube Rock Trail* runs approximately 3.5 mi to the *Appalachian Trail* near Brown Gap. It skirts Hickory Ridge to cross Rube Rock Branch and at 1 mi, then turns NE on L of Tom Hall

Branch. At 2.9 mi it reaches the first of a number of knobs on Harmon Den Mountain. It must be backtracked, or use an access route from the *Appalachian Trail*, either to join the *Groundhog Creek Trail* at 2.3 mi L, or go 3 mi R to Max Patch Road.)

Turn L on old railroad grade up Groundhog Creek. At 1.3 mi cross Chestnut Orchard Branch, followed by Ephraim Branch. At 2.3 mi reach Groundhog Creek Shelter, a stone shelter with five bunks. A spring is nearby. Continue ahead for 0.2 mi more to reach the *Appalachian Trail* at Deep Gap, also called Groundhog Creek Gap. (It is 5.6 mi NE to Max Patch Rd, NC 1182, and 7.8 mi SW to Pigeon River and I-40.) USFS Trail #315.

Hurricane Creek Trail   123

Length: 12.2 mi rt (!9.2 km), moderate; *USGS:* Lemon Gap, Fines Creek; *Trailhead:* I-40 at Hurricane Creek, FSR 233.

Directions and Description: On I-40 from the Welcome Center and Rest Area, go W for 2.6 mi to Hurricane Creek and park near driveway, using care not to block vehicular entrance.

Hike 0.7 mi to private homes on R; the L side is the Harmon Den Wildlife Management Area boundary line. Continue on road, which becomes more of a jeep road, with a few mudholes and numerous creek fordings. Forest vegetation is low elevation southern Appalachian hardwoods, white pine, and hemlock. At 2.5 mi enter a grazing meadow; cross for 0.1 mi and reach another grazing meadow at 3 mi cross for 0.2 mi. At 3.5 mi pass an abandoned house on R; continue upstream over increasingly difficult jeep road, which is, however, ideal for backpackers and horseback riders. Wildflowers are profuse on this old road and wild grapes are found by the meadow brooks, which are stocked with trout. Bear, bobcat, deer, raccoon, and smaller mammals are in the wildlife area. Continue on gradual incline to Meadow Fork Gap at 6.1 mi; reach jct with Max Patch Road. Return by the same route or use one of the three other access routes from the crossroads. One runs R on SR 1182 in Madison County, becoming SR 1334 in Haywood County, to Fines Creek at 7.5 mi. From there it is 3.8 mi to I-40 on SR 1338. Another route goes NW for 3.6 mi on Meadow Fork Road, SR 1175, to fork over bridge and then proceeds 2 mi to NC 209. The NW route follows Max Patch Road, SR 1182, for 3.3 mi to FSR 148 in Harmon Den at Little Creek Gap, and then proceeds 1.6 mi more to the Tennessee state line at Max Patch. Hurricane Creek Road is also known as Haynes Creek Road, FSR 233.

SECTION II

GRANDFATHER RANGER DISTRICT

Curtis Creek Area, McDowell County

Young's Ridge Trail   124

Length: 4.4 mi (7 km), moderate; *USGS:* Marion, Black Mtn; *Trailhead:* Old Fort Picnic Area (or SR 1400 Parking Overlook in Ridgecrest).

Directions and Description: (This trail includes the former *Kitsuma Peak Trail* [USFS Trails #205 and 276].) From Old Fort take old SR 10 for 5 mi to Old Fort Picnic Area on L.

Park and follow trail upstream on the L through a ravine dark with heavy hemlock shade. (On the R there is a 0.5-mi loop trail near the Swannanoa River.) Goats beard grows on the damp banks. Following switchbacks reach top of ridge at 0.9 mi. Turn R, and continue W up and down knobs to Kitsuma Peak (3,195 ft) at 3.4 mi. Views of Greybeard Mtn and Mt Mitchell Wildlife Management Area are impressive. Descend on switchbacks to open lane by fence of I-40, and FS boundary line, at 4.2 mi. At 4.4 mi reach SR 1400 Parking Overlook at Ridgecrest. (Overlook gate closes at 8 PM. Check with Blue Ridge Baptist Conference Center across the street for information on parking.) Elev gain, 1,565 ft. Vehicle switching necessary, or backtrack. USFS Trail #206.

Mackey Mountain Trail   125

Length: 8 mi (12.8 km), moderate; *USGS:* Marion (W); *Trailhead:* Jct of Curtis Creek Rd and Sugar Cove Rd.

Directions and Description: (This trail is to be combined with *Mackey Creek Trail* [USFS Trail #215] for a total trip of 14 mi. Inquire at Ranger office for information.) From Old Fort go 1 mi E on US 70 to Curtis Creek Rd, SR 1227, and turn L. Follow road 4 mi to R on FSR 482. Go 5 mi on this road to jct with FSR 1188, Sugar Cove Rd.

Trailhead is on R. Camping is allowed along this trail, but water may be infrequent. Begin on old logging road going through oaks, maples, and laurels; follow a bear sanctuary boundary line marked with orange blazes for 5 mi. Bears or evidence of them may be seen. Follow ridge and decend steeply to Clear Creek Rd, SR 1422. In descent, motorcycle trails may cause confusion. Elev change, 1,700 ft. Vehicle switching necessary. (At the Curtis Creek Primitive Campground the *Hickory Branch Trail* [USFS Trail #213] is being developed for a distance of 2 mi. It will follow Hickory Branch part of the way.) USFS Trail #216.

Buck Creek Area, McDowell County

Woods Mtn Trail   126

Length: 13 mi rt (20.8 km), moderate; *USGS:* Celo, Little Switzerland; *Trailhead:* Hazelwood Gap on the Blue Ridge Parkway svc rd near mp 344.

Directions and Description: From Buck Creek Gap at jct of NC 80 and the Blue Ridge Parkway, mp 344.1, follow sign up svc rd parallel with Parkway for 0.7 mi to Hazelwood Gap.

Turn R on trail, opposite large oak, and skirt S side of knob. At 0.9 mi ridge becomes a narrow spine covered with blueberries, turkey grass, laurel, and chinquapins. Dominant trees on the trail at this point are oaks and pitch pine. Scenic views of Table Rock, Hawksbill, and Armstrong Valley are found at 1.3 mi and 3.6 mi. Other views along the ridge include Mackey Mtn, Mt Mitchell, and Lake Tahoma. A number of unmarked spur trails, most of which deadend, exist along the ridge. (The USFS is considering incorporating *Betsey's Ridge Trail* and the connecting section of *Little*

Buck Creek Trail to *Woods Mtn Trail*. Also, a trail to connect the eastern terminus of *Woods Mtn Trail* to FSR 469 is proposed by the USFS.) At 6.2 mi pass jct with *Little Buck Creek Trail*, and reach dismantled lookout tower site (3,646 ft) at 6.5 mi. Backtrack, or use *Little Buck Creek Trail* (USFS Trail #219) down the mtn to FSR 470. (Another way out is to backtrack for 2.2 mi on the *Woods Mtn Trail* to the jct, R with *Bad Fork Trail* [USFS Trail #227], a primitive, rarely used, 4-mi trail down the N side of the Woods Mtn range to the Armstrong Fish Hatchery. Road access to the Hatchery is off NC 266-A, between Little Switzerland and Woodlawn on US 221). USFS Trail #218.

Little Buck Creek 129

Length: 5.8 mi rt (9.3 km), strenuous, *USGS:* Little Switzerland, Marion; *Trailhead:* Little Buck Creek Rd.

Directions and Description: At jct of US 70 and NC 80 (NW of Marion), go 4 mi N on NC 80 to Lake Tahoma on R. Turn R on Little Buck Creek Rd, SR 1436, and go N for 1.5 mi to FS gate (FSR 470). Park.

Follow old logging road through hemlocks and hardwoods by Firescald Creek for 0.4 mi. At Slim Creek avoid trails to left and turn sharply R, climbing E above the creek. Trail is steep along spur of Betsey Ridge, going L to jct with *Woods Mtn Trail* at 2.9 mi. Camping permitted at jct. At 3.3 mi hike E on Woods Mtn. Peak offers outstanding views of Black Mtn, Marion, and Little Switzerland. Return by the same route. Elev gain, 1,900 ft. USFS Trail #219.

Wilson Creek Area, Burke and Avery Counties

Steel's Creek Trail 130

Length: 8 mi (12.8 km), easy; *USGS:* Chestnut Mtn; *Trailhead:* New Gingercake Rd.

Directions and Description: From NC 181 near Barkhouse Picnic Area, go SW on FSR 496, New Gingercake Rd for 1.5 mi to trailhead on L.

Descend on old logging road among rhododendron slicks to Steel's Creek. Trail crisscrosses the creek and joins Steel's Creek Rd, FSR 228. Turn R from road and exit at NC 181, 0.3 mi N of Pisgah Forest boundary sign. Excellent camping spots on the trail. Descent, 1,100 ft. Vehicular switching is necessary — or, backtrack for 8 mi. USFS Trail #237.

Wilson Creek Trail, Wilson Creek Access Trail, and Wilson Creek Access Trail   131-133

Length: 7.2 mi (11.5 km), moderate; *USGS:* Grandfather Mtn, Chestnut Mtn; *Trailhead:* FSR 45 near Bark Camp Ridge.

Directions and Description: From community of Edgemont near Mortimer Rec Area on NC 90, go N 1.5 mi to Forest boundary and FSR 45. It is 2 mi to *Wilson Creek Access Trail* (USFS Trail #264) on L.

Park and hike 0.8 mi to join the *Wilson Creek Trail*. Since the trail crosses the creek a number of times, wading is necessary. (This is supposed to be among the best trout streams in the state.) After 6.2 mi jct with *Wilson Creek Access Trail* (USFS Trail #258-A) is reached on L. Follow R for 1 mi to FSR 192 on L; follow it for 1.5 mi to FSR 192. Vehicle switching necessary — or, backtrack. Elev gain, 500 ft. USFS Trails #258, 264, and 258-A.

Harper Creek Trail   134

Length: 5 mi (8 km), strenuous; *USGS:* Chestnut Mtn; *Trailhead:* NC 1328 S of Mortimer Rec Area.

Directions and Description: From NC 1328 on Wilson Creek, ascend steeply, pass *Yellow Buck Trail* (USFS Trail #265) on R and *Raider Camp Trail* (USFS Trail #277) on L, and reach Harper Falls at 0.5 mi. Continue upstream to South Harper Creek. From North Harper Creek Falls to South Harper Creek Falls the trail is rough and difficult. From the falls near Kawana the trail begins steeply and then levels out, reaching FSR 58 at 5 mi. Vehicle switching is necessary, or backtrack completely, or take one of the connecting trails. (There is a shorter route using *Raider Camp Trail* [USFS Trail #277] from South Harper Creek Falls. A spectacular view of the

200-ft. falls is found on a short spur of *Raider Camp Trail.* Follow the trail on, rejoining the *Harper Creek Trail,* and proceed to NC 1328). USFS Trail #260.

Lost Cove Trail   137

Length: 7.5 mi (12.2 km), strenuous; *USGS:* Chestnut Mtn; *Trailhead:* Old Game Warden station.

Directions and Description: Take FSR #981 from NC 90 at Edgemont and go up Rockhouse Creek to parking area near jct of FSR 192 near Roseborough and old Game Warden station.

Climb R to crest of Timber Ridge and turn R. *Timber Ridge Trail* (USFS Trail #261) is L, a 1.3 mi connector along the ridge. Follow ridge to top of Bee Mtn. Descend steeply to Lost Cove Creek and parking area at terminus of FSR 464A. For 2.5 mi follow Lost Cove Creek, an excellent trout stream. Keep L at Hunt Fish Falls (USFS Trail #263), a short trail of 0.7 mi ascending to parking area on FSR 464. Continue on even contour to base of Timber Ridge, climb, go R of Timber Ridge Trail, and descend to Gragg Prong Creek. Follow the trail upstream for 1.5 mi by a number of waterfalls, and return to parking area. USFS Trail #262.

Hunt Fish Falls Trail   139

Length: 1.4 mi rt (2.2 km), moderate; *USGS:* Chestnut Mtn; *Trailhead:* FSR 464.

Directions and Description: Near Edgemont on NC 90, take FSR 464 to first parking area. Trail descends by switchbacks to Hunt Fish Falls and reaches jct with *Lost Cove Trail* (USFS Trail #262) at 0.7 mi. Backtrack to origin. USFS Trail #263.

North Harper Creek Trail   140

Length: 6.9 mi (11 km), easy to moderate; *USGS:* Chestnut Mtn; *Trailhead:* On FSR 58 at North Harper Creek.

Directions and Description: Turn R on first gravel road 0.5 mi N of jct of NC 181 and 183. Go 1.3 mi to FSR 464. Long Ridge Church is opposite intersection. Turn R and go 2.3 mi to jct with FSR 58,

Kawana Rd. Take FSR 58 for 0.4 mi, and reach North Harper Creek trailhead on L.

The trail follows the trout stream, crossing it 17 times. Camping sites are found along the stream. End of trail is at jct with *Harper Creek Trail* (USFS Trail #260). If not backtracking the entire 6.9 mi, the shortest way out to a road is to backtrack 0.6 mi, and turn R for 0.8 mi to FSR 464 on Persimmon Ridge (USFS Trail #270). Vehicle switching would be necessary. USFS Trail #266.

Simmons Ridge Trail   143

Length: 4.5 mi (7.2 km), moderate; *USGS:* Chestnut Mtn; *Trailhead:* Near North Harper Creek Camp.

Directions and Description: See directions above to get to FSR 58. Take FSR 58 for 0.8 mi, past *North Harper Creek Trail*, to trailhead on R. Follow old logging road to top of Headquarters Mtn, a climb of 770 ft. Continue on old logging road to gap between North Harper and South Harper Creek watersheds. Cross dirt road, follow part of ridge on old railroad grade to FSR 58 parking area near Kawana. Backtrack, hike FSR 58 back, or employ vehicle switching. USFS Trail #267.

Greentown Trail and Raven Cliff Trail   142-143

Length: 13.2 mi rt (21.2 km), moderate to strenuous; *USGS:* Grandfather Mtn, Chestnut Mtn; *Trailhead:* Near FSR 496 on NC 181.

Directions and Description: From NC 181 near Barkhouse Picnic Area, trail is across the road near FSR 496. Follow old logging road down the ridge to Upper Creek, and then go down the creek for 1.5 mi. Turn L at Burnthouse Branch (*Raven Cliff Trail* [USFS Trail #268A] turns R for 1.2 mi to parking area on FSR 197.) Campsite is found at the head of Burnthouse Branch and trail jct with FSR 198. Cross into Avery County and follow a long ridge to jct with *Raider Camp Trail* (USFS Trail #277), near South Harper Creek Falls, for a total hike of 6.6 mi. Backtrack another 6.6 mi, or take L and go 1.6 mi to parking area on FSR 58 near Kawana. For the latter vehicle switching is required. USFS Trails #268 and 268A.

Upper Creek Falls Trail   144

Length: 1.6 mi rt (2.5 km), moderate; *USGS:* Grandfather Mtn; *Trailhead:* Parking area on NC 181 near Cold Springs.

Directions and Description: From jct of NC 183 and 181, go 4.1 mi down the mountain on NC 181 to parking area on L. Descend on switchbacks through hardwoods and rhododendron to creek. Cross creek; ascend steeply to base of falls at 0.8 mi. Rocks can be slippery. Return by same route. USFS Trail #268B.

Persimmon Ridge Trail   145

Length: 3 mi (4.8 km), moderate to strenuous; *USGS:* Chestnut Mtn; *Trailhead:* FSR 58 near parking area at Kawana.

Directions and Description: From jct of NC 183 and 181, go S on NC 181 for 0.8 mi, turn L on Mortimer Rd, and stay on gravel road for 2.3 mi to FSR 464. Turn R and go 2.3 mi to Kawana Rd, FSR 58. Turn R and go 3.5 mi to trailhead on L.

Climb a short distance to top of Persimmon Ridge (2,785 ft); descend steeply 1.5 mi through hardwoods. At 2 mi cross jct of North Harper Creek and North *Harper Creek Trail.* Ascend steeply for 0.3 mi, and then gradually for 0.5 mi to jct on R with *Yellow Bucks Trail* (USFS Trail #265). Keep L on logging rd to FSR 464 at 3 mi. Backtrack or use vehicle switching. USFS Trail #270.

Big Lost Cove Cliffs Trail   146

Length: 3 mi rt (4.8 km), easy; *USGS:* Chestnut Mtn; *Trailhead:* FSR 464 near North Harper Creek.

Directions and Description: From FSR 464 near North Harper Creek camping area follow old logging road to Big Lost Cove Ridge on generally level contours, and descend to cliff at 1.5 mi. Some of the rock faces can be scaled. View spans 180° and is mainly of Grandfather Mtn. Return by same route. USFS Trail #271.

Little Lost Cove Cliffs Trail   147

Length: 3 mi rt (4.8 km), moderate; *USGS:* Chestnut Mtn; *Trail-head:* FSR 464 near North Harper Creek.

Directions and Description: From FSR 464 jct with FSR 58 near North Harper Creek, go on FSR 464 for 1.6 mi to trailhead on R. Begin trail on old logging road, go through orchard, ascend steeply, enter predominately oak forest, and reach summit of cliffs (3,400 ft). Excellent 360° views and a number of spur trails. Descend to parking area at FSR 464 at 1.5 mi. Return by same route or take FSR 464 route of 1.4 mi to L. USFS Trail #271A.

Raider Camp Trail   148

Length: 7.4 mi rt cb (11.8 km), strenuous; *USGS:* Chestnut Mtn; *Trailhead:* SR 1328 near Mortimer Rec Area.

Directions and Description: To reach this trail, another trail must be used to enter and to exit. Distance could vary from 5.2 mi if going to Kawana parking area at FSR 58, or go the same distance to a campsite area on FSR 198 requiring vehicle switching, or backtrack to SR 1328 for a total hike of 7.4 mi.

On the Wilson Creek Rd (SR 1328), 1 mi S of Mortimer Rec Area, enter on *Harper Creek Trail* (USFS Trail #260), crossing Harper Creek and bearing to the L. *Yellow Bucks Trail* (USFS Trail #265) is to the R. At 1.4 mi reach *Raider Camp Trail;* follow upstream through hemlocks and rhododendron. Pass *Phillips Branch Trail* (USFS Trail #278) on L. Continue ahead, ascending. Reach short spur near South Harper Creek Falls for spectacular view of 200-ft falls over a granite wall. *Greentown Trail* (USFS Trail #268) is L. Descend on switchbacks along main trail to jct with *Harper Creek Trail* (USFS Trail #260) near base of falls. Elev change, 1,000 ft. USFS Trail #277.

Phillips Branch Trail   149

Length: 3 mi (4.8 km), moderate; *USGS:* Chestnut Mtn; *Trailhead:* SR 1328 at Phillips Branch.

Directions and Description: On Wilson Rd, SR 1328, 2 mi S of Mortimer Rec Area, enter on W side of road and go 1 mi up creek, bearing R toward ridge of young timber. *Raider Camp Trail* (USFS Trail #277) jct is at 1.5 mi. Backtrack, or return R on *Raider Camp Trailhead:* Parking area at Lettered Rock Ridge.   79

Trail, joining *Harper Creek Trail* (USFS Trail #260), and return to SR 1328 at 3 mi. USFS Trail #278.

Thorpe Creek-Schoolhouse Ridge Trail   **150**

Length: 5.8 mi (9.3 km), moderate; *USGS:* Chestnut Mtn; *Trailhead:* Mortimer Rec Area.

Directions and Description: At jct of NC 90 and SR 1328, enter Mortimer Rec Area and go to back of campground. Follow trail up Thorpe Creek for 2.4 mi, passing waterfalls and going through forest of birches, hemlock, and rhododendron. Reach headwaters and climb to Wilson Ridge, bearing L through oaks in an open forest. Continue on loop and down Schoolhouse Ridge to campground at 5.8 mi. (A number of trails which connect as short cuts in this loop trail have been made by hikers from the camp.) USFS Trail #279.

Burke County

Linville Gorge Wilderness Area

The Linville Gorge Wilderness Area has 7,600 acres of wild, rugged, and scenic country, which makes it a distinct challenge to the climber, hiker, and camper. Over twelve miles the Linville River's white water cascades in a descent of more than 2,000 feet before it flows into Lake James. The area is named in honor of explorer and naturalist William Linville, who, with his son, was killed by Indians in the Gorge in 1766.

The Gorge is rich in both plant and animal life, which is protected by regulations. Permits are required to use the 25 miles of trails because the demand is greater than the natural area can accommodate. Camping is allowed in designated areas only.

Free entrance permits may be obtained at the District Ranger's Office, P.O. Box 519, Marion, NC 28752, or by phone at 704-652-4841. Permits may also be obtained at the Texaco Station, P.O. Box 68, Linville Falls, NC 28647, or by phone at 704-765-6989. Permits must be in the hiker's possession at all times while in the wilderness zones. Permits are not required for the following trails: *Gingercake, Hawksbill, Table Rock,* and *Shortoff.* Hunting and fishing are permitted under North Carolina Wildlife Resources Commission regulations.

Hawksbill Mtn Trail   151

Length: 0.8 mi rt (2.2 km), moderate; *USGS:* Linville Falls;

Directions and Description: At jct of NC 183 and 181 near Blue Ridge Parkway, go S on NC 181 for 3 mi to FSR 210 (also known as Old Gingercake Acres Rd, SR 1265), and turn R. Turn L at first fork. At 2.1 mi reach *Devil's Hole Trail* parking area. Go 1.3 mi farther and park on L; trail is on R. Ascend steeply on Lettered Rock Ridge through laurel, turkey grass, and bristly locust to rough rock formation at the summit (4,030 ft). Excellent views into the Gorge. Return by same route. USFS Trail #217.

Spence Ridge Trail   152

Length: 3.4 mi rt (5.4 km), strenuous; *USGS:* Linville Falls; *Trailhead:* Parking area on R at Spence Ridge.

Directions and Description: See above, but go 1 mi farther on FSR 210 from *Hawksbill Mtn Trail.* Park on side road at R. *Spence Ridge Trail* descends steeply with some switchbacks for 1.7 mi to the Linville River. Return by the same route or cross the River and connect with the *Linville Gorge Trail* (USFS Trail #231). A permit is required for this trail. Elev descent, 700 ft. USFS Trail #233.

Table Rock Trail   153

Length: 1.6 mi rt (2.6 km), moderate; *USGS:* Linville Falls; *Trailhead:* Parking area at Table Rock.

Directions and Description: See above, but go 1.1 mi farther on FSR 210 from Spence Ridge to FSR 210B. The North Carolina Outward Bound School is located nearby on the R. Keep R after 0.5 mi turn R on FSR 99. Ascend steeply to the Table Rock parking area.

Hike N on designated trail for 0.8 mi, ascending on switchbacks, rocky in places, to the bald summit and to a lookout tower (3,909 ft). Views are outstanding in every direction, particularly into the Gorge and toward the Piedmont. Return by the same route. The *North Table Rock Trail* connects with this trail, and it is 2 mi N to jct with *Spence Ridge Trail* and FSR 210. USFS Trail #242.

Shortoff Mtn Trail   155

Length: 9.4 mi rt (15 km), moderate; *USGS:* Ashford, Linville Falls; *Trailhead:* Parking area and picnic grounds at Table Rock.

Directions and Description: From the parking area at Table Rock, following trail sign, descend W and then turn S to ridge — narrow in places — and reach the Chimneys (3,557 ft) at 1.2 mi. The area is a mixture of spires, overhanging cliffs, fissures, and 600-ft precipices. Continue on ridge and descend gradually to Chimney Gap (2,509 ft). Ascend gradually to 3,000 ft, and follow generally even contours to Shortoff Mtn at 4.7 mi. Return by same route. (Poisonous snakes in the Linville Wilderness are the copperhead and timber rattler.) USFS Trail #235.

Pine Gap Trail and Bynum Bluff Trail   156-157

Length: 2.6 mi rt cb (4.2 km), strenuous; *USGS:* Linville Falls; *Trailhead:* Parking area at Pine Gap Trail entrance.

Directions and Description: USFS permit required for these trails.

At jct of US 221 and NC 183 in Linville Falls, go E 0.8 mi on NC 183 to jct with SR 1238 (Kistler Memorial Highway) and turn R. Go 0.9 mi to Pine Gap parking area on L.

Descend on steep wall of Linville Gorge to jct of *Bynum Bluff Trail* (USFS Trail #241) at 1 mi. Turn R and ascend, steeply at first and then more gradually, to SR 1238 parking area. Return on gravel road to origin at 2.6 mi. USFS Trails #247 and 241.

Babel Tower Trail   158

Length: 2.4 mi rt (3.8 km), strenuous; *USGS:* Linville Falls; *Trailhead:* Parking area at Babel Tower Trail entrance.

Directions and Description: USFS permit required for this trail.
At jct of NC 183 and SR 1238, go S 2.7 mi on gravel road, SR 1238, to *Babel Tower Trail* parking area on L.

Descend on switchbacks, but generally on crest of ridge, through hardwoods, heather, rhododendron, and leucothoe to cliff overlooking a horseshoe bend in the roaring Linville River at 1.2 mi. Elev descent, 920 ft. Return by the same route for 2.4 mi; or, hike up river to *Pine Gap Trail* at 2.5 mi for exit trail from *Linville Gorge Trail;* or, go down river to *Conley Cove Trail* at 3.6 mi for exit trail from *Linville Gorge Trail.* (The latter route is a loop, including hiking on SR 1238, of 8.7 mi.) USFS Trail #240.

Conley Cove Trail   159

Length: 2.8 mi rt (4.5 km), strenuous; *USGS:* Ashford, Linville Falls; *Trailhead:* Parking area at Conley Cove Trail entrance.
Directions and Description: USFS permit required for this trail.
From jct of NC 183 and SR 1238, go S 5.2 mi on gravel road, SR 1238, to *Conley Cove Trail* parking area on L.

Descend on switchbacks, then pass cave and water supply at 0.4 mi. Trail is well graded and nicely designed through a forest of oak, pine, cucumber trees, silverbell, and wildflowers. Reach jct with *Linville Gorge Trail* at 1.4 mi. Elev descent, 1,000 ft. Return by same route. A longer hike can be made up or down river. If going down river, the exit at *Pinch In Trail* (USFS Trail #228) is steep, primitive, and includes a climb out of 1,800 ft. Topo maps are recommended if one uses the Gorge Trails. USFS Trail #229.

Linville Gorge Trail   160

Length: 13.2 mi cb (21.1 km), strenuous; *USGS:* Ashford, Linville Falls; *Trailhead:* Parking area at Pine Gap parking entrance.
Directions and Description: USFS permit required for this trail.
From jct of NC 183 and SR 1238, go S 0.9 mi on gravel road, SR 1238, to Pine Gap parking entrance on L.

Descend to cliffside of Gorge near the river and jct with *Bynum Bluff Trail* at 1 mi. Continue down river through virgin spruce and

hardwoods, with chokeberry, yellow root, and a variety of rhododendron species as an understory. The river has brown and rainbow
trout. Deer, ruffled grouse, and, occasionally, bear are likely to be
seen up the ridges.

At 3.5 mi reach jct with *Babel Tower Trail*. Excellent scenic
views of the river are found at 4.0 mi, and of Hawksbill Mtn at 5.5
mi. Reach spring and campground at 5.6 mi. Jct with *Spence Ridge
Trail*, from the eastern side of the Gorge is reached at 6.4 mi. At 7.1
mi there is a jct with *Conley Cove Trail*, the last graded exit up to the
rim for 1.4 mi. The *Linville Gorge Trail Extension* continues down
river from stream crossing and jct at *Conley Cove Trail* with less
up-and-down walking but on more rugged and remote terrain. At
11.6 mi trail reaches jct (may be difficult to locate) with *Pinch In
Trail*. Ascend for 1,800 ft on rough climb to SR 1238 parking area at
13.2 mi. It is 7.4 mi on SR 1238 back to origin at Pine Gap, and 8.3
mi to jct with NC 183. Vehicle switching may be necessary. USFS
Trail #231.

Cabin Trail, Sandy Flats Trail, and Pinch In Trail   161-163

These trails are primitive and strenuous spur trails which descend
into the Gorge from SR 1238, joining the *Linville Gorge Trail* at the
Linville River. They are steep, extremely rough, and heavily overgrown in sections. Their locations are as follows: *Cabin Trail*,
length 0.8 mi, with 1.9 mi on SR 1238 from NC 183; *Sandy Flats
Trail*, length 1 mi, with 3.7 mi on SR 1238 from NC 183; and, *Pinch
In Trail*, length 1.6 mi, with 8.3 mi on SR 1238 from NC 183. USFS
permits are required on these trails. USFS Trails #246, 230, and
228.

Linville Falls Trails   164

Entrance trails to Linville Falls are listed in the chapter on Blue
Ridge Parkway trails. The Falls provides a spectacular scene and
gives an idea of the Gorge's development for wilderness hikers.
From the western side of the Falls, a well-used trail descends 0.6 mi
from the parking area at the jct of NC 183 and SR 1238. At the upper
falls, trails extend to views on the western side of the Gorge. The

Falls area was donated to the government by John D. Rockefeller, Jr. to be part of the National Park Service System.

North Catawba Area, McDowell County

Overmountain Victory Trail   165

In celebration of the bicentennial (1780-1980) of the "Overmountain Men," a section of trail in the Pisgah National Forest, Grandfather Mountain District, was planned, constructed, and designated a National Historic Trail in 1980.

When Major Patrick Ferguson of the Loyalist Army sent word to the frontier mountain men, warning them that if they further resisted British authority he would destroy them with fire and sword, the mountain men immediately responded. They mustered 1,000 men from Virginia, Tennessee, and North Carolina and marched to Kings Mountain, South Carolina, where they defeated the Loyalists. Major Ferguson was killed in the battle. Marching for twelve days from Sycamore Shoals in Tennessee, they passed along the route of this trail on September 30, 1780.

Length: 3 mi (4.8 km), moderate; *USGS:* Linville Falls, Ashford; *Trailhead:* Jct of FSR 493 and SR 1560.

Directions and Description: From jct of US 221 and SR 1560 near Ashford, go S 2.5 mi to gated FSR 493.

Park, follow signs, and begin climb on old road, to reach FSR 106 on crest of ridge at 1.5 mi. Descend through white pines and rhododendron slicks to Yellow Creek at 1.9 mi. Cross stream at 2.4 mi, and reach Kistler Memorial Highway, gravel FSR 1238, at 3 mi. USFS parking lot is nearby.

Woodlawn Fitness Trail   166

Length: 0.5 mi (0.8 km), easy; *USGS:* Little Switzerland; *Trailhead:* Parking lot at picnic area.

Directions and Description: From Marion take US 221 N 6.5 mi to Woodlawn Picnic Area on L, near SR 1451. Follow switchbacks through open forest to beginning of fitness trail, a wood chip-covered trail of fourteen stations that provides a European method for informal exercises or serious training. Complete loop and return to parking area at 0.5 mi.

Support Facilities: Suggested commercial campgrounds for the Curtis Creek, Buck Creek, and North Catawba areas are: Buck Creek Campground — from jct of US 70 and NC 80 go N on NC 80 for 2 mi to Tom's Creek Rd and cross bridge; full svc, limited rec; open April 1-November 1; Tel: 704-724-4888. Twin Lakes Campground — from jct of US 221 and US 70 go 8 mi W on US 70 and turn L (S) for 0.3 mi; full svc, limited rec; open May 1-October 1; Tel: 704-724-4117.

For Linville Gorge area: Linville Falls Trailer Lodge and Campground, P.O. Box 203, Linville Falls, NC 28647. Tel: 704-765-2681. From jct of US 221 and Blue Ridge Parkway mp 317-318, go 500 ft S on US 221, then 1 mi SW on SR 1100. Full svc, rec fac. Open April 15-October 15.

Campgrounds in the Steel Creek and Wilson Creek areas are: Daniel Boone Family Campground, Tel: 704-433-1200, and Steele Creek Park, Tel: 704-437-9873, on NC 181 near jct with NC 126. Call for information. Developed camping in the Pisgah National Forest is at Mortimer Recreation Area near jct of NC 90 and SR 1328 W of Lenoir.

SECTION III

PISGAH RANGER DISTRICT

Bent Creek Area, Buncombe County

Lake Powhatan Recreation Area

Bent Creek Trails

The Lake Powhatan Recreation Area offers camping, swimming, fishing, nature study, and hiking. It has three interconnecting loop trails totaling 3.7 mi. Two other trails, *Explorer Trail* — 3 mi long — and *Sleepy Gap* and *Grassy Mtn Loop Trail* — 7 mi long — also connect the campground trails. *Grassy Mtn Loop Trail* also connects with the *Shut-In Trail*. Campground entrance from the Parkway is at mp 393.6. Turn at exit with sign to I-26 and NC 191 at the French Broad River bridge and go 0.3 mi to NC 191. Turn L and go 0.3 mi to Bent Creek Ranch Rd, SR 3484; turn L at sign for Pisgah National Forest Recreation Area, Lake Powhatan. Go another 0.3 mi and turn L as SR 3484 becomes FSR 806. Entrance is another 2 mi.

Homestead Trail   167

Length: 1.1 mi (1.7 km), easy; *USGS:* Ashville, Skyland, Dunsmore Mtn; *Trailhead:* Parking area near Lake Powhatan beach.

Directions and Description: From beach parking area, follow hiking sign around the lake under hardwood and white pine forest to an area where Dr. Carl A. Schenck — see *Cradle of Forestry Trail* — had a lodge from which he managed the Pisgah National Forest area (previously the Biltmore Forest). Cross stream at FSR 480 and return around the lake, or backtrack.

Deerfield Loop Trail and Pine Tree Loop Trail   168-169

Length: 2.4 mi cb (3.8 km), easy; *USGS:* See above; *Trailhead:* Lake Powhatan parking area near beach.

Directions and Description: From beach parking area follow E side of *Deerfield Loop Trail* toward South Ridge Rd; loop back W to jct with *Pine Tree Loop Trail*, passing a number of wildlife openings among pines and rhododendron. Turn R on new trail on the S side of Bent Creek and return to the camp road near the beach. Trails are not marked or color-coded; therefore, a map from the campground office helps clarify trail connections.

Explorer Loop Trail   170

Length: 3 mi (4.8 km), easy; *USGS:* See above; *Trailhead:* Pine Tree Loop Trail near Bent Creek Gap Rd parking area.

Directions and Description: From the trail sign on Bent Creek Gap Rd, follow sign to *Explorer Loop Trail* or enter from *Pine Tree*

Loop Trail. Trail loops between Bent Creek and South Ridge Rd. Since the campground is about 1 mi NE, this trail can be used for connecting with all the other loops of the campground area.

Sleepy Gap and Grassy Mountain Trail   171-172

Length: 1.2 mi (1.9 km), moderate; *USGS:* See above; *Trailhead:* Explorer Loop Trail jct.

Directions and Description: From the jct of the *Explorer Loop Trail* near the *Pine Tree Trail* jct, cross South Ridge Rd, climb steeply to Sleepy Gap on the Parkway at mp 397.3 (2,930 ft), and make a loop back to South Ridge Rd. Go R or continue to *Explorer Loop Trail*.

Ferrin Knob Trail   173

Length: 2.4 mi rt (3.8 km), moderate; *USGS:* See above; *Trailhead:* Near Pisgah Ledge Overlook on Parkway.

Directions and Description: (This trail is part of the *Shut-In-Trail* from Bent Creek to Pisgah Mtn.) Go to Pisgah Ledge Overlook at mp 399.7 and park. Trail entry is 0.4 mi S at Bent Creek Gap, mp 400.3, at NW corner of overpass. Follow old jeep road up N side of ridge with good views of Asheville and the Biltmore Estates. At fork, turn sharply L and reach summit at 1.2 mi (4,000 ft). Firetower at the summit has been dismantled. Backtrack to parking area. This trail can be followed N on the *Shut-In Trail* to connect with the trails at Lake Powhatan.

Davidson River Area, Transylvania County

Farlow Gap and Lanning Ridge Trail   174

Length: 6.9 mi (11 km), moderate to strenuous; *USGS:* Shining Rock; *Trailhead:* Parking area at Cove Creek Group Camp.

Directions and Description: From Ranger Sta go 3.5 mi on US 276 and turn L on Davidson River Rd, FSR 475. At 3.5 mi turn R to Cove Creek Camp and parking area.

Follow sign of *Lanning Ridge Trail* to jct with *Cove Creek Trail*. Continue on *Lanning Ridge Trail* through mature forest of beech and oaks; it is near old railroad artifacts. There is a jct at 2.6 mi with *Daniel Ridge Trail*, a spur leading to the Old Fish Hatchery. Continue on old roadbed near abandoned mica mines, cross Daniel Ridge and Shuck Ridge, and reach Farlow Gap at 6.9 mi. Jct with *Art Loeb Trail* is here. Ascent, 1,800 ft. Backtrack, or hike down FSR 229 to Gloucester Gap (3.3 mi) and vehicle at FSR 475. FSR 229 is rough, requiring 4WD. USFS Trail #106.

Looking Glass Rock Trail   175

Length: 6.2 mi rt (9.5 km), strenuous; *USGS:* Shining Rock; *Trailhead:* Davidson River Rd parking area on FSR 475.

Directions and Description: From jct of US 276 and FSR 475 go 0.4 mi to parking area on L side of road. Trailhead is on R. A popular trail, eroded in spots along the switchbacks, it climbs steadily to summit (3,969 ft), for magnificent views of the Pisgah National Forest and Blue Ridge Parkway areas. The granite dome, particularly on the S, NW, and N sides, is a challenge to rock climbers. Major vegetation consists of oak, birch, laurel, and rarer species — such as the Carolina hemlock. Ascent, 1,369 ft. Backtrack. USFS Trail #114.

Cat Gap Trail and Horse Cove Loop Trail   176-177

Length: 5 mi (8 km), moderate to strenuous; *USGS:* Shining Rock; *Trailhead:* Parking lot at the Fish Hatchery.

Directions and Description: At jct of US 276 and FSR 475, go 2 mi to Pisgah Forest National Fish Hatchery; park. Follow sign W of the fish rearing tanks and office to Cedar Rock Creek and Picklesimer Fields. Trail on R is *Butter Gap Trail*. Ascend to Cat Gap (3,350 ft) at 2.3 mi. Jct with *Art Loeb Trail* is at Cat Gap. Turn L and N and follow a steep section to Horse Cove, around John Rock Mtn, along part of John Rock Branch, and back to parking lot at 5 mi. USFS Trails #120 and 151.

Butter Gap Trail   178

Length: 6.6 mi rt (10.6 km), moderate; *USGS:* Shining Rock; *Trailhead:* Parking lot at Fish Hatchery.

Directions and Description: At Pisgah Forest National Fish Hatchery follow *Cat Gap Trail* — see preceding directions — for 0.8 mi to Picklesimer Field and turn R. Follow up W side of Grogan Creek to Butter Gap and jct with *Art Loeb Trail* at 3.3 mi. Backtrack or make a loop by following the *Art Loeb Trail* to Cat Gap and descending back to the Fish Hatchery. A spur trail going E at Butter Gap leads to the summit of Cedar Rock (4,056 ft), a granite peak similar to Looking Glass Rock. Rock is dangerous in wet or icy weather. USFS Trail #123.

Black Mtn Trail   179

Length: 7.7 mi (12.3 km), strenuous; *USGS:* Shining Rock, Pisgah Forest; *Trailhead:* Pisgah Work Center.

Directions and Description: On US 276, 0.3 mi SE of Ranger Sta, park outside the fence of Work Center. Follow trail sign and climb steadily on what has become a popular overnight trail. Cross Little Hickory Knob and Hickory Knob, and reach Pressley Gap at 2.8 mi. Views on the ridges are better during leafless seasons. Climb to summit of Black Mtn (4,386 ft) at 3.9 mi, descend to Clawhammer Mtn (4,100 ft), and go on to Buckhorn Gap and shelter at 5.8 mi. *Buckhorn Gap Trail* crosses at the Gap. Continue NW to Club Gap at 6.9 mi Jct with *Avery* and *Buckwheat Knob Trails* is here. Turn R to parking area on FSR 477, or go to the parking area at the Cradle of Forestry at 7.7 mi. Elev change, 2,086 ft. Vehicle shuttle necessary. USFS Trail #127.

Pisgah Ecology Trail   180

Length: 0.6 mi (1 km), easy; *USGS:* Pisgah Forest; *Trailhead:* Pisgah Ranger Sta.

Directions and Description: From jct of US 276, US 64, and NC 280, go W on US 276 for 1.2 mi to Pisgah Ranger Sta on R. Follow sign for graveled loop trail, pass 21 interpretive stations — some on elevated walkways, and return to parking lot by Andy Cove Creek.

Coontree Loop Trail 181

Length: 3.7 mi (5.9 km), easy to moderate; *USGS:* Shining Rock; *Trailhead:* Coontree Picnic Area parking lot.

Directions and Description: From Pisgah Ranger Station go N on US 276 for 3 mi. Park, cross road to trail entrance, and follow N up Coontree Creek through a stand of ironwood. At 0.2 mi loop begins. Take R prong, follow old road, and ascend to Coontree Gap (2,960 ft). Turn L at jct with *Bennett Gap Trail* and follow crest. No views. Turn L to sign, descend steeply, and rejoin loop at jct at 3.3 mi. Elev change, 1,000 ft. USFS Trail #144.

Art Loeb Trail 182
Sections I, II, III, and Spur Trail

Named in honor of the late Arthur J. Loeb, hiking enthusiast and dedicated officer of the Carolina Mountain Club, the *Art Loeb Trail* is 28.3 mi long, the longest and most challenging of the trails in the Pisgah Ranger District. Its elevation gain is nearly 4,000 ft, with another 3,000 ft of up-and-down between cols and gaps. It begins at the Davidson River (2,160 ft) near the Schenck Job Corps Center and ends at Cold Mtn (6,030 ft) in the Shining Rock Wilderness Area. Another 6.6 mi of hiking is necessary to reach the nearest exit at the Daniel Boone Camp on the *Deep Gap Trail*.

Although the full trail requires quite a bit of exertion, usually taking three or four days for the experienced backpacker, it is divided in three sections with connecting or loop trails, thus allowing for return, supply points, or vehicle switching. *Section III* requires a permit for the Shining Rock Wilderness Area. Jointly maintained by the Carolina Mountain Club and the U.S. Forest Service, the trail is marked with a yellow stenciled hiker silhouette.

The trail passes through a wide variety of hardwoods and conifers, wildflowers and shrubs. Mammals common to the area are black bear, deer, gray fox, bobcat, red squirrel, and woodchuck. Among the songbirds are Carolina junco, winter wren, nuthatch, raven, and tanager. Wild turkey and ruffled grouse are also in the area.

Length: 28.3 mi cb (45.3 km), strenuous; *USGS:* Pisgah Forest, Shining Rock, Sam Knob, Cruso; *Trailhead:* Parking area on SE side of Davidson River.

Directions and Description: From the Pisgah Ranger Station go E 0.3 mi to a point 1.2 mi W of jct of US 276, US 64, and NC 280. Turn at the sign of Davidson River Campground, and before the bridge turn L. Proceed 0.2 mi to parking area near the swinging bridge; park.

Cross swinging bridge, turn L, and follow yellow marker on a river plain through bee balm and cone flowers, virgin oaks and poplars. Cross bridge at 0.5 mi, turn R and then L to begin ascent W on Shut In Ridge. Ascending through rosebay rhododendrons, reach crest at 2.9 mi. Descend to Neil Gap at 3.3 mi. *North Slope Trail* turns R to Davidson River Campground, a distance of 3.2 mi. *Camp Strauss Trail* turns L at 4.2 mi.

Climb to Chestnut Knob (3,840 ft), and descend to Cat Gap and trail jct at 6.3 mi. *Horse Cove Gap Trail* turns R, going 2.2 mi to Fish Hatchery on FSR 475. *Cat Gap Trail* turns R also, going 2.3 mi to Fish Hatchery. At 6.9 mi pass the *Cedar Rock Spur Trail* over Cedar Rock Mtn (4,056 ft). Cedar Rock Mtn is a partially exposed massif with exceptional views, but it can be dangerous for climbing in wet or icy weather or when the pine needles are slippery. Cross a stream at 7 mi, circle S of Cedar Rock, and reach an A-frame shelter at 8.6 mi. Two streams are nearby. Ascend to Butter Gap at 8.8 mi, a jct of seven roads and trails. *Butter Gap Trail* descends N 2.7 mi to the Fish Hatchery, and *Cedar Rock Spur Trail* goes R up the ridge. Continue L on ridge through open woods of hickory, oak, maple, locust, and sourwood, with undercover of buckberry. Reach summit of Chestnut Mtn, cross road at 11.6 mi, reach summit of Rich Mtn at 11.8 mi, and descend to Gloucester Gap (3,250 ft) at 12.3 mi.

Begin *Section II* by crossing FSR 5095. Cross FSR 229 at 12.8 mi, and again at 13.8 mi. Begin multiple switchbacks up Pilot Mtn, and reach the summit (5,040 ft) at 14.4 mi. Vegetation at summit is chinquapin, bush honeysuckle, mountain laurel, blueberry, and chestnut oak. Views are impressive. Descend through yellow birch and other hardwoods to Deep Gap, follow FSR 229 for 0.1 mi, and reach an A-frame shelter at 15.2 mi. Climb Sassafras Knob, with groundcover of galax, wood betony, azalea, and young mountain ash. Descend to Farlow Gap at 16.1 mi. *Farlow Gap Trail* turns R for 6.9 mi to connect with FSR 137 and the *Lanning Ridge Trail,* to reach FSR 475. Ascend to Shuck Ridge through oak, beech nut, and spruce; reach Blue Ridge Parkway mp 421.2 at 17.7 mi. Turn L on road and go 90 yd to trail up embankment. (Trail may be easy to miss in thick vegetation.) Ascend on highly eroded and exceptionally steep trail to crest of ridge at 18 mi. On a narrow trail through fir and spruce, pass Silvermine Bald and reach FSR 816 at 19.1 mi. (L on road it is 0.3 mi to small stream and 0.5 mi to parking area for entrance to *Art Loeb Spur Trail* to Black Balsam. To R on road it is 1 mi to Parkway.)

Section III begins when one crosses FSR 816 and ascends through heath bald area to grassy bald summit of Black Balsam Knob (6,214 ft), the highest peak in the Pisgah Ranger District, at 19.5 mi. Continue N on ridge and ascend to Tennent Mtn at 20.7 mi. Descend and follow old road entry into the Wilderness Area to Ivester Gap and the boundary of the Shining Rock Wilderness Area at 21.4 mi. (For entry into the Wilderness Area a permit is required in advance from the Ranger District Office or cooperators.) At 22.6 mi reach Flower Gap and skirt E of Flower Knob on old railroad bed through an umbrella of beech nut, with bush honeysuckle, wild orchids, and sundrops in sunny areas. A spring is found at 23 mi on the R. Proceed to Shining Rock Gap at 23.2 mi, pass an overused camping area, and reach jct with other trails. *Little East Fork Trail* descends W 5.9 mi to the Daniel Boone Camp. *Shining Creek Trail* descends E 4.2 mi to US 276. *Old Butt Knob Trail* ascends to the E side of Shining Rock, goes on to Dog Loser Knob, and crosses Old Butt Knob before descending to US 276. Ascend to Shining Rock (5,940 ft) for views of the snow white quartz outcrops, and reach jct with *Old Butt Knob Trail* at 23.5 mi. Area has abundant laurel, bristly locust, fetterbush, blueberry, and fly poison.

Continue on old railroad bed W of Shining Rock to Crawford Creek Gap, ascend over rough trail to Stairs Mtn (5,869 ft) at 24.5 mi, and descend on the spine of the Narrows to Deep Gap at 26.1 mi. On the L is the 4.2 mi *Deep Gap Trail* to the Daniel Boone Camp on SR 1129. Ascend to Cold Mtn (6,030 ft) at 27.7 mi; this is the northern terminus of the *Art Loeb Trail*. Backtrack to Deep Gap and take either the *Deep Gap Trail* or return on the *Art Loeb Trail* to other exits. (The *Art Loeb Spur Trail* of 0.6 mi runs from the parking area at the end of FSR 816 off the Parkway W of Black Balsam Knob.) USFS Trail #141.

Moore Cove Trail 187

Length: 1.4 mi rt (2.2 km), easy; *USGS:* Shining Rock; *Trailhead:* Near Looking Glass Falls bridge on US 276.

Directions and Description: Go 1 mi W of Looking Glass Falls on US 276 and park near bridge, between highway and river. Hike across the stone bridge, turn R on steps, and begin steep climb of 150 ft to trail on railroad grade. Cross stream on footlogs in rhododendron area. Trail may be muddy in rainy season. Abundant wildflowers. Reach 45-ft Moore Creek cascades at 0.7 mi. Return by same route. USFS Trail #318.

Avery Creek Trail 188

Length: 8.4 mi rt (13.4 km), moderate; *USGS:* Shining Rock; *Trailhead:* Club Gap.

Directions and Description: From US 276 at Cradle of Forestry, hike gravel road past caretaker's residence to *Club Gap Trail.* At 0.8 mi go straight ahead, S. *Buckwheat Trail* is R and *Black Mtn Trail* is L. Follow old road and Avery Creek to jct with FSR 477 at 4.2 mi. Trail is a typical creek trail with good campsite choices. Backtrack; or, hike R up FSR 477 to Bennett Gap and take the *Buckwheat Trail* to Club Gap; or continue hiking on FSR 477 to jct of US 276 or Cradle of Forestry, for approximately 5 mi and a total of nearly 9 mi rt. USFS Trail #327.

Daniel Ridge Trail 189

Length: 2.4 mi rt (3.8 km), easy; *USGS:* Shining Rock; *Trailhead:* Old Fish Hatchery on FSR 137.

Directions and Description: At jct of US 276 and FSR 475, take FSR 475 to FSR 137 and turn R. Go 0.8 mi to Old Fish Hatchery; park. Trail has scenic waterfalls, large broadleaf trees, and hemlocks. Wildflowers plentiful. Trail connects at 1.2 mi with *Lanning Ridge Trail.* Backtrack. USFS Trail #330.

Thrift Cove Loop Trail and Starnes Branch Loop Trail   190-191

Length: 5.1 mi cb (8.2 km), moderate; *USGS:* Pisgah Forest; *Trailhead:* Pisgah Work Center on US 276.

Directions and Description: On US 276, 0.3 mi SE of Ranger Sta. Park outside the fence of Work Center. Follow signs for *Black Mtn Trail*; after 1.2 mi, *Black Mtn Trail* turns L and a Wildlife Rd turns R. *Thrift Cove Trail* goes straight ahead, turning later at the upper end of the cove. At least three examples of timber management can be seen on the return trail. At 3.2 mi there is a jct with *Starnes Branch Trail*. To return to Work Center go straight ahead, or take sharp L and follow *Starnes Branch Trail* in a loop to return to the Work Center. Area has mature forest and white pines. Combined loops total 5.6 mi. USFS Trails #356 and 329.

North Slope Loop Trail   192

Length: 2.4 mi (3.8 km), easy; *USGS:* Pisgah Forest; *Trailhead:* Davidson River Amphitheatre parking lot.

Directions and Description: At Davidson River Campground off US 276 near Ranger Sta, park on L in campground. Trail begins along the river upstream, past the campground and English Chapel; it follows an old logging road through hardwood and hemlocks. At Neil Gap jct, turn sharp L and return to campground. USFS Trail #359.

Cove Creek Trail and Caney Bottom Trail   193-194

Length: 4.6 mi rt (7.4 km), moderate; *USGS:* Shining Rock; *Trailhead:* Cove Creek Group Campground.

Directions and Description: At jct of US 276 and FSR 475, go 3.5 mi W on FSR 475. Keep L when road forks. Park outside gate of Cove Creek Camp, hike up road, branch off to L at yellow blaze of *Lanning Ridge Trail*, take a sharp R, follow rim of campground, pass L of waterfall, and reach jct with FSR. Follow road to *Caney Bottom Creek Trail*, turn R, and follow on the L side of the creek to return to campground. USFS Trails # 361 and 329.

Pressley Cove and Clawhammer Cove Trail   **195**

Length: 8.5 mi (13.6 km), moderate to strenuous; *USGS:* Pisgah Forest, Shining Rock; *Trailhead:* Parking area on FSR 477.

Directions and Description: At jct of US 276 and FSR 477, Avery Creek Rd, 0.4 mi NW of Ranger Sta, go 1.8 mi to trailhead; park. Loop can be made by following trail up Clawhammer Cove on modern logging road to Buckhorn Gap at 4 mi. Then follow *Black Mtn Trail* S to Pressley Gap, or hike 1 mi back from parking area to Pressley Cove trail entrance, hiking up cove to Pressley Gap, and turn L on the *Black Mtn Trail* to reach Buckhorn Gap and then descend on the logging road to parking area and vehicle. Elev change, 2,000 ft. Entry gates to FSR 447 are locked each night from 8 P.M. and are opened at 7 A.M.

Support Facilities: Davidson River Campground has 113 camp sites with picnic tables and regular facilities. It is the only campground in the Pisgah Ranger District with hot showers. It is located 1.3 mi W on US 276 from jct of US 276, US 64, and NC 280; it is 0.2 mi E on US 276 from the Pisgah Ranger District headquarters. A commercial campground in the area is Little River Camp Resort, Route 2, Box 241, Pisgah Forest, NC 28768. Tel: 704-877-4475. From jct of US 64 and US 276 go 3.5 mi E on US 64, then turn S on SR at Ponrose Grocery and go 6 mi, following signs. Full svc, rec fac. Open May 15-Labor Day.

Pink Beds Area, Transylvania and Henderson Counties

Buck Spring Trail   **196**

Length: 6.2 mi (9.9 km), moderate; *USGS:* Shining Rock, Cruso; *Trailhead:* Pisgah Inn parking lot on Parkway.

Directions and Description: From parking lot at Inn enter the trail at sign behind the dining hall, SW. The trail descends with switchbacks through two plant zones — at the entry of the trail a Canadian zone of fir and spruce, and near the end mature Appalachian trees of birch, poplar, oak, and maple. Cross 13 creeks, wind around 10 ridges with outstanding views of the Pink Beds, and reach the last stream at 5.8 mi. US 276 is at 6.2 mi. Descent, 1,200 ft. Vehicle switching needed, or backtrack. USFS Trail #104.

Laurel Mtn Trail   197

Length: 7.4 mi (11.8 km), moderate; *USGS:* Dunsmore Mtn; *Trailhead:* Buck Spring Overlook on the Blue Ridge Parkway, mp 407.7.

Directions and Description: From the overlook parking area go SW on *Buck Spring Trail* spur, taking the first L at 0.3 mi. Avoid the second trail 100 yd ahead on *Buck Spring Trail*, since it is an access route to *Pilot Rock Trail*. Descend steadily through thick oaks and laurels; pass along crests, slopes, and gaps such as Turkey Spring, Good Enough, Sassafras, Johnson, and Yellow. Avoid R at Turkey Spring Gap, and avoid L at the fork in Good Enough Gap. Trail may be heavily overgrown in places. Reach Yellow Gap Rd, FSR 1206, in Yellow Gap at 7.4 mi. Descent, 2,000 ft. Vehicle switching necessary. USFS Trail #121.

Buckwheat Knob Trail and Avery Creek Trail   198

Length: 6.7 mi (10.7 km), moderate; *USGS:* Shining Rock; *Trailhead:* Bennett Gap parking area.

Directions and Description: At FSR 477 near entrance to Cradle of Forestry, go 2.4 mi to Bennett Gap parking area. Park and proceed N up to Buckwheat Knob. Descend into Club Gap — see *Club Gap Trail* description — to trail jct. Turn R on *Avery Creek Trail*, gradually descending along the creek on old road with excellent camping spots. At jct with FSR 477 turn R and ascend on road for 2 mi to Bennett Gap parking area to complete loop. Elev change, 1,400 ft. USFS Trails #127 and 327.

Club Gap Trail and Buckwheat Knob Loop Trail   199

Length: 4.5 mi (7.2 km), moderate; *USGS:* Shining Rock; *Trailhead:* Parking area on FSR 477 near US 276.

Directions and Description: From US 276 turn onto Avery Creek Rd, FSR 477 — it is 9.5 mi from Ranger Sta — and go 0.3 mi to parking area. Proceed N to vicinity of Cradle of Forestry caretaker's residence, turn R. Ascend on switchbacks to Club Gap at 0.8 mi, and reach jct with *Avery Creek Trail*. Turn R, cross under power line, and ascend to Buckwheat Knob at 1.9 mi. Descend, reaching FSR 477 at 2.4 mi. Turn R and hike road back to parking area. USFS Trail #127.

Bennett Gap Trail   200

Length: 2.9 mi (4.6 km), moderate; *USGS:* Shining Rock, Pisgah Forest; *Trailhead:* Avery Creek Rd, FSR 477, parking area.

Directions and Description: From the Pisgah Ranger Station, go 9.5 mi W to Avery Creek Rd, near the Cradle of Forestry, and turn R. Go 2.4 mi to sign at Bennett Gap; park. Hike S into open field. Follow ridge line, and climb Coontree Mtn and follow ridge. Pass two jct with *Coontree Trail* on R. Turn L at fork, at 2.9 mi before descent to Avery Creek Rd. Backtrack, or use vehicle switching. Descent, 1,200 ft. USFS Trail #138.

Thompson Creek Trail   201

Length: 1.3 mi (2.1 km), moderate; *USGS:* Dunsmore Mtn, Cruso; *Trailhead:* Parking lot at Pisgah Inn.

Directions and Description: At Blue Ridge Parkway mp 408.6 parking lot, follow sign at L of Pisgah Inn and begin steep descent past the Flat Laurel Gap. L is access trail to *Pilot Rock Trail*. Continue ahead, with excellent views of Pink Beds area, descending through mature alluvial forest to Yellow Gap Rd, FSR 1206. Descent, 1,700 ft. Vehicle switching needed, or backtrack. USFS Trail #132.

Pilot Rock Trail   202

Length: 3.6 mi (5.8 km), moderate; *USGS:* Dunsmore Mtn, Cruso; *Trailhead:* Parking lot at Pisgah Inn on Blue Ridge Parkway at mp 408.6

Directions and Description: From the parking lot of Pisgah Inn, go L of Inn to trail signs and descend S on *Thompson Creek Trail* for

0.2 mi to jct with *Pilot Rock Trail* spur. Turn L . Reach jct with *Turkey Gap Trail* at 1.3 mi. Turn R. Reach Pilot Rock (4,000 ft) for excellent views of Pink Beds and Mills River Valley. Descend by switchbacks to Grassy Lot Gap on Yellow Gap Rd, FSR 1206. Descent, 1,700 ft. Return by same route or use vehicle switching. USFS Trail #321.

Pilot Cove Trail and Slate Rock Creek Trail 203-204

Length: 5.4 mi (8.6 km), moderate; *USGS:* Dunsmore Mtn; *Trailhead:* Parking area on Yellow Gap Rd, FSR 1206.

Directions and Description: Turn off US 276 E onto Yellow Gap Rd, FSR 1206 at 11.5 mi from Ranger Sta and go 4.5 mi to parking area and primitive camping area at Pilot Cove. Backtrack on road for 300 yd to trail entry on R. Ascend for 1.2 mi to summit of Slate Rock Ridge (2,800 ft), and descend on old railroad grade along NE side of Slate Rock Creek through hardwoods, spruce, and rhododendrons. Reach Yellow Gap Rd at 4 mi, and return R on FSR 1206 for loop to vehicle at 5.4 mi. USFS Trail #358.

Pink Beds Loop Trail 205

Length: 5 mi (8 km), easy; *USGS:* Pisgah Forest, Shining Rock; *Trailhead:* Parking area at Pink Beds picnic area.

Directions and Description: Enter the Pink Beds picnic area from US 276 near and N of the Cradle of Forestry; park in the area near trail sign. The trail may also be entered at the middle point of the loop at the Gaging Sta on Wolf Ford Rd, FSR 476. Follow trail on old logging and railroad grades with easy elevation gains for most of its length; it passes through hardwood forest.

Bradley Creek Trail 206

Length: 3.3 mi (5.2 km), moderate; *USGS:* Pisgah Forest, Dunsmore Mtn; *Trailhead:* Turkey Pen Gap parking lot.

Directions and Description: Follow Turkey Pen Gap Rd, FSR 297, from NC 280 at Transylvania and Henderson County line to

Turkey Pen Gap; park. Start on the road down to the South Mills River; go 0.8 mi. Turn R for 0.2 mi on old road grade by the side of the river. Cross the South Mills River and begin climb to Pea Gap. Descend through wildlife openings, and follow Bradley Creek to the Hendersonville Watershed Intake. Exit, or consider use of *Laurel Creek Trail, Squirrel Gap Trail,* or *Vineyard Gap Trail* for loop. USFS Trail #351.

Shining Rock Area, Haywood and Transylvania Counties

Shining Rock Wilderness

Permits are required to hike or camp in the 13,600-acre Shining Rock Wilderness; they are available in advance from the following locations: Pisgah Ranger Station, 1.5 mi W of jct of US 64-276 and NC 280 on US 276; Riverside Grocery on US 64 2 mi E of Ranger Station; Lake Logan Grocery at jct of NC 215 and SR 1129, 4.7 mi S on NC 215 from jct of US 276 and NC 110; and, Cruso Grocery in Cruso, 5.2 mi W on US 276 from the Shining Rock Wilderness at Big East Fork parking area. Information is available from the District Ranger, P.O. Box 8, Pisgah Forest, NC 28768. Tel: 704-877-3265.

Deep Gap Trail   207

Length: 3.8 mi (6 km), moderate to strenuous; *USGS:* Cruso, Waynesville; *Trailhead:* Camp Daniel Boone parking area.
Directions and Description: From jct of NC 215 and Blue Ridge Parkway, go N 13 mi on NC 215 to SR 1129 and turn R. Lake Logan Grocery is across the bridge on NC 215. Proceed 3.8 mi to Camp Daniel Boone parking area (BSA, Asheville); park. Ascend steeply on switchbacks to crest of ridge at 1.1 mi; then gradually ascend on NW slope of Shining Rock Ledge through laurel, buckeye, birch, and spruce. Reach Deep Gap and jct with *Art Loeb Trail* at 3.8 mi. Backtrack, or use *Art Loeb Trail* for loop with *Little East Fork Trail.* USFS Trail #101.

Little East Fork Trail   208

Length: 5.4 mi (8.6 km), strenuous; *USGS:* Waynesville, Sam
Knob, Shining Rock; *Trailhead:* Camp Daniel Boone parking area.

Directions and Description: See above for directions to parking
area. From parking area hike up road, avoiding road to L at bridge;
cross bridge R and turn L through Boy Scout camps named for a
variety of Indian tribes. Enter Shining Rock Wilderness Area on old
logging road at 0.3 mi, cross Cathey Cove Creek, and at 1.2 mi cross
Hemlock Branch. The Little East Fork Pigeon River cascades on L.
At 2.8 mi cross river and begin switchbacks or climb to jct with
Shining Rock Trail at 4.9 mi. Turn L on old railroad grade and reach
Shining Rock Gap at 5.4 mi. Backtrack, or take the *Art Loeb Trail* N
for a loop on the *Deep Gap Trail*, a total of 12.1 mi rt. Ascent, 2,240
ft.

Case Camp Trail   209

Length: 2.8 mi rt (4.5 km), moderate; *USGS:* Shining Rock;
Trailhead: On FSR 475-B.

Directions and Description: From the Pisgah Ranger Station, go
N on US 276 for 9 mi, turn L on Headwater's Rd, FSR 475-B, and
proceed for 0.8 mi to parking. Follow blue-blazed trail in sloping
ascent on N side of Case Camp Ridge through forest of hardwoods
and conifers to the Blue Ridge Parkway at mp 415.9. Backtrack.
USFS Trail #119.

Courthouse Trail   210

Length: 3.6 mi rt (5.8 km), strenuous; *USGS:* Sam Knob; *Trailhead:* End of FSR 140.

Directions and Description: From the jct of the Blue Ridge
Parkway and NC 215 go 6.7 mi on NC 215 to Courthouse Creek Rd,
FSR 140. Turn L and follow gravel road for 1 mi to fork; bear L and
continue for another 3 mi to end of road. Park and enter the trail,
ascending by Coalney Creek for 1 mi. Trail becomes exceptionally
steep and rocky near the end — the true headwaters of the French
Broad River. Reach the Parkway between Devil's Courthouse Over-

look and the tunnel. Vegetation on the trail is chiefly birch, beech, oak, and buckeye, with scattered fir and spruce. Return by the same route or use vehicle switching at the Parkway at mp 422.4. USFS Trail #128.

Summey Cove Trail 211

Length: 4 mi (6.4 km), moderate; *USGS:* Sam Knob; *Trailhead:* NC 215 at Bee Tree Fork.

Directions and Description: From the jct of the Blue Ridge Parkway and NC 215 go S 5.4 mi on NC 215 to bridge at Bee Tree Crossing; park. Begin steep climb up Big Fork Ridge for 0.4 mi to gap. Descend steeply to Summey Cove, with views of Devil's Courthouse and Pilot Mtn. Follow gentle trail on old railroad bed. Spur trail at 1.7 mi leads to Courthouse Falls. Reach Courthouse Rd, FSR 140, at 2 mi. Backtrack or use vehicle switching. USFS Trail #129.

Shining Rock Gap Trail 212

Length: 2 mi (3.2 km), easy; *USGS:* Shining Rock; *Trailhead:* Ivestor Gap at Wilderness boundary.

Directions and Description: Access to this trail can be from the *Art Loeb Trail* or from the Black Balsam parking area at the end of FSR 816, 1.5 mi from mp 420.2 on the Blue Ridge Parkway. From the parking area hike or drive 4WD 2.2 mi to Ivestor Gap. (Vehicles not permitted beyond Ivestor Gap.) Follow the old railroad grade for 2 mi to Shining Rock Gap. Pass between borders of yellow birch, beech nut, laurel, and bush honeysuckle. Backtrack, or loop 1.7 mi on the *Art Loeb Trail*. USFS Trail #143.

Old Butt Knob Trail 213

Length: 4.3 mi (6.9 km), moderate to strenuous; *USGS:* Cruso, Shining Rock; *Trailhead:* Summit of Shining Rock.

Directions and Description: See above for directions to summit of Shining Rock. From the snow-white quartz of Shining Rock's summit (5,940 ft) and jct with the *Art Loeb Trail*, go R (facing as one would following the 0.2 mi up from Shining Rock Gap), descending to Beech Spring Gap; then climb to Dog Loser Knob, and descend again to Spanish Oak Gap. Ascend Old Butt Knob at 2 mi. Descent is extremely steep from 3 to 3.6 mi. Reach Shining Creek Gap and begin switchbacks to Big East Fork parking area on US 276 at 4.3 mi. Vehicle switching may be necessary. USFS Trail #332.

Big East Fork Trail and Greasy Cove Trail   214-215

Length: 6.7 mi cb (10.7 km), strenuous; *USGS:* Shining Rock; *Trailhead:* Big East Fork parking area at Shining Rock Wilderness Area on US 276.

Directions and Description: From jct of US 276 and Blue Ridge Parkway, take US 276 NW for 2.9 mi to Big East Fork parking area; park. Proceed up the East Fork Pigeon River on old railroad grade. There are excellent camping and fishing locations along the way. Forest vegetation is mainly hardwoods, with an understory of rhododendron, purple raspberry, moose wood, and buckeye. Reach Bridges Camp at 3.4 mi. Begin at this point on the *Greasy Cove Trail*, ascending steeply on the *Greasy Cove Prong* to Grassy Cove Gap at 4.7 mi. At 6 mi reach old railroad bed, and then come to jct with *Art Loeb Trail* in Ivestor Gap at 6.7 mi. Hike 2 mi out to parking area on FSR 816 for vehicle switch, or return on the same trail or other loop routes such as *Shining Creek Trail* or *Old Butt Trail*. USFS Trails #357 and 362.

Shining Creek Trail   216

Length: 4.2 mi (6.9 km), strenuous; *USGS:* Shining Rock; *Trailhead:* Big East Fork parking area on US 276.

Directions and Description: Ascend on *Old Butt Trail* and *Shining Creek Trail* for 0.7 mi to Shining Creek Gap. Turn L and continue ascent. Pass Daniel Cove at 2 mi, reach North Prong. Trail has rocky sections, waterfalls, and wildflowers. Near the summit fir and spruce replace the oaks and maples. Ascend with switchbacks to Shining Rock Gap at 4.2 mi. Ascent, 2,340 ft. Backtrack, or use other trail for loop. USFS Trail #363.

Fork Mountain Trail   **217**

Length: 6.1 mi (9.8 km), moderate; *USGS:* Sam Knob, Waynesville, Shining Rock; *Trailhead:* Between FSR 816 parking area and
Ivestor Gap.

Directions and Description: At mp 420.2 on the Blue Ridge
Parkway, take FSR 816 for 1.5 mi to parking area. Hike N on old
railroad grade for 1.7 mi to jct with *Fork Mtn Trail* on L. (Summer
vegetation may have obscured the trail, making it difficult to follow.
Except for some inclines at knobs, the trail is on an even contour line
for the first 4 mi.) Follow trail W and at 1.6 mi reach jct with *Fire
Scald Ridge Trail* on L. Skirt N side of Birdstand Mtn along the
Shining Rock Wilderness boundary, reaching Cathey Ridge at 3.5
mi. At 4 mi begin descent on switchbacks to Turnpike Creek. Follow
creek to West Fork Pigeon River, bearing R and reaching the river
crossing at 6.1 mi. Since footbridge has been swept away, rock hop
across and ascend to NC 215. (River may be impassable at high
water.) Sunburst Campground is 0.2 mi R on NC 215 and the BRP is
8.4 mi L on NC 215. Vehicle switching is necessary. Elev change,
2,620 ft.

Fire Scald Ridge Trail   **218**

Length: 2.8 mi (4.5 km), strenuous; *USGS:* Sam Knob; *Trailhead:* On NC 215, 5.3 mi N from Parkway.

Directions and Description: From Parkway go N for 5.3 mi to
narrow space for parking against a rock wall L on a curve; park.
Cross road and climb over guard rail, and then descend steeply
through wildflowers and tall basswood, poplar, and locust to the
rapids and pools of West Fork Pigeon River at 0.1 mi. If river is
high, crossing can be made on double steel cables. Across the river
climb exceptionally steep trail, faint in places, to fork on old road at
0.3 mi. Bear L or R for loop. If L, follow up creek for a short
distance on unmaintained trail, climbing steeply to *Fork Mtn Trail* at
1.1 mi. Bear R on return loop through heavy undergrowth in places
to origin at 2.8 mi. Some of the vegetation is sweet pepper bush,
arrow wood, rhododendron, mosses, and liverwort. Upon return to
highway it is 3.3 mi R (N) to Sunburst Campground.

Sam Knob Trail   219

Length: 6.4 mi rt (10.2 km), moderate to strenuous; *USGS:* Sam Knob; *Trailhead:* Parking area on NC 215 near Parkway.

Directions and Description: From the Parkway go N on NC 215 for 0.9 mi to a hiking sign on R. Turn R and park. Climb over earth and rock hummocks, cross Bubbling Spring Branch, and follow old railroad grade with borders of bush honeysuckle, fir, maple, mountian ash, and wild cherry. Skirt Little Sam Knob and reach jct at 2 mi. Take L to base of Sam Knob, ascending NW on S side of mtn for outstanding views of Shining Rock area, Plott Balsam, and Pisgah game lands. (It is 0.4 mi more to N summit.) An alternate and shorter route is from the parking area on FSR 816 off Blue Ridge Parkway at mp 420.2. Drive 1.5 mi from Parkway to parking area, then proceed W on old road, turning R at two forks to base of Sam Knob. Ascend on SW side to both S and N summit as described above. Backtrack.

South Mills River Area,
Transylvania and Henderson Counties

Big Creek Trail   220

Length: 4.9 mi (7.8 km), moderate to strenuous; *USGS:* Dunsmore Mtn; *Trailhead:* Hendersonville Reservoir, FSR 142.

Directions and Description: At jct of NC 280 and 191 at Mills River intersection, go 1 mi, turn L at signs for North Mills River Campground, and drive 5 mi on SR 1345 to FSR 479 on R. Go another 2 mi, then turn L on FSR 142. Follow road to reservoir; park.

Trail begins on old railroad grade behind the reservoir and follows up Big Creek. At 2.8 mi the large marks on an old chestnut tree are reputed to be the claw marks of a black bear. At 3 mi trail becomes steeper, alternating between a ridge trail and a slope trail. Vegetation during the ascent ranges from birch and poplar to spruce and chestnut oak. Reach old road bed at Little Pisgah Ridge tunnel on the BRP at mp 406.9; this is at 4.9 mi. Backtrack or use vehicle shuttle. USFS Trail #102.

Buckhorn Gap Trail   221

Length: 4.6 mi (7.3 km), moderate; *USGS:* Pisgah Forest, Shining Rock; *Trailhead:* Gaging station on FSR 476.

Directions and Description: From US 276 11 mi N of Ranger Sta, turn R on FSR 1206, Yellow Gap Rd, and go 3 mi to R before turning on FSR 476, Wolf Ford Rd. Continue for 1.5 mi to Gaging Station; park.

Begin hike on *South Mills River Trail* and turn R (W) on *Buckhorn Gap Trail* at 1.5 mi. Climb to Buckhorn Gap and jct with *Buckwheat Trail*. Continue W and join the *Avery Creek Trail;* branch off at a sign on an old skid road and reach FSR 477, Avery Creek Rd, a vehicle exit to US 276. USFS Trail #103.

South Mills River Trail   222

Including the following connecting trails:

Cantrell Creek Trail (USFS Trail #148)   223

Horse Cove Trail (USFS Trail #325)   224

Mullinax Trail (USFS Trail #326)   225

Poundingmill Trail (USFS Trail #349)   226

Wagon Gap Trail (USFS Trail #360)   227

Length: 12 mi (19 km), moderate; *USGS:* Pisgah Forest; *Trailhead:* Turkey Pen gap parking area.

Directions and Description: This trail crosses the South Mills River thirteen times, eight at which the river must be forded; the fordings come after passing the Cantrell Creek Lodge site. Since crossing the river can be difficult or impossible after heavy rains, caution is advised. The trail also serves as a horse trail and is frequented by fishermen looking for trophy water angling. Nine other trails connect with the *South Mills River Trail*, providing numerous loop possibilities.

From jct of US 276-64 and NC 280, proceed NE on NC 280 for 5 mi to Henderson and the Transylvania county line. Turn L between two private homes on FSR 297, Turkey Pen Rd, and go 1.2 mi to parking area; park.

Follow wide road at end of parking area, turning L at the horse trail sign by a single poplar tree, and descend for 0.4 mi to the river. (A longer route, 0.8 mi long, is to follow the old road to the river.) Cross the swinging bridge.

At 0.6 mi *Mullinax Trail* intersects on R and follows seeded road, rough in places, for 0.9 mi; this is both horse and hiking trail. It connects with *Squirrel Gap Trail*.

Continuing up South Mills, at 1.9 mi the *Poundingmill Trail* turns R and follows up Poundingmill Branch on a moderate grade for 1.5 mi to jct with *Squirrel Gap Trail*.

At 3 mi the *Wagon Road Gap Trail* turns L for 0.7 mi, where it reaches jct with *Turkey Pen Gap Trail*.

The entire trail follows on old railroad grade; most of the trestles have vanished. Second growth oaks and poplars are the chief forest trees; outstanding displays of purple rhododendron and wildflowers are frequent.

Reach Cantrell Creek Lodge area at 3.9 mi; here in 1903 Dr. Carl Schenck housed his students of forestry. The building was moved to the Cradle of Forestry as an exhibit in 1978.

From the Cantrell site the *Cantrell Creek Trail* turns R (N), following an old railroad grade through at least a dozen creek crossings and some rough sections for 1.9 mi to jct with *Squirrel Gap Trail*. (After 0.9 mi on the *Cantrell Creek Trail,* the *Horse Cove Gap Trail* connects L to *Squirrel Gap Trail*, after a moderate climb of 0.7 mi.)

From the Cantrell site continue up the South River to Wolf Ford at 9.5 mi, and reach a connection with *Squirrel Gap Trail* on the R. (The horse trail turns L and rejoins the hiking trail at 11 mi, near Billy Branch.) At 10.6 mi the *Buckhorn Gap Trail* intersects on the L, ascending to Buckhorn Gap and descending to the Avery Creek Rd for a total distance of 4.6 mi. Continue up South Mills to exit at Gaging Station on FSR 476 for a total of 12 mi. A loop trail may be used for return to Turkey Pen Gap — or use vehicle shuttle. USFS Trail #133.

Squirrel Gap Trail   **228**

Length: 7.5 mi (12 km), moderate; *USGS:* Pisgah Forest; *Trail-head:* Pea Gap on Bradley Creek Trail.

Directions and Description: To reach *Squirrel Gap Trail*, the hiker must hike part of another trail for access. For example, from the W terminus hike 2.4 mi on the *South Mills Trail* from FSR 476, or hike the *Bradley Creek Trail* from the Hendersonville Water Intake, or from Turkey Pen Gap take the *Vineyard Gap Trail* for 3.3 mi, or also from Turkey Pen Gap take the *Bradley Creek Trail* to Pea Gap for a walk of 1.7 mi. The latter route of entry is used here.

From NC 280 jct with Turkey Pen Rd, FSR 297, follow FSR to Turkey Pen Gap; park. Hike down old logging road L on *South Mills Trail* for 0.4 mi, but do not cross bridge. Take old road down river, cross at county line at 0.9 mi, and ascend on *Bradley Creek Trail* to Pea Gap at 1.7 mi. Turn L and begin on *Squirrel Gap Trail*. Follow trail used by both horses and hikers for 1.5 mi. Jct with *Mullinax Trail* is on L at 0.7 mi; reach *Laurel Creek Trail* at 1.5 mi. (Going R on rough, rarely used connection of 1.8 mi leads to *Bradley Creek Trail*.) Then reach *Poundingmill Branch Trail,* which descends L to *South Mills Trail* at 1.5 mi. Continue ahead through forest of hardwood, laurel, and rhododendron, winding in and out of coves and gaps. Reach highest point, Laurel Gap (3,480 ft), at 2.5 mi. At 4 mi reach jct with *Cantrell Creek Trail* (L), and then come to *Horse Cove Gap Trail* (L) at 5.4 mi. reach Wolf Ford at jct of *South Mills Trail* at 7.5 mi. Backtrack, or exit for 2.4 mi on *South Mills Trail* to FSR 476. USFS Trail #147.

Turkey Pen Gap Trail   **229**

Length: 5.5 mi (8.5 km), moderate to strenuous; *USGS:* Pisgah Forest; *Trailhead:* Turkey Pen Gap parking area.

Directions and Description: From Turkey Pen Gap parking area at end of FSR 297, look for sign, W, on L of road. Follow dry ridge over Simpson Gap, Sharpy Mtn, and Sandy Gap to jct with *Wagon Road Trail* (R) at 2.3 mi. Continue on ridge over McCall Mtn, down to Deep Gap, and ascend to Muleshoe Gap, reaching *Black Mtn Trail* jct at 5.5 mi. Backtrack, or take *Black Mtn Trail* out (N) to

Cradle of Forestry or S to Ranger Work Center on US 276. USFS
Trail #322.

Vineyard Gap Trail   230

Length: 3.3 mi (5.3 km), moderate; *USGS:* Pisgah Forest; *Trailhead:* Turkey Pen Gap parking area.

Directions and Description: From Turkey Pen Gap parking area
at end of FSR 297, look for sign on R of road (E), opposite *Turkey
Pen Gap Trail,* and follow ridge to Vineyard Gap at 1.9 mi. Descend
and cross South Fork Mills River at confluence with Bradley Creek
at approximately 2.4 mi. Exit at 3.3 mi at jct of *Bradley Creek Trail.*
Backtrack, or use loop with *Bradley Creek Trail* or *Mullinax Trail.*
USFS Trail #324.

Fletcher Creek Trail and Middle Fork Trail   231-232

Length: 8.4 mi rt cb (13.4 km), easy; *USGS:* Dunsmore Mtn;
Trailhead: Hendersonville Reservoir.

Directions and Description: From NC 191-280,turn at sign for
North River Campground on SR 1345 and go 5 mi to FSR 479. Turn
to L on Hendersonville Reservoir Rd, FSR 142, and park at reservoir. Both trails begin at the N end of the dam. *Fletcher Creek
Trail* crosses the creek a number of times, intersects with other
trails, and dead ends at 2.4 mi. Backtrack to *Middle Fork Trail* (and
return to parking area) or turn sharply R and hike 1.8 mi on old
logging road to dead end of the trail. Backtrack to *Fletcher Creek
Trail* and return to parking area. USFS Trails #350 and 352.

Trace Ridge Trail   233

Length: 3.1 mi (5 km), moderate to strenuous; *USGS:* Dunsmore
Mtn; *Trailhead:* Hendersonville Reservoir Rd.

Directions and Description: From NC 191-280, turn at sign of
North River Campground on SR 1345 and go 5 mi to FSR 479. Turn
L on Hendersonville Reservoir Rd, FSR 142, and go 0.5 mi. Look
for old road on R, unmarked and rarely used, but sometimes emp-

loyed by horse traffic. Follow up a dry ridge of regenerated hard-woods and pines. After 3.1 mi reach the Parkway at mp 401.5, SW of but near Ferrin Knob Tunnel #3 and Beaverdam Gap. Return by the same route or use vehicle shuttle. USFS Trail #354.

Cradle of Forestry Area, Transylvania County

Forest Festival Trail   **234**

Length: 1 mi (1.6 km), easy; *USGS:* Shining Rock; *Trailhead:* Parking lot.

Directions and Description: From the Blue Ridge Parkway jct with US 276, drive 4 mi S to entrance of the Cradle of Forestry. Hike from the parking lot on paved trail suitable also for wheelchairs. Trail features exhibits of forestry management and steam-powered logging equipment, based on Dr. Carl A. Schenck's Biltmore Forest Fair of 1908. Open April 1 through October.

Cradle of Forestry Campus Trail   **235**

Length: 1 mi (1.6 km), easy; *USGS:* Shining Rock; *Trailhead:* Parking lot.

Directions and Description: Driving directions as given above except follow sign L at the Visitors Center to paved historic trail through the first forestry school area in America, founded by Dr. Carl A. Schenck. A German forester employed by George Vanderbilt to manage his vast forest empire, Schenck became the father of American forestry management because of his work in this area from 1897 to 1909. The school opened in 1898 and graduated its first class in 1913. Trail is a National Recreational Trail and a National Historic Site. Open April 1 through October. USFS Trail #319.

SECTION IV
TOECANE RANGER DISTRICT

South Toe Area, Yancey County

Woody Ridge Trail   236

Length: 4 mi rt (6.4 km), moderate to strenuous; *USGS:* Mt Mitchell, Celo; *Trailhead:* Gate of USFS timber access road #5528.

Directions and Description: From Micaville at jct of US19E and NC 80, go S on NC 80 for 6 mi to Lower Whiteoak Creek Rd. Turn R and go 2 mi to Upper Whiteoak Creek Rd. Turn R, and go 0.5 mi to Woody Ridge trailhead at gate.

Begin hike at the gate, paralleling Shuford Creek for 0.2 mi, and then begin climb to Woody Ridge. Trail switchbacks steeply, straightens out, and ascends to summit of Horse Rock (6,140 ft) at 2 mi. Trail is not blazed and may be overgrown and difficult to follow. This walk offers an excellent example of vegetation change — from southern softwoods to northern hardwoods to spruce and fir. No camping or water on the climb. Return by same route for total of 4 mi. Elev change, 2,980 ft. USFS Trail #177.

Colbert Ridge Trail   237

Length: 7.4 mi rt (11.8 km), strenuous; *USGS:* Mt Mitchell, Celo; *Trailhead:* Parking area at trail sign on SR 1158.

Directions and Description: From Micaville at jct of US19E and NC 80, go S on NC 80 for 10 mi to community of Hamrick (near Carolina Hemlock Recreation Area). Turn R onto Colbert Creek Rd, SR 1158. At 0.5 mi parking for trailhead is on R.

Follow white-blazed trail, ascending gently at first. Rock outcroppings provide scenic views. At 2.7 mi ascend switchbacks on E side of Winter Star Mtn. Reach spring on L at 3.3 mi, and Deep Gap (5,700 ft) at 3.7 mi. Shelter and tent camping. Hike can continue S on *Black Mtn Crest Trail* for 3.9 mi to parking lot at Mt. Mitchell, or hiker can return to Colbert Creek Rd for total of 7.4 mi. Elev change, 2,950 ft. USFS Trail #178.

Black Mountain Crest Trail   238

Length: 12 mi (19.2 km), strenuous; *USGS:* Mt Mitchell, Celo, Burnsville; *Trailhead:* Mt Mitchell summit picnic area.

Directions and Description: Sections of this trail were formerly called *Deep Gap Trail* and *Celo Knob Trail.* The trailhead is in Mt Mitchell State Park, and vehicles must be registered with Park Ranger if left overnight.

Leave parking lot near summit of Mt Mitchell on what is considered to be one of the most rugged and difficult trails in the state. Follow orange-blazed trail over rocky terrain; hiking and climbing can be slow, but on a clear day the scenic grandeur is unmatched. Ascend to Mt Craig (6,645 ft), named in honor of Governor Locke Craig, at 1 mi. Then climb Big Tom Mtn at 1.1 mi N (6,593 ft), named in honor of Thomas Wilson. (See Mt Mitchell State Park description for a full account of peak names in this area). There is a jct at 1.6 mi with *Big Tom Gap Trail.* Continue on crest among ferns, thornless blackberry, Clinton's lily, moose wood, and the fragrance of spruce and fir to summit of Balsam Cone (6,611 ft) at 1.9 mi, and then ascend Cattail Peak (6,583 ft) at 2.5 mi. Enter boundary of Pisgah National Forest, ascend to Potato Hill at 3 mi, and reach Deep Gap Shelter at 3.9 mi. Shelter has four large wood bunks, tent camping in area, and water 300 yd down the mountain in front of shelter. Jct with *Colbert Ridge Trail* R comes next at 4 mi, and then reach summit of Deer Mtn (6,200 ft) at 4.5 mi and jct with old road L at 6.2 mi. Continue ahead on old road, skirting W of Gibbs Mtn and Horse Rock. Leave old road at 7.2 mi, and reach summit of Celo Knob (6,427 ft) at 7.4 mi. Turn L and begin descent into Bowlens Creek watershed on old logging road at 7.6 mi, passing spring on R at 7.8 mi, crossing stream at 8.8 mi, passing dangerous open mine shaft on L at 9.5 mi, and coming to gate at 10.3 mi. Note unique four-trunked treeat 10.4 mi. From 11 mi, follow cascading Bowlens Creek to Bowlens Creek Rd, SR 1109, at 12 mi. On Bowlens Creek Rd R, it is 2.4 mi to NC 197 and then R 0.7 mi to jct of US 19E in

Burnsville. Elev change, 3,580 ft. Vehicle shuttle necessary. USFS Trail #179.

Lost Cove Ridge Trail   240

Length: 3.3 mi (5.3 km), moderate to strenuous; *USGS:* Celo, Marian (W); *Trailhead:* Milepost 350.4 W on BRP.

Directions and Description: From mp 350.4 at Flinty Gap (4,782 ft) on the Blue Ridge Parkway, stop at parking lot and cross road to climb switchbacks to Green Knob Lookout Tower (5,070 ft), with outstanding 360° views. Turn R and descend on a white-blazed trail between FSR 472 and Big Lost Cove Creek. Trees are hardwoods and conifers. No water on trail. At 2.7 mi trail descends steeply to FSR 472. Cross road, then South Toe River, and enter Black Mountain Recreation Area at 3.3 mi. No camping on trail, but camping and picnicking permitted in Recreation Area. USFS Trail #182.

Bald Knob Ridge Trail   241

Length: 2.8 mi (4.5 km), easy to moderate; *USGS:* Montreat; *Trailhead:* Parking lot at mp 355 on BRP.

Directions and Description: From parking area at mp 355 (5,200 ft) on the Blue Ridge Parkway, descend 0.1 mi on white-blazed trail to FS boundary, and then follow Bald Knob Ridge on N of Left Prong South Toe River. At 1 mi begin switchbacks. Trail passes through park-like stands of virgin red spruce and Fraser's fir. Reach FSR 472 at 2.8 mi. Return by same route or have vehicle at FSR 472. USFS Trail #186.

Mt Mitchell Trail   242

Length: 5.6 mi (9 km), strenuous; *USGS:* Mt Mitchell, Celo; *Trailhead:* Near campground amphitheatre.

Directions and Description: Also see *Mt Mitchell Trail* description in Mt Mitchell State Park section.

Go 3.5 mi from NC 80, FSR 472, jct near Mt. Mitchell Golf Course to Black Mountain Campground, or travel 5 mi down the mountain from Blue Ridge Parkway at Deep Gap on FSR 472. Begin hike near bridge, walk across meadow, and pass amphitheater at upper level near campground host's residence. Follow blue-blazed, well-graded trail past *Devil's Den Forest Walk* at 0.1 mi. Large banks of meadow rue are passed 0.9 mi. Jct with *Long Arm Ridge Trail* R is reached at 1.2 mi, and *Open Ridge Trail* comes in R at 1.7 mi. Cross Creek at 2.7 mi, and reach jct L with *Higgins Bald Ground Trail*. Spruce forest predominates for 0.4 mi. Continue on switchbacks to jct with *Buncombe Horse Range (and Hiking) Trail* (formerly *Maple Camp Trail*) at 3.9 mi. Turn L and at 4 mi turn R into forest. (Camp Alice Trail Shelter is 200 ft L; it has wire bunks for ten and picnic table.) Ascend steeply over rough and eroded trail for 1.6 mi to summit of Mt. Mitchell and parking lot. Elev change, 3,884 ft. Vehicle switching necessary. USFS Trail #190.

Big Tom Gap Trail   243

Length: 0.5 mi (0.8 km), strenuous; *USGS:* Mt Mitchell; *Trailhead:* Access from either Buncombe Trail or Black Mtn Crest Trail jcts.

Directions and Description: Follow this blue-blazed trail as a rough, steep, primitive, unmaintained connection between the *Black Mtn Crest Trail* and the *Buncombe Horse Range Trail*. Trail crosses unstable rock rubble, high-elevation spruce and fir forest between Big Tom and Balsam Cone mtns.

Buncombe Horse Range Trail   244
Includes: **Old Maple Camp Trail**

Length: 17.5 mi (28.2 km), easy to moderate; *USGS:* Mt Mitchell, Celo, Montreat; *Trailhead:* Buncombe Horse Range parking area on SR 1159.

Directions and Description: This trail is used both as a horseback-riding and hiking trail.

From the community of Hamrick on NC 80 (10 mi S of Micaville), turn R on Colbert Creek Rd, SR 1158, and go 1 mi to jct with SR 1159. Turn L, and go 1 mi to trailhead sign (2,920 ft).

The white-blazed trail skirts the S edge of Middle Creek Natural Area, with switchbacks near Maple Camp Creek; it ascends the Maple Camp Ridge and goes on to Maple Camp Bald. At 3.5 mi pass through burned-over area, enter old railroad tramway path at 4 mi, and continue for 2.9 mi to jct with *Mt Mitchell Trail*. Reach Camp Alice Shelter at 7 mi (5,782 ft), and come to end of *Old Maple Camp Trail*. Shelter has ten wire bunks, picnic shed, and horse corral. Water is nearby.

Continue on old railroad tramway right-of way, and at 8 mi reach jct with access road to NC 128 near Mt Mitchell State Park entrance. Continue on tramway, pass E of Potato Knob, and turn off tramway at 13.3 mi. Descend through spruce-fir forest, and follow old logging road to Right Prong South Toe River at bridge on FSR 472 (3,560 ft). Small area for parking. USFS Trail #191.

Brian Bottom Trail   246

Length: 1 mi (1.6 km), easy; *USGS:* Celo, Marion (W); *Trailhead:* Entrance bridge at Black Mtn Recreation Area.

Directions and Description: From bridge at the Black Mtn Recreation Area off FSR 472 (N 5 mi from Deep Gap on Blue Ridge Parkway), go up the river in a loop from the bridge for 1 mi. Trail crosses two rustic locust bridges. Vegetation is representative of river area. (This is also a bicycle trail.) USFS Trail #1006.

Hemlock Trail   247

Length: 1 mi (1.6 km), easy; *USGS:* Celo; *Trailhead:* Swimming area at Carolina Hemlocks Recreation Area.

Directions and Description: From Micaville jct of NC 80 and US 19E, go S 10 mi to Carolina Hemlocks Recreation Area on NC 80. Begin R at the swimming beach, follow along South Toe River, cross road, and enter the *Nature Trail Loop* by the campground. Part of the trail is interpretive. Area has camping, comfort station, picnicking, swimming, and fishing. Open April 15-November 1. USFS Trail #1003.

Support Facilities: In addition to the USFS campgrounds, Black Mtn and Carolina Hemlocks Recreation Area on NC 80, the following commercial campgrounds for the South Toe area are recommended. Toe River Campground — from jct of US 19E and NC 80 in Micaville, go S on NC 80 for 4 mi and turn 1 mi E on SR 1152 to Toe River. Address is P.O. Box 766, Micaville, NC 28755. Tel: 704-675-5111. Full svc, rec fac. Open March 15-September 15. Clear Creek Camping Park — from jct of US 19E and NC 80 in Micaville, go S on NC 80 for 10 mi and turn L on gravel road for 0.5 mi. Address is Rt. 5, Box 189, Burnsville, NC 28714. Tel: 704-675-4510. Full svc, limited rec. Open May 1-October 31.

Cloudland Trail   248

Length: 3 mi rt (4.6 km), easy; *USGS:* Carvers Gap, White Rocks Mtn; *Trailhead:*Parking lot #1.

Directions and Description: Take SR 1348 for 1.8 mi at jct with NC 261 at Carvers Gap on the Tennessee-North Carolina state line. Turn R to parking lot #1. Follow trail sign W on the crest of Roan Mtn through spruce and fir, mountain avents and rhododendron, heavy moss on trees and ground, and parking lots #2 and #3. Climb to Roan High Bluff (6,267 ft) at 1.5 mi for superb views of Bald and Unaka mtns. Return by same route. USFS Trail #1000.

Roan Mtn Gardens Trail   249

Length: 1 mi (1.6 km), easy; *USGS:* See above; *Trailhead:* Parking lot #2 near picnic area.

Directions and Description: Follow triple loop paved trail from Roan Mtn Gardens parking lot #2 through an extraordinary display of purple rhododendron and flame azalea. One of the trails has sixteen interpretive signs, and another loop passes through a large grassy bald area with rhododendron — usually at their flowering peak the last of June. Area easy for handicapped. USFS Trail #1002.

Support Facilities: Roan Mtn State Resort Park — from jct of US 19E and TN 143S go 5 mi on TN 143 from the town of Roan Mtn. Tel: 615-772-4178. Full svc, limited rec.

Flat Top Area, Yancey County

Devil's Creek Trail   250

Length: 6 mi rt (9.6 km), easy to moderate; *USGS:* Chestoa; *Trailhead:* Jct of FSR 278 and FSR 5506 at Devil's Creek Gap.

Directions and Description: From the town of Sioux on US 19W, go W 5 mi, turn on FSR 278 (Flat Top Mtn Rd), and go 1 mi to jct of FSR 1278 and FSR 5506 at Devil's Creek Gap; trailhead is here. Follow the timber access route at trailhead for 1 mi, and continue around flanks of Flat Top Mtn. Trail ends at Lost Cove and jct with *Lost Cove Trail* (see below). Water available, but no camping. Lost Cove is a private, isolated area, accessible to the inhabitants in the early 1900's only by foot or rail. There are many legends about the "lost" inhabitants and the "bear woods." USFS Trail #188.

Lost Cove Trail   252

Length: 4 mi rt (6.4 km), easy; *USGS:* Chestoa; *Trailhead:* FS timber access road #4404 entrance.

Directions and Description: From the town of Sioux on US 19W, go W 1 mi to Harmiller Gap. Turn R on SR 1415 for 1 mi; where it branches into three roads. Take L fork, which is FSR 278. Go 2.5 mi to Lost Cove trailhead at timber access FSR 5505 entrance. Enter gate on foot, follow road for 0.5 mi, and reach Joe Lewis Fields, where outstanding views of the Nolichucky River gorge can be found. Descend by switchbacks, and join *Devil's Creek Trail* near lost Cove at 2 mi. Return by same route, or take *Devil's Creek Trail*.

Support Facilities: No camping allowed on the trail. A public campground in the area is Rock Creek Campgrounds, Cherokee National Forest; it is 6 mi E on FSR 30 from the town of Erwin, Tennessee. Tel: 615-743-5871. (U.S. Forest Service office is on Johnson City highway outside Erwin.) USFS Trail #196.

Elk Falls Area, Avery County

Big Falls Trail   253

Length: 0.5 mi rt (0.8 km), easy to moderate; *USGS:* Elk Falls;
Trailhead: Parking lot at Big Falls.
   Directions and Description: From Elk Park on US 19E, go W and
turn R on FSR 190 (Elks Falls Rd). Go 6 mi to Big Falls parking lot.
Begin hike on timber access road to Elk River, and descend to
bottom of the 50-ft falls with amphitheater-like walls. Camping is
not permitted. Return by the same route. USFS Trail #1007.

Big Ivy Area, Buncombe County

Big Butte Trail   254

Length: 7 mi (11.3 km), moderate to strenuous; *USGS:* Mt
Mitchell, Montreat; *Trailhead:* East side of road at Cane River Gap.
   Directions and Description: From Burnsville on NC 197, go SW
16 mi to top of Cane River Gap. Or, from Barnardsville on NC 197
go NE 10 mi. Begin at parking area and ascend on white-blazed trail
with switchbacks along the Yancey-Buncombe county line. Reach
Mahogany Knob, then Flat Spring Knob at 2.3 mi, and come to Flat
Spring Gap at 2.5 mi. Primitive campsite and water available here.
Ramps, a long-lasting, garlic-tasting wild onion, is massed in sections throughout this trail area. Bypass Big Butte (5,920 ft), but
climb Little Butte Knob at 4.1 mi. Reach Point Misery at 5.5 mi, and
the Blue Ridge Parkway at 7 mi. Parking area is Balsam Gap. Some
of the vegetation on this trail consists of birch, beech, spruce, fir,
hickory, maple, trillium, along with grassy groundcovers. USFS
Trail #161.

Halfway Trail   255

Length: 6.2 mi rt (9.9 km), moderate; *USGS:* Montreat, Craggy
Pinnacle; *Trailhead:* Parking lot at Craggy Gardens Visitors Center.

Directions and Description: Begin at the N end of the parking lot at Craggy Gardens Visitors Center, which is at mp 364.1 on the Blue Ridge Parkway. Skirt Craggy Knob on white-blazed trail, and turn L at 0.5 mi. Descend, cross stream at 0.9 mi, and pass through canopy of moosewood under yellow birches and by wildflowers such as twistedstalk and merrybells. Cross stream at 2.4 mi, and reach impressive Cascade Falls at 1.8 mi. Use cable for safety. Descend steeply to 2.3 mi, and cross stream at 2.4 mi. Turn sharp L at 2.7 mi, and descend on switchbacks. Trail to R is *Bullhead Ridge Trail,* leading to primitive camping area near FSR 74 and Dillingham. Turn R by large boulders at 2.9 mi. Reach 70-ft Douglas Falls at 3.1 mi. Return by the same route, or hike 0.5 mi on well-graded trail to FSR 74 parking lot. FSR 74 winds down the mtn for 8.7 mi and to Dillingham Rd, SR 2173, which then goes for 5 more mi to Barnardsville and NC 197. Elev change, 1,114 ft. USFS Trail #162.

Straight Creek Trail and Corner Rock Trail 256

Length: 3.5 mi (5.6 km), easy to moderate; *USGS:* Mt Mitchell; *Trailhead:* Parking area at jct of FSR 5552 and NC 197.
Directions and Description: From Cane River Gap on NC 197, go S to sign and FSR 5552 on L. Park. Follow timber road for 1 mi. Climb switchbacks to Big Butte Gap, and descend on a series of switchbacks to another timber access road, FSR 5551. Follow *Corner Rock Trail* to Corner Rock, a balancing rock, at 3.4 mi. FSR 74 and parking area at 3.5 mi. USFS Trail #169.

Shope Creek Trail 257

Length: 2.2 mi (3.5 km), moderate; *USGS:* Craggy Pinnacle; *Trailhead:* Blue Ridge Parkway mp 375.
Directions and Description: From jct of US 70 and Blue Ridge Parkway in Asheville, go N on Parkway to mp 375 parking overlook (4,350 ft). Park. Descend on ridge along National Forest boundary for 0.5 mi. Turn R to Shope Creek, cross creek, and continue descent on steep slopes through a ravine. Reach FSR 5532 and jct gates at 2.2 mi. Check with Toecane Ranger District in Burnsville

before using area for camping or parking of vehicles at S end of trail at Slope Creek Rd. USFS Trail #1004.

Bullhead Ridge Trail   258

Length: 2 mi rt (3.2 km), easy; *USGS:* Craggy Pinnacle; *Trailhead:* Parking area at end of FSR 74.

Directions and Description: From dead end of parking area FSR 74, 9.2 mi from paved SR 2173 to Dillingham, ascend on Bullhead Ridge through splendid stands of virgin maple, birch, and eastern hemlock to jct with *Halfway Trail* (USFS Trail #162). Return by same route, or turn R and descend to Douglas Falls. Turn R and follow graded trail 0.5 mi for loop back to parking lot. Primitive and scenic camping area. USFS Trail #1005.

Snowball Trail   259

Length: 8 mi rt (12.8 km), moderate; *USGS:* Craggy Pinnacle; *Trailhead:* Gated FSR 63 and Blue Ridge Parkway.

Directions and Description: Turn off Parkway at Craggy Picnic Area, mp 367.7, and park in the vicinity of gated FSR 63, Barnardsville Rd. Enter trail L of gate and go up ridge to reach side of Snowball Mtn (5,494 ft) via switchbacks at 0.7 mi. Descend and continue NW on main ridge through birch forest and rich displays of wildflowers. Summer growth may be heavy. Avoid trails and jeep roads from ridge L to Camp Sequoyah or R to FSR 63. Pass Hawkbill Rock and reach Little Snowball Mtn (4,720 ft) at 4 mi. Outstanding views of French Broad River and the Craggies. Spring water near summit. Return by the same route.

CHAPTER IV

UWHARRIE NATIONAL FOREST

Montgomery, Randolph, and Davidson Counties

In the center of the state, the nearly-50,000-acre Uwharrie National Forest spreads into three counties; it is chiefly in Montgomery, but more than 8,000 acres lie in Randolph County and another 1,000 acres are in Davidson County. The large forest area is broken into a patchwork by private properties and approximately 300 miles of county, state, and private roads. More than 185 miles are forest roads. Elevation is rarely over 900 ft, but some hills provide a climb of 500 ft for the hiker.

Badin Lake Recreational Area and Lake Tillery form the forest's western boundary. Outdoor recreation facilities are provided for fishing for largemouth bass, bream, and white bass; hunting for grouse, duck, and deer; boating and canoeing; and, camping. There are also trails for hikers, horseback riders, and ORV's.

Although there are no virgin sections of forest, there are a few large trees near ravines and stream banks. Most of the hardwoods are oak, poplar, and gum, with a subcanopy of sourwoods. Among the conifers are Virginia yellow pines, long and short leaved pines, and loblolly. Among the 700 species of plants, wildflowers are abundant.

Access to the forest can be from NC 109 N and S; NC 24-27 between Albermarle and Troy; NC 47 and 49 from the NW; and NC 134 between Asheboro and Troy. The forest headquarters is 2 mi E of Troy on NC 24-27.

Uwharrie Trail

Southern Section

Length: 20.5 mi (32.8 km), easy to moderate; *USGS:* Albermarle (SE), Troy; *Trailhead:* Parking lot on NC 24-27 at jct with FSR 517.

Directions and Description: At parking lot, enter scrub oaks on L and descend on narrow white-blazed trail through forests of hardwoods and yellow pines. Skirt E of mountain slope. At 2 mi pass side trail on R which leads 0.5 mi to Woodrum Camp, a primitive campsite and wilderness area. Cross Island Creek at 4.5 mi, and reach *Dutchman's Trail* a 9.5-mi yellow-blazed wilderness trail which forms a 19-mi loop from the trailhead at NC 24-27 and FSR 517 to Yates Camp and back, at 5.1 mi.

Continue through forest, where deer and wild turkey may be seen. Unlikely to be seen is the red-cockaded woodpecker — an endangered species which builds its nest in live pine trees. Pass side trail, which goes R 0.5 mi to Yates Camp, at 8.9 mi, and cross SR 1146 at 9.0 mi. At 9.3 mi cross creek, and cross it again at 10.3 mi. Follow downstream on R for 0.5 mi, then turn R from steep, rocky climb to reach summit at 10.8 mi. Turn sharp R off logging road at 11.1 mi, and cross NC 109 at 11.9 mi.

At 12.4 mi spring is on L. Cross stream at 12.8 mi and 13.9 mi. Cross Spencer Creek hiking bridge at 14 mi. Ascend and pass a bed of running cedar at 14.1 mi. Intersect with W *Morris Mtn Camp Trail* at 14.3 mi. To Morris Mtn Camp it is 1 mi. No water at the campsite. Ascend and reach summit at 14.6 mi, reach FSR 549 at 15 mi. Cross road and at 17 mi cross two streams on bridges a few feet apart. Cross SR 1134 at 18.1 mi. Reach high ridge at 19.2 mi, and continue to rocky peak of Dark Mtn (940 ft) at 19.4 mi. Here is an excellent western view. After a rocky descent, reach landscaped parking area and SR 1306 at 20.5 mi. (Ophir is L 1.8 mi, Flint Hill is R 2.8 mi, and NC 134 is reached at 7 mi. Trail continues across Barnes Creek bridge with sharp R, but the Forest Service has not opened it to general public use at the time of this report. (See below), Vehicle switching necessary.

Middle Section

Length: 5.4 mi (9.6 km), easy to moderate; *USGS:* Troy, Asheboro (Eleazer); *Trailhead:* Parking lot at SR 1306 near Barnes Creek bridge, 1.8 mi E of Ophir.

Directions and Description: This section of trail is not open to the general public at the time of this report. Parts of the trail cross private lands. Information on this section can be received by contacting the Uwharrie Trail Club, P.O. Box 2073, Asheboro, NC 27206, whose members maintain the trail.

From parking lot cross Barnes Creek bridge, and turn sharp R. Turn L after 50 ft, ascending steeply for 0.3 mi. Skirt rocky mountainside E and reach crest of ridge at 0.4 mi. Continue ascent to summit (800 ft), follow ridge, and descend to SR 1108 at 2.4 mi. (Near Randolph County line it becomes 1305 W.) Cross road and continue through private land. Reach SR1109 near Dewey Luther property at 4.4 mi and continue N. Follow gravel road through pasture and open fields to SR 1143 at 5.4 mi. (SR 1107 is L at 2 mi, and NC 49 is at 7 mi. Ulah on US 220 is 11 mi R on SR 1143 and SR 1142). Vehicle switching recommended.

"Birkhead Trail," Northern Section

Length: 7.2 mi (11.5 km), easy to moderate; *USGS:* Asheboro (Eleazer); *Trailhead:* Intersection of SR 1109 and 1143.

Directions and Description: Follow white-blazed trail N on gravel SR 1109 for 0.6 mi to end of state maintenance at Strieby Church; descend on FSR 6523 to South Prong Creek at 0.9 mi. Reach forest boundary at 1.6 mi, campsite and water at 1.7 mi, and then ascend. At 2.1 mi cross log bridge over North Prong Creek. Bingham Graveyard Camp #6 is on R at yellow blaze at 2.8 mi. At 3.8 mi on L are ruins of John Watson Birkhead (1858-1933) plantation. Reach Camp #5 on scenic ridge to W at 4.2 mi. Wild quinine in abundance here. Rattlesnakes are also seen along these ridges and on Coolers Knob. Camp #1-B, with water, is on L at 5.3 mi. At 6 mi is Coolers Knob, with a scenic view E at 50 yd. At 6.3 mi turn R from old road with blueberries and bristly locust. Descend, cross Talbotts Creek at 7 mi, and reach SR 1142 at 7.2 mi. This is the northern terminus of the *Uwharrie Trail*. (There is no parking lot here.) To reach NC 49 take L for 2 mi, and to get to Asheboro take R for 6 mi NE. Vehicle switching necessary.

Badin Lake Trail   261

Length: 5.6 mi (9 km), easy; *USGS:* Albermarle (NE); *Trailhead:* Cove Boat Ramp parking lot.

Directions and Description: From NC 109 and 1153 jct, 1.5 mi NW from the town of Uwharrie, take NC 1153 0.4 mi to FSR 576. Turn R and go 2.9 mi to FSR 597; turn R. At 0.3 mi turn L on 597B to Cove Boat Ramp.

From parking lot hike N, taking either the lakeside L or the switchbacks R on the yellow-blazed loop trail. If ascending R, reach jct with *Dutch John Trail* at 0.6 mi. Turn L, continuing through forest of hardwoods; cross roads at 0.9 mi and 1.4 mi. Pass stream and skirt rocky side of hill at 1.6 mi. (Short loop is L at 1.9 mi.) Reach lake cove at 2 mi and scenic end of point at 2.8 mi. Turn L and reach large rock slopes by the lake at 3.7 mi. Area has abundant cedars, mosses, and wildflowers. Continue by lakeside, cross road at 4.3 mi, and reach jct with short trail at 5.1 mi. Return to parking lot at 5.6 mi.

Dutch John Trail   262

Length: 3.4 mi (5.4 km), easy; *USGS:* Albermarle (NE); *Trailhead:* Dutch John Campground on FSR 553.

Directions and Description: From NC 109 and 1153 jct, 1.5 mi NW from the town of Uwharrie, take NC 1153 0.4 mi to FSR 576. Turn R and go 1.5 mi to FSR 553. Turn L and reach Dutch John Campground on R after 2 mi.

From campground follow trail adjacent to Dutch John Creek for 1.3 mi. Reach FSR 576 at 2.7 mi, cross road and reach FSR 597 at 3.4 mi. To reach Cove Boat Ramp cross the road, hike 280 yd to jct of *Badin Lake Trail*, take L, and reach Cove Boat Ramp parking lot at 4.2 mi. Return to Dutch John Campground by same route.

Densons Creek Trail 263

Length: 3.5 mi rt cb (5.6 km), easy; *USGS:* Troy; *Trailhead:* Parking lot behind Uwharrie National Forest ranger station headquarters.

Directions and Description: On NC 24-27, 2 mi E of Troy, enter driveway to parking lot. Follow signs to beginning of both short and long loops of interpretive trail. At 0.3 mi turn L for 1-mi-long trail to Densons Creek, or turn R on short loop along high bank and reach jct with *Densons Creek Trail* at 0.6 mi. *Densons Creek Trail* is 2.3 mi long. Return uphill to parking lot at 0.9 mi for short loop and hike 2.6 mi for long loop. Trails have abundance of milky quartz.

Dutchman's Creek Trail and Morris Mountain Trail 264-265

The *Dutchman's Creek Trail* was constructed as an alternate route for use as a figure-eight loop when hiking the southern section of the *Uwharrie Trail*. It is a 9.5-mi yellow-blazed trail which begins at the opposite end of the parking lot for the *Uwharrie Trail*. Because it connects with the *Uwharrie Trail* at the halfway point, the hiker could make a loop of approximately 9 mi, instead of the full 19 mi.

The *West Morris Mountain Trail* is a 2.3 mi loop trail from the Morris Mtn Campground. It includes 0.7 mi of the spur from the *Uwharrie Trail* mentioned under the *Uwharrie Trail* description, Southern Section. The remaining 1.6 mi can be hiked from the spur or begun at the campground on FSR 549 near jct with SR 1303.

Other Trails in the Uwharrie

Old maps show a number of trails not listed above which have been abandoned or which have grown over with vegetation. Some have been designated as bike trails or ORV trails. Most are in the Badin Lake area and have such names as *Daniel Trail, Big Buck*

Trail, *Long Leaf Pine Trail*, *Rattlesnake Trail*, *Saw Dust Trail*, *Second Creek Trail*, *Lost Man Trail*, *Prison Camp Trail*, and *Iron Mine Trail*, to name a few. A current map of the trails and trail developments should be requested from the Headquarters Office (see ''Information'' below).

Support Facilities: Primitive camping facilities are available in the Forest. The nearest private campgrounds are: Asheboro East KOA, Route 6, Box 535, Asheboro, NC 27203. Tel: 919-629-4069. Open all year. Full svc, rec fac. Approach 5 mi E on US 64-NC 49. Holly Bluff Family Campground, Rt 3, Box 412, Asheboro, NC 27203. Tel: 919-857-2761. Open April 1 to Nov 1. Full svc, rec fac. Approach is 8 mi S of Asheboro on NC 49. Twin Harbor Camping Resort, P.O. Box 638, Mt. Gilead, NC 27306. Tel: 919-439-6129. Open all year. Full svc, rec fac. Approach is from NC 24-27 at Pee Dee River; turn E on NC 73, go 1.1 mi, then turn W on SR 1111 for 1 mi.

Information: Uwharrie National Forest District Ranger, Route 1, Box 237, Troy NC 27371. Tel: 919-576-3591.

TRAILS IN THE NATIONAL
PARK SYSTEM

APPALACHIAN FOOT TRAIL

GEORGIA TO MAINE

N.C.S.H.C.

CHAPTER V

APPALACHIAN NATIONAL SCENIC TRAIL

The Appalachian National Scenic Trail 266

The 2,100-mile *Appalachian Trail* along the crest of the Appalachian mountains from Georgia to Maine (or from Maine to Georgia) is the world's most famous hiking trail. It traverses all or portions of 14 states and is protected by the National Trails System Act of 1968, to which supplemental amendments were made in 1970. Its maintenance, however, is essentially dependent on more than 32 organized clubs and hundreds of volunteer workers.

It was Benton MacKaye of Shirley Center, Massachusetts, who first conceived of such a supertrail. In response, clubs affiliated with the New York-New Jersey Trail Conference constructed the first section of the *A.T.* in the Bear Mountain area of the Palisades Interstate Park in 1922. Interest in a contiguous trail spread to New England, where the older Appalachian Mountain Club and the Dartmouth Outing Club were influential in permanent trail connections.

In 1926 the leadership of Arthur Perkins of Hartford, Connecticut, translated MacKaye's dream into reality, but it was Myron H. Avery of Lubec, Maine, who, more than any other person, was instrumental in implementing and coordinating the agreement with government agencies and thousands of volunteers to complete the *Trail*. He served as chairman of the Appalachian Trail Conference (A.T.C.) from 1930 to 1952.

The 293 miles of the *A.T.* in North Carolina frequently weave back and forth on the Tennessee border, for instance reaching US 19E at Elk Park after ascending to the boundary from Fontana Dam in the Smokies. It is jointly maintained by private clubs of the A.T.C., the U.S. Forest Service, and the National Park Service. The Nantahala Hiking Club maintains 59.4 mi from the Georgia-North Carolina state line to the Nantahala River at Wesser on US 19. From there the Smoky Mountain Hiking Club maintains 95.2 mi to Davenport Gap at NC 284-TN 32. For the next 87.9 mi, the Carolina Mountain Club maintains the *A.T.* to Spivey Gap, US 19W. At that point the Tennessee Eastman Hiking Club maintains 53.8 mi to Elk Park, as well as 62.4 mi exclusively in Tennessee, which takes the *Trail* to the Virginia state line.

Because the *Trail* runs over private property, the threat of the chain being broken by industrial and residential development has been a serious concern of the Appalachian Trail Conference and other hiking organizations. In a June, 1981, land acquisition report, it was stated that nearly 575 miles of *A.T.* were still unprotected; 21 miles of this were in North Carolina and Tennessee. A major advantage for *Trail* protection in North Carolina has been the location of trail sections in the Nantahala and Pisgah National Forests and in the Great Smoky Mountain National Park. This has also been true in Georgia, with its Chattahoochee National Forest, and in Tennessee in the Cherokee National Forest.

Hikers on the *Appalachian Trail* should acquire the sixth edition of the *North Carolina-Georgia Appalachian Trail Guide* and the sixth edition of the *Tennessee-North Carolina Appalachian Trail Guide*. If not available in the local bookstore, the guidebooks can be ordered from the Appalachian Trail Conference, P.O. Box 236, Harpers Ferry, West Virginia 25425. Tel: 304-535-6331.

The following information is only a reference listing of some of the prominent features of the *Appalachian Trail* system in North Carolina. Detailed information is in the guidebooks mentioned above.

Milepoint	Location and Description
	The first 79.54 mi. of the *A.T.* are in Georgia, beginning at Springer Mtn.
0.00	Bly Gap, NC-GA state line (3,840 ft). Nearest all-weather road is 8 mi S on US 76 in Georgia.
1.52	Court House Bald (4,650 ft).
2.90	Muskrat Creek Shelter.
3.94	Jct L with *Chunky Gal Trail*.
7.09	Deep Gap (4,330 ft). Forest service road 71 leads 6 mi L to US 64.
7.59	Standing Indian Lean-to.
9.59	Standing Indian Mountain (5,490 ft). A rocky heath bald with excellent views of Georgia and the Tullulah River gorge.
12.39	Beech Gap (4,508 ft).
15.59	Carter-Gap Lean-to (4,550 ft).
21.59	Albert Mtn (5,280 ft). Firetower and outstanding views of Coweeta Experimental Forest.
21.99	Big Spring Gap Lean-to.
27.19	Rock Gap Lean-to (3,750 ft).
28.56	Wallace Gap (3,738 ft). US 64. Town of Franklin is 15 mi E.
35.46	Siler Bald Lean-to and Siler Bald Mtn (5,216 ft). Named in honor of William Siler, great grandfather of Rufus Morgan.
37.58	Wayah Gap (4,180 ft). Cross SR 35.
39.85	Jct L with yellow-blazed *Bartram Trail*.
41.38	Wayah Bald Observation Tower and John B. Byrne Memorial.

Milepoint	*Location and Description*
41.99	R jct with *Bartram Trail* and *Big Locust Trail*.
43.68	Licklog Gap (4,408 ft).
46.78	Cold Springs Lean-to.
47.48	Copper Bald (5,249 ft), scenic view of Nantahala River Valley.
47.88	Tellico Bald (5,130 ft).
48.38	Black Bald (5,000 ft).
48.78	Rocky Bald (5,180 ft), heath bald of rhododendrons and azaleas.
51.70	Tellico Gap (3,850 ft), road.
52.70	Wesser Bald Firetower (4,627 ft).
56.10	Wesser Creek Lean-to (*A.T.* route changed to W route).
59.43	US 19, Wesser, NC (1,650 ft), lodging, groceries, and restaurant.
59.53	Cross Nantahala River bridge.
61.63	Tyre Top (3,760 ft).
62.13	Grassy Gap (3,050 ft).
62.93	The Jump-Up, near extraordinary view of Nantahala River Valley.
65.33	Sassafras Gap Lean-to.
66.43	Cheoah Bald (5,062 ft).
70.73	Stekoah Gap (3,165 ft).
79.24	Cable Gap Lean-to.
80.24	High Top (3,786 ft).
82.04	Walker Gap (3,450 ft).

Milepoint	*Location and Description*
84.64	NC 28, Fontana Dam, NC, lodging, groceries, restaurant, recreational facilities, post office. Permit required for hiking in the Smokies.
86.04	Cross Fontana Dam. New shelter constructed.
90.38	Shuckstack Mtn (4,020 ft). Shuckstack Tower for scenic views.
91.68	Birch Spring Shelter (3,830 ft).
96.18	Mollies Ridge Shelter (4,600 ft) near Devils Tater Patch.
98.28	Russell Field Shelter (4,400 ft). *Russell Field Trail* descends L 3.5 mi toward Cades Cove Campground, Tenn.
100.68	Spence Field Shelter (4,890 ft). *Eagle Creek Trail* descends R leading to Fontana Lake. Bote Mtn Rd leads L 6.6 mi to Cades Cove Rd in Tenn.
101.08	Side Trail R, *Jenkins Ridge Trail* leading S in N.C.
101.78	Rocky Top (5,440 ft).
102.48	East Peak of Thunderhead (5,530 ft).
102.98	Beechnut Gap (4,840 ft).
104.88	Starky Gap (4,530 ft).
106.68	Derrick Knob Shelter (4,880 ft).
106.98	Sams Gap (4,840 ft). *A.T.* goes R, *Greenbrier Ridge Trail* descends L 5.1 mi to Tremont Rd, Tenn.
108.98	Cold Spring Knob (5,240 ft).
109.28	*Miry Ridge Trail* exits L to Elkmont Campground, Tenn.
109.78	Buckeye Gap (4,820 ft).

Milepoint	*Location and Description*
112.08	Silers Bald Shelter (5,440 ft). Two shelters. Scenic view of Mt. Le Conte NE.
112.48	*Welch Ridge Trail* descends R to High Rocks Fire Tower and connects with Hazel Creek trails in N.C.
113.78	Double Springs Gap Shelter (5,590 ft). *Goshen Prong Trail* exits L to Little River Rd in Tenn.
116.08	Mt. Buckley (6,580 ft).
116.58	Clingmans Dome (6,643 ft), highest elevation on the entire *A.T.* Tower provides panoramic views.
119.48	Mt. Collins (6,190 ft) and Mt. Collins Shelter. *Sugarloaf Mtn Trail* exits L in Tenn. *Fork Ridge Trail* exits R in N.C.
122.38	Indian Gap. *Road Prong Trail* exits L 3.3 mi to Chimney Tops parking area in Tenn.
124.09	Newfound Gap (5,040 ft) and highway (formerly US 441).
125.79	*Sweat Heifer Trail* exits R 3.6 mi to Kephart Prong Shelter (5,830 ft).
126.79	*Boulevard Trail* (6,030 ft) exits L to Mt. Le Conte and the Jumpoff.
127.09	Ice Water Spring Shelter (5,900 ft).
128.19	Charlies Bunion (5,400 ft). Outstanding view of the Smokies and Mt. Le Conte. Crowded by visitors; dangerous in icy weather.
128.49	Dry Sluice Gap (5,380 ft). *Richland Mtn Trail* exits R to connect with *Bradley Fork* and *Kephart Prong Trails* in N.C.
130.49	False Gap Shelter (5,230 ft).
133.09	Bradleys View (5,800 ft)

Milepoint	*Location and Description*
134.39	Pecks Corner Shelter (5,850 ft). *Hughes Ridge Trail* exits R, 11.8 mi to Smokemont Campground in N.C.
137.09	Mt. Sequoyah (5,980 ft).
138.46	Mt. Chapman (6,220 ft).
139.29	Tri-Corner Knob Shelter (5,920 ft). *Balsam Gap Trail* exits R 5.8 mi to Laurel Gap Shelter in N.C.
140.59	Mt. Guyot Spur (6,180 ft) leads to summit of Mt. Guyot (6,621 ft).
144.09	*Maddron Bald Trail* exits L to *Snake Den Mtn* and *Indian Camp Creek Trails* in Tenn.
145.49	Camel Gap (4,700 ft). *Yellow Creek Trail* goes R 5.2 mi to Walnut Bottoms in N.C.
146.99	Cosby Knob Shelter (4,800 ft).
147.79	Low Gap (4,240 ft) *Low Gap Trail* exits R 2.3 mi to Walnut Bottoms in N.C. ; *Cosby Creek Trail* exits L 2.5 mi to Cosby Campground in Tenn.
149.79	Mt. Cammerer side trail goes L 0.6 mi to summit (5,025 ft).
153.99	Davenport Gap Shelter (2,200 ft).
154.84	Davenport Gap, TN 32, NC 284 roads (1,975 ft).
156.79	Big Pigeon River bridge (1,400 ft) and I-40.
164.39	Snowbird Mtn (4,263 ft). Excellent scenic views.
167.09	Groundhog Creek Shelter.
169.79	Max Patch Mtn (4,629 ft). Panoramic view of the Smokies.
173.59	Lemon Gap, NC 1182 and TN 107 roads (3,550 ft).
174.79	Walnut Mtn Shelter.

Milepoint	Location and Description
180.79	Garentlo Gap and road (2,500 ft).
184.19	Deer Park Mtn Shelter.
187.39	Hot Spring, NC (1,326 ft). Lodging, groceries, post office, restaurant. Roads US 25 and 70 and NC 209.
188.79	Lovers Leap Rock. Scenic view of the French Broad River.
195.49	Rich Mtn Firetower (3,643 ft). Panoramic views of Black Mtn range and the Smokies.
198.19	Spring Mtn Shelter.
201.79	Allen Gap (2,234 ft). Roads NC 208 and TN 70.
228.99	Sams Gap (2,800 ft). Road US 23.
234.59	Big Bald (5,516 ft). Grassy bald with spectacular views.
236.99	Little Bald (5,185 ft).
240.29	Spivey Gap (3,200 ft). Road US 19W.
244.89	No Business Knob Shelter.
247.19	Temple Hill Gap (2,850 ft).
250.49	Nolichucky River (1,700 ft). Erwin, Tenn. Lodging, groceries, restaurants, post office.
254.79	Curley Maple Gap Shelter (3,080 ft).
258.89	Indian Grave Gap (3,360 ft).
259.99	US Forest Service Rd 230.
261.19	Beauty Spot (4,337 ft).
264.29	Unaka Mtn (4,709 ft).
266.99	Cherry Gap Shelter.
269.69	Iron Mtn Gap. TN 107 and NC 226 roads (3,723 ft).

Milepoint	*Location and Description*
277.79	Hughes Gap (4,919 ft). The town of Buladean is R on NC 26 5.3 mi, and the town of Burbank is L 3.2 mi.
280.49	Roan High Knob (6,285 ft). Cloudland Rhododendron Gardens. Entire summit forested with evergreens — fir, spruce, heather. New shelter constructed.
282.39	Carvers Gap (5,512 ft). TN 143 and NC 261 roads.
283.99	Grassy Ridge Shelter.
286.79	Yellow Mtn Gap (4,682 ft). Site of John Sevier's "Overmountain Men" and historic Bright's Trace.
288.49	Big Yellow Mtn (5,459 ft). Grassy balds with extra-ordinary views.
289.99	Hump Mtn (5,587 ft). Superb panorama of Doe River Valley NW, Whitetop and Mt. Rogers in Virginia, Beech Mtn to NE, and Grandfather Mtn to E.
293.09	US 19E, Elk Park, NC. Lodging, groceries, restaurants, post office to R 1.5 mi. *A.T.* continues 65 mi NW through Tenn. to Damascus, VA.

◄ BLUFF MOUNTAIN TRAIL ►

◄ BLUFF MTN. SUMMIT	0.8 MI.
◄ BLUFF LODGE	2.0 MI.
◄ CAMPGROUND	3.3 MI.
◄ BRINEGAR CABIN	4.8 MI.
BLUFF VIEW OVERLOOK 1.2 MI. ►
GRASSY GAP TRAIL 1.5 MI. ►
BASIN COVE OVERLOOK 2.5 MI. ►

CHAPTER VI

BLUE RIDGE PARKWAY

THE BLUE RIDGE PARKWAY TRAIL SYSTEM

The Blue Ridge Parkway, a 470-mile scenic highway that averages 3,000 feet in elevation and runs along the crest of the southern Appalachians, is a link between the Shenandoah National Park in Virginia and the Great Smoky Mountains National Park in North Carolina and Tennessee.

Recreational facilities for fishing, camping, bicycling, picnicking, horseback riding, and hiking are provided for the public at special areas. In addition, historic exhibits, museums, parks, and preservation areas of mountain culture are numerous.

The Parkway's 241 miles through North Carolina begins at milepost 217 at Cumberland Knob Park. More than 87 trails, graded or rugged, provide 120 miles of hiking from parks, lookouts, and campgrounds. Some of the trails join a network of trails in the adjacent National Forests.

For information on the trail system, contact Blue Ridge Parkway Superintendent, National Park Service, P.O. Box 7606, Asheville, NC 28807. Tel. 704-258-2850.

Cumberland Knob
Surry County, mp 217.5

Cumberland Knob is a 1,000-acre forest and park one mile from the Virginia state line. Picnic areas and a Visitor's Information

Center are open from May 1 through October. No camping is available. Elevation, 2,740 ft. Galax, VA, is 8 mi N on NC-VA 89.

Cumberland Knob Trail 267

Length: 1.7 mi (2.7 km), easy; *USGS:* Cumberland Knob; *Trailhead:* Parking lot.

Directions and Description: Follow signs to Information Center, turn R, and reach summit (elev, 2,855 ft) at 0.3 mi. Circle Knob and return through picnic areas, or descend on the *Gully Creek Trail*.

Gully Creek Trail 268

Length: 2.7 mi (4.3 km), moderate; *USGS:* See above; *Trailhead:* See above.

Directions and Description: Follow the *Gully Trail* from L of the Visitor's Center, descending on a well-graded trail with switchbacks to Gully Creek at 0.8 mi. Trail crisscrosses the stream and begins ascent on switchbacks at 1.3 mi. Scenic knob at 1.9 mi. Return by Cumberland Knob, or take shorter trail to R and back to parking lot.

Fox Hunters Paradise Trail 269
mp 218.6, near NC 18 exit

Length: 0.2 mi (0.3 km), easy; *USGS:* See above; *Trailhead:* Parking lot at overlook.

Directions and Description: From the parking lot the short trail provides a scenic view of forests in western Surry County.

Little Glade Mill Pond Trail 270
mp 230.1, near US 21 exit

Length: 0.3 mi (0.5 km), easy; *USGS:* Glade Valley; *Trailhead:* Parking lot.

Directions and Description: From parking overlook take loop trail and return by picnic area.

Doughton Park
Wilkes County, mp 238.5-244.7

Doughton Park is named in honor of Robert Lee Doughton, a leader and advocate for establishing and developing the Blue Ridge Parkway. The Park has a lodge (open May through October), service station, camp store, campground, backcountry camping, picnic area, nature studies, special exhibits, fishing, and 32 one-way miles for hiking. The following trails can begin at a number of points for interconnecting loops. Check the Doughton Park Trail System signboards, particularly the one at Alligator Back Overlook. Permits are required for overnight camping.

Cedar Ridge Trail   271

Length: 11 mi rt (17.6 km), moderate to strenuous; *USGS:* Whitehead, Glade Valley; *Trailhead:* Campground.

Directions and Description: From the campground go E 1.1 mi on orange-blazed trail to Brinegar Cabin jct, continue ahead, and begin descent for 4.4 mi, reaching Absher Rd at 5.5 mi. Return by the same route for a trip of 11 mi, or take the *Flat Rock Ridge Trail* for a total of 17.6 mi, or take the *Blue Ridge Primitive Trail* for a total of 15 mi.

Flat Rock Trail   272

Length: 11.7 mi rt (18.7 km), moderate to strenuous; *USGS:* See above; *Trailhead:* Basin Cove Overlook.

Directions and Description: This trail can be taken from the campground for a loop of 18 mi, or it can be used from other points. From the overlook go R on blue-blazed trail for 5 mi to Absher-McGrady Rd, and return by the same route — or, ascend by the Cove Creek Fire Rd, for a total distance of 11.7 mi.

Bluff Ridge Primitive Trail   273

Length: 15.7 mi rt (20.8 km), strenuous; *USGS:* See above; *Trailhead:* Parking lot at service station.

Directions and Description: From the service station cross the road and ascend following yellow blazes through the picnic area and to the shelter at 1.8 mi (3,796 ft). Descend to Basin Creek and jct with Cove Creek and Cove Creek Fire Rd at 6.5 mi. Return by the same route — or, take R and ascend by Cove Creek Fire Rd, past Bluff Mtn Overlook and to Alligator Overlook at 13.1 mi. Climb steeply to shelter and return to service station at 15.7 mi. This trail can also terminate at Absher-McGrady Rd (1,425 ft).

Fodder Stack Trail   274

Length: 1.4 mi rt (2.2 km), easy; *USGS:* See above; *Trailhead:* Lodge parking lot.

Directions and Description: From the parking lot at the Lodge go NE to impressive view of the Martin and Janie Caudill homestead and Basin Creek watershed. Views also from Wildcat Rock.

Jumpinoff Rocks Trail   275
mp 260.3, near NC 16 exit

Length: 1.0 mi (1.6 km), easy; *USGS:* Horse Gap; *Trailhead:* Parking lot.

Directions and Description: Follow trail signs through forest to scenic view at rocky cliffs above forested valley.

The Lump Trail   276
mp 264.4, near NC 16 exit

Length: 0.3 (0.5 km), easy; *USGS:* Horse Gap; *Trailhead:* Parking lot.

Directions and Description: Climb grassy bald for sweeping 360° scenic view.

Cascades Trail   277
mp 271.9, near US 421 exit

Length: 1.2 mi (1.9 km), easy; *USGS:* Glendale Springs; *Trailhead:* Parking lot.

Directions and Description: Follow loop trail through forest of hardwoods and rhododendron to Falls Creek on well-graded trail.

Plant labels allow for self-guided interpretive tour. There is also an area for picnicking at the E.B. Jeffress Park.

Tompkins Knob Trail   **278**
mp 272.5, near US 421 exit

Length: 0.6 mi (1.0 km), easy; *USGS:* Deep Gap; *Trailhead:* Parking lot.
Directions and Description: Turn L at parking lot and pass by the Cool Springs Baptist log Church in a loop.

Moses Cone Memorial Park
Watagua County, mp 292.7-295, near US 321 exit

The 3,600-acre mountain estate of Moses H. Cone was donated to the National Park Service in 1950 for the pleasure of the public. There are more than 25 miles of carriage trails, depending on whether one prefers one-way trips or loops, and cross-trail connections are numerous. A Crafts Center occupies part of the mansion. Fishing is provided at a Trout Lake N near Shulls Mill Rd and a Bass Lake S near US 221.
Length: 25 mi (40 km), moderate; *USGS:* Boone; *Trailhead:* Parking lot at Cone Manor.
Directions and Description: Request Blue Ridge Parkway map for directions for the following trails:

Rich Mountain Carriage, Horse, and Hiking Trail—4.3 mi   **279**
Flat Top Mountain Carriage, Horse, and Hiking Trail—3.0 mi **280**
Watkins Carriage, Horse, and Hiking Trail—3.3 mi   **281**
Black Bottom Carriage, Horse, and Hiking Trail—0.6 mi   **282**
Bass Lake Carriage, Horse, and Hiking Trail—1.8 mi   **283**
Deer Park Carriage, Horse, and Hiking Trail—0.8 mi   **284**
Maze Carriage, Horse, and Hiking Trail—2.3 mi   **285**
Duncan Carriage, Horse, and Hiking Trail—2.7 mi   **286**
Rock Creek Bridge Carriage, Horse, and Hiking Trail—1.0 mi **287**
Trout Lake Hiking and Horse Trail—1.0 mi   **288**
Figure Eight Self-Guided Trail (Craftsman's Trail),
    with herbs for medicine and handicrafts—0.7 mi   **289**

Julian Price Memorial Park
Watagua County, mp 295.1-298, near US 221 exit

A 4,344-acre plateau of forests, fields, lakes, and campgrounds. Elev, 3,400 ft. With more than 12 miles of hiking trails — the longest (4.9 mi) is *Boone Fork Trail*. Unnamed treadways in the Price Picnic Area and Campground area total 3.0 mi. Fishing at Price Lake.

Green Knob Trail   290

Length: 2.3 mi (3.7 km), easy; *USGS:* Boone; *Trailhead:* Sims Lake parking lot.
Directions and Description: From Sims Lake parking lot descend to lake, cross bridge, and circle L. Follow up R side of Sims Creek and cross under the Parkway bridge at 0.7 mi. Cross stream and reach summit (3,930 ft) at 1.5 mi. Descend to Parkway, cross, and return to parking lot.

Price Lake Loop Trail   291

Length: 2.4 mi (3.8 km), easy; *USGS:* See above; *Trailhead:* Price Lake parking lot.
Directions and Description: Follow signs counterclockwise around the lake. Cross Cold Prong Stream at 0.7 mi, Boone Fork Creek at 0.9 mi, and Laurel Creek at 1.6 mi. Trail is well-graded except where some spots are wet due to nearby marsh areas. Hardwoods and rhododendron tunnels. Mountain trout fishing. Return to parking lot across dam and bridge at 2.4 mi.

Boone Fork Trail   292

Length: 4.9 mi (7.8 km), easy, *USGS:* See above; *Trailhead:* Picnic area or campground.
Directions and Description: Begin in picnic parking lot, cross Boone Fork Creek to trail system sign, and enter woods for clockwise loop. Ascend to campground at 0.6 mi. Leave campground

NW, and continue ascent to 3,515 ft. Descend to Bee Tree Creek. Turn R at 2.6 mi at confluence with Boone Fork Creek. Follow up the Creek on the R to the sign for Old Lake Bed area at 4.7 mi. Return to parking lot at 4.9 mi.

Gwyn Memorial Trail 293
mp 298.6, near US 221 exit

A short 0.1-mi garden trail in honor of Rufus Lenoir Gwyn (1877-1963), whose efforts were influential in the location of the Parkway through the Blue Ridge. Trail is at jct with Holloway Mtn Rd 1 mi from US 221.

Beacon Heights Trail 294
mp 305.2, near US 221 exit

Length: 0.3 mi (0.5 km), easy; *USGS:* Grandfather Mtn; *Trail-head:* Parking lot.
Directions and Description: Cross gravel road and ascend rocky trail to summit (4,205 ft). Spectacular views of Pisgah National Forest, Brown Mtn., Hawkbill and Table Rock mtns, Grandfather and Grandmother mtns.

Grandmother Mtn Trail 295
mp 307.4, near US 221 exit

A short 0.2-mi ascent trail to the Park Service boundary from the Grandmother Mtn parking lot.

Flat Rock Trail 296
mp 308.2, near NC 181 exit

Length: 0.7 mi (1.1 km), easy; *USGS:* Grandfather Mtn; *Trail-head:* Parking lot.
Directions and Decription: Ascend well-graded self-guiding loop nature trail. Signs provide geological and biological information. Summit supplies outstanding views of Grandfather Mtn, Linville Valley, Black Mtn, and Roan Mtn.

Linville Falls
Burke County, mp 315.5-316.5, near US 221 exit

The Linville Falls area of the Parkway includes six short trails for a total of 3.3 mi. (Other trails of the Linville Gorge Wilderness are listed under the Pisgah National Forest Section.) On the Parkway there is a picnic area with 100 sites, a camp store, two campgrounds with a total of 190 sites, and an Information Shelter.

Linville Falls Trail   297

Length: 2 mi (3.2 km), easy; *USGS:* Linville Falls; *Trailhead:* Parking lot.

Directions and Description: Cross Linville River bridge and follow wide trail to Upper Falls. Ascend through hemlocks and rhododendron to choice of three lookouts for outstanding views of Linville Falls. (This trail is also known as *Erwins Trail*—to Erwins Lookout at 1 mi.)

Linville Gorge Trails   298-299

Length: 1.8 mi (2.9 km), moderate; *USGS:* See above; *Trailhead:* See above.

Directions and Description: Leave parking lot on L, and ascend through rhododendron and hemlocks to jct with *Plunge Basic Overlook Trail* and *Linville Gorge Trail* at 0.4 mi. Turn R and descend to overlook for superb view of Falls. On return, turn R at sign for *Gorge Trail,* and descend steeply to rocky bank at basin of Falls at 0.9 mi. Return on same trail to parking lot.

Duggers Creek Trail   300

Length: 0.3 mi (0.5 km), easy; *USGS:* See above; *Trailhead:* See above.

Directions and Description: Follow the signs E of the parking lot for an interpretive loop trail over Duggers Creek and back to parking lot.

Camp Creek and Linville River Trails   301

Length: 1.0 mi (1.6 km), easy; *USGS:* See above; *Trailhead:* See above.

Directions and Description: From picnic area and campground follow the signs between River Bend Overlook, Camp Creek Overlook, and return to point of origin.

Chestoa View Trail   302
mp 320.8, near US 221

Length: 0.8 mi (1.3 km), easy; *USGS:* Linville Falls; *Trailhead:* Parking lot.

Directions and Description: From parking lot enter paved trail and follow loop L through mature hardwoods and numerous wildflowers including large areas of Bowman's roots; take gravel trail to return, passing scenic views of the Linville Wilderness area.

Crabtree Meadows Campground
Yancey County, mp 339.5, near NC 80

Crabtree Meadows has a restaurant that is open May through October; with it is a gift shop, camp store, and service station. The campground has tent and trailer sites with all necessary conveniences except hot water and electricity. Crabtree Falls is the central feature of the campground. The area has a total of 5 trail miles, including the campground and picnic trails and the *Falls Trail.* The nearest lodging is at Little Switzerland, 5.5 mi N at mp 334.

Crabtree Falls Trail   303

Length: 2.5 mi (4 km), moderate; *USGS:* Little Switzerland, Cello; *Trailhead:* Campground parking lot.

Directions and Description: Follow posted directions N to 0.4 mi and begin at steps. Reach waterfalls at 0.8 mi and cross bridge to begin climb. At 1.4 mi cross Crabtree stream and walk through banks of trillium at 1.7 mi. Follow L at all trail jcts until jct with original trail is reached; return to parking lot at 2.5 mi.

Woods Mountain Ridge Trail   **304**
mp 344.1, near NC 80 exit

Length: 2 mi (3.2 km), moderate; *USGS:* Mt Mitchell, Cello, Marian; *Trailhead:* Buck Creek Gap Parking Overlook.

Directions and Description: This trail is an old service road connecting Buck Creek Gap at NC 80 (3,373 ft) and Black Mtn. Parking Overlook (3,892 ft); it is not to be confused with the 6.4 mi *Woods Mtn. Trail* in Pisgah NF. Follow signs from Buck Creek Gap, ascending to reach jct with *Woods Mtn. Trail* (USFS) R at 0.7 mi. The *Woods Mtn Trail* follows a rocky spine covered with blueberries and chinquapins SE and E. (See *Woods Mtn Trail* description under Pisgah NF, Grandfather District.) Continue on road for 1.3 mi and reach Parkway at 2 mi.

Green Knob Trail   **305**
mp 350.4, near NC 80 exit

Length: 1.2 mi rt (1.9 km), moderate; *USGS:* Cello, Marian (W); *Trailhead:* Green Knob Parking Overlook.

Directions and Description: From parking overlook (4,761 ft) follow trail N and across the Parkway, up switchbacks to reach firetower at 0.6 mi. Outstanding view of the Black Mountain range. Trail to R is *Lost Cove Ridge Trail* (USFS Trail #182); it runs for 3.3 mi, descending to Black Mtn Recreation Area. (See Pisgah NF, Toecane District.)

Bald Knob Ridge Trail   **306**
mp 355.0, near NC 80 exit

This is a terminus point (0.1 mi) of the *Bald Knob Ridge Trail* (USFS Trail #186), which descends 2.8 mi toward Black Mtn Recreation Area on a white-blazed trail to FSR 472. (See Pisgah NF, Toecane District.)

Big Butte Trail   **307**
mp 359.8, near NC 80 exit

This is a terminus point (0.2 mi) of the *Big Butte Trail* (USFS Trail #161), which descends for 7 mi into Buncombe County and to NC 150

197 W. This trailhead is near the highest point on the Parkway north of Asheville (5,676 ft), at mp 358.5. (See Pisgah NF, Toecane District.)

Craggy Gardens Trails   308-310
mp 364-367, near US 70 exit

Craggy Gardens has three trails — *Pinnacle, Self-Guiding,* and *Bear Pen Gap* — in the Parkway area. A fourth trail, the *Halfway Trail,* has a terminus point at the Visitor Center and descends 3.1 mi to Douglas Falls. (See Pisgah FS, Toecane District.) The Gardens has picnic sites with tables, grills, water, and comfort stations. The Visitor Center has exhibits and Parkway information. The central attraction, though, is the purple rhododendron, blooming in mid-June, which covers Craggy Dome, the Pinnacle, and the Flats.

To hike the *Pinnacle Trail* (0.8 mi rt), follow signs from the parking lot at Craggy Garden Parking Overlook up switchbacks to summit with 360° scenic views (5,840 ft). For the *Craggy Gardens Self-Guiding Trail,* follow signs from the Visitor Center to the picnic area, for a one-way distance of 0.8 mi. The *Bear Pen Gap Trail* is 0.2 mi long and runs through the picnic area.

Rattlesnake Lodge Trail   311
mp 374.4, near US 70 exit

Length: 4.8 mi rt (7.7 km), strenuous; *USGS:* Craggy Pinnacle; *Trailhead:* Parking area near Tanbark Tunnel.

Directions and Description: From parking area ascend steeply for 0.4 mi by stream on an orange-blazed trail to ruins of the summer home of Dr. Chase P. Ambler, an Asheville physician who built the lodge in 1900. At L the carriage road leads down the mountain to Ox Creek Rd and return by the Parkway to parking, for a distance of 2.3 mi. Spring water. Turn R, reach old chimney at 0.6 mi, and follow switchbacks — sometimes steep and rocky — through hardwoods. Wildflowers, including the indigo bush, are plentiful. Foot trail becomes a manway. Reach Rich Knob (4,930 ft) at 2.4 mi. Elevation gain is 1,600 ft. Return by same route. (Hikers with maps may wish to continue to Potato Field Gap and the Parkway.)

Shut-in Trail   **312**

mp 393.6, near NC 191 exit

Length: 17.3 mi (27.7 km), strenuous; *USGS:* Asheville, Duns-more Mtn; *Trailhead:* Bent Creek parking lot.

Directions and Description: This trail climbs 3,681 ft, and provides infrequent or no water.

Turn off the Blue Ridge Parkway at NC 191 jct (sign for I-26) and immediately turn L on FSR 479. Take first gravel rd L at 0.1 mi to Bent Creek trailhead (2,040 ft).

Follow hiking trail sign up switchbacks and through rhodo-dendron thicket (water here) to reach old road at 0.4 mi. Turn L at 1.1 mi. Reach gravel road at 1.7 mi, and turn L. Leave road and begin ascent at 1.8 mi. Reach crest at 2.5 mi and Parkway at 3.5 mi; this is Walnut Cove (2,915 ft). Ascend and skirt NW of Grassy Knob (3,318 ft) to reach Sleepy Gap (2,930 ft), mp 397.3, at 5.2 mi. From Sleepy Gap continue into forest of hardwoods to Chestnut Cove (3,035 ft) at 6.1 mi. From Chestnut Cove Gap follow signs, descending into Chestnut Cove and skirting N of Cold Knob to reach mp 400.3 at Bent Creek Gap (3,270 ft) at 9 mi.

From Bent Creek Gap enter old road by gate and ascend. Excellent views of city of Asheville and Craggy Mtns at 9.2 mi. Reach summit of Ferrin Knob (4,064 ft) at 10.2 mi, then descend on ridge through oaks and locust. Turn R at 10.5 mi and reach Beaver Dam Gap (3,570 ft) at 10.9 mi. Reach Stoney Bald (3,750 ft) at 12 mi, and continue from Stoney Bald to Big Ridge Overlook (3,820 ft) at 13.2 mi. Continue on to Mills River Valley Overlook (4,085 ft) at 14.3 mi, and then to Elk Pasture Gap (4,235 ft) and jct with NC 151 at 15.4 mi. Begin climb to plateau through large oaks and dense groundcover; reach crest of Little Pisgah Mtn at 16.9 mi. (Take side trail R for 1.2 mi one-way to Mt. Pisgah, 5,721 ft. Continue and descend to Buck Spring Gap parking lot at 17.3 mi. (To exit at the Pisgah Inn, continue across parking lot to trail steps and take the *Buck Spring Trail* for 1.1 mi.) Vehicle switching necessary.

Mount Pisgah
Haywood, Buncombe, and Transylvania Counties, mp 407-409

The mile-high Mt. Pisgah complex has modern motel and dining facilities, and is open May through October. There is a service station, a picnic area with facilities, and a large campground for trailers and tents with all facilities except hot water and electricity. The area is part of an original 100,000-acre estate owned by the late George W. Vanderbilt, and it has become the nucleus of what is now the Pisgah National Forest. More than 10 miles of trails interconnect among the parking lots.

Mt. Pisgah Trail   313

Length: 2.4 mi rt (3.8 km), moderate to strenuous; *USGS:* Cruso, Dunsmore; *Trailhead:* Mt Pisgah parking lot.

Directions and Description: From the parking lot enter trail at sign for Mt. Pisgah (named for the Biblical mountain range where Moses saw the Promised Land) and begin ascent at 0.4 mi. Climb rocky route to summit (5,721 ft) at 1.2 mi. Panoramic views of Pigeon River and Blue Ridge range. Return by same route.

Buck Spring Trail   314

Length: 2.2 mi rt (3.5 km), easy; *USGS:* See above; *Trailhead:* Parking lot in front of Pisgah Inn.

Directions and Description: Follow trail sign N on the NE side of the ridge for 0.3 mi, and then go through a natural garden of wildflowers, shrubs, banks of bluets, weather sculptured chestnut oaks, and rhododendron slicks. Reach Buck Spring Gap parking lot at 1.1 mi. Return by the same route. (This trail is also part of the 6.2-mi *Buck Spring Trail,* which veers SW to US 276. See Pisgah FS, Pisgah Ranger District.)

Mt. Pisgah Campground Trail 315

Length: 2.0 mi rt (3.2 km), easy; *USGS:* See above; *Trailhead:* Campground entrance.

Directions and Description: From the campground follow the posted sign on the W side of the Parkway through the picnic area and the Canadian forest zone of fir, spruce, and hemlock to the Mt. Pisgah parking lot. Return the same way or take the *Buck Spring Trail*.

Thompson Creek Trail 316

This is the N terminus of the *Thompson Creek Trail* which descends steeply 0.8 mi to Parkway boundary lines and Yellow Gap Rd, FSR 1206. Entry is from the posted sign at the N end of the Pisgah Inn, which is also the jct with the *Buck Spring Trail*.

Frying Pan Mtn Trail 317

Length: 4 mi rt (6.4 km), moderate; *USGS:* See above; *Trailhead:* Campground entrance.

Directions and Description: Follow posted sign, ascending to Big Bald where azaleas, filberts, and leather flowers thrive. Reach Frying Pan Gap (4,931 ft) at 1.3 mi. Follow gravel road to summit of Frying Pan Mtn (5,450 ft) and firetower at 2 mi. Panoramic views.

Graveyard Fields Loop Trail 318
mp 418.8, near NC 215 exit

Length: 2.3 mi rt cb (3.7 km), easy; *USGS:* Shining Rock; *Trailhead:* Parking overlook at mp 418.8.

Directions and Description: Park at overlook (5,120 ft) and examine the trail design board. Enter paved trail through dense rhododendron; it runs to rocky area and bridge over Yellowstone Prong at 0.2 mi. Cross and turn R for trail to Second Falls at 0.3 mi; return, staying on the W side of the creek to Upper Falls at 1.2 mi, then proceed through semi-open area. Here fallen tree trunks were covered with gray moss and spruce needles, once appearing to be a graveyard and giving the area its name. The trunks were destroyed by fire in 1925. Return on loop section by crossing stream or backtracking to the parking area.

Devil's Courthouse Trail   319
mp 422.4, near NC 215 exit

Length: 0.8 mi rt (1.3 km), easy; *USGS:* Sam Knob; *Trailhead:* Parking lot at mp 422.4.

Directions and Description: Park at parking lot (5,462 ft) and follow sign and paved trail to L for 0.1 mi to spot near Parkway tunnel. Climb heavily used trail to summit at 0.4 mi (5,720 ft). Views are spectacular on clear days; it is possible to see mountains in North Carolina, South Carolina, Georgia and Tennessee. Open area has rhododendron, laurel, and wildflowers. SE side of rock face is used by rock climbers. Return by same route to parking area.

Tanasee Bald-Herrin Knob Trail   320
mp 423.5, near NC 215 exit

Length: 2.4 mi rt (3.8 km), easy; *USGS:* Sam Knob; *Trailhead:* Courthouse Valley Overlook.

Directions and Description: From jct of Blue Ridge Parkway and NC 215 go S for 0.3 mi to Courthouse Valley Parking Overlook (5,362 ft) on L, and park. Trail begins at SW corner behind picnic table. Follow narrow trail under beech nut, fir, hawthorne, arrow wood, and birch, with groundcover of ferns, galax, and sorrel. Take R fork at 0.5 mi. To L is 0.3-mi spur trail to Tanasee Bald. At 0.6 mi enter a summertime natural garden of berries, fragrant wildflowers, birds, and butterflies. At 0.7 mi climb steeply to SW slope of Herrin Knob (5,720 ft). This rocky bluff is naturally landscaped with laurel, orchids, and moss. Descend to Parkway, mp 424.2, at 1.2 mi. Backtrack, or hike the Parkway for 0.8 mi as a loop.

Grassy Ridge Trail, Buckeye Gap Trail, and Haywood Gap Trail   321-323

These trails can be entered or exited from the Parkway; they connect with trails of the Pisgah Ranger District of the Pisgah National Forest.

Grassy Ridge Trail (across the Parkway from the *Tanasee Bald-Herrin Knob Trail*) begins at mp 424.2 on the R (N) side of Parkway at Mt. Hardy Gap. Enter under dense stand of beech and yellow birch and climb rocky switchbacks to N side of Mt. Hardy. Reach jct of faint trail R on Fork Ridge at 0.6 mi. (Fork Ridge is in the Pisgah Ranger District and has a number of bald areas.) Turn L up ridge to bald summit of Mt. Hardy (6,110 ft) at 0.8 mi. From summit lescend W through fir and spruce forest with carpets of moss and wood sorrel. Reach faint trail on R at 1.2 mi; here *Grassy Ridge Trail* descends to old road at 0.5 mi. Continue straight, W, to Wolf Bald at 1.5 mi. Descend to trail jct at 1.9 mi. (Turn L to Parkway's Rough Butt Bald Overlook at mp 425.4.)

Turn R for 100 yd to *Buckeye Gap Trail*. Turn L and go 150 yd to Parkway at mp 425.5. The trailhead at the Parkway is at a cabled gate under a large beech tree and a partially fallen tree; it is 2 mi. from Mt. Hardy Gap. The trail R from the Buckeye Gap Trail jct leads 2.9 mi — or 3.8 mi on a longer route — N as *Grassy Ridge Trail* to *Haywood Gap Trail*. Some hikers call the *Grassy Ridge Trail* from Parkway mp 425.5 the *Buckeye Gap Trail*.

Haywood Gap Trail begins or ends on the Parkway at mp 426.5 (5,225 ft) on the R (N) side of Parkway at Haywood Gap. Entry is at a tall locust tree stump by a fallen locust. Parts of this trail are filled with nettles in the summer. Descent on this trail is near Haywood Gap Stream for approximately 2.5 mi. Reach jct with *Grassy Ridge Trail* at Grassy Ridge Branch. Wet, rocky, and sometimes a manway, the trail continues by the Middle Prong to an old road at the "cattle crossing." For the next 3.1 mi the road winds along the river through birch, poplar, locust, oak, maple, primrose, fox grape vines, spruce, and beebalm. This area connects with other trails often used by ORV's and equestrians. Exit at Sunburst Recreation Area, with facilities for picnicking and camping, on NC 215. The USFS considers this trail area as primitive, since the trails are presently not maintained.

Bear Pen Gap Trail and
Gage Bald-Charley Bald Trail   324-325
mp 427.6, near NC 215 exit

Length: 6 mi rt (9.6 km), moderate; *USGS:* Sam Knob; *Trailhead:* Bear Pen parking lot, mp 427.6.

Directions and Description: Only 0.2 mi of the *Bear Pen Gap Trail* is on the Parkway boundary, but it is the easiest route to the *Gage Bald-Charley Bald Trail.* In the parking lot (5,560 ft) go to L (S) corner of parking area and through gate at 0.1 mi. Continue on old road under a canopy of birch and beech nut, making a L turn at each jct until reaching Bear Pond in Wet Camp Gap at 1.3 mi. Follow old road to Gage Bald at 1.8 mi. Continue along ridge to Charley Bald (5,473 ft) at 3 mi. Open points at the balds in this area provide views of the Smokies, parts of the Pisgah National Forest, and a vast expanse of the Nantahala National Forest. It is part of the Mead property, acquired by the USFS in 1981.

Richland Balsam Trail   326
mp 431.4, near NC 215 and US 19-A, US 23 exit

Length: 1.4 mi rt (2.2 km), moderate; *USGS:* Sam Knob; *Trailhead:* Parking lot at Richland Balsam Overlook.

Directions and Description: At NW corner of parking area follow sign up the interpretive trail. The trail runs through a damp Canadian zone-type forest, chiefly of balsam. Other trees and shrubs are mountain ash. Rowan tree, yellow birch, red spruce, pin cherry, witherod, and blueberry. Groundcover has golden moss and wood sorrel. Some of the birds heard in the area are veery, junco, and winter wren. Reach the summit (6,410 ft) at 0.6 mi, and return on the loop to the parking area. An old trail *Lickstone Ridge Trail,* heavily overgrown, leads to Double Springs Gap, Lickstone Gap, and Wolf Pen Mountain.)

Old Bald Trail   327
mp 434, near US 19-A and US 23 exit

Length: 0.8 mi (1.3 km), easy; *USGS:* Hazelwood; *Trailhead:* Parking space near mp 434.

Directions and Description: On R of Parkway (N side) follow old gated road in open blueberry field past elderberry and sassafras to fork at 0.3 mi. (Road R at gate is *Old Bald Ridge Trail*, which descends to Quinland and Hazelwood. "No Tresspassing" signs have been posted on it by the town of Waynesville.) Continue straight up the field near a fence to the grassy summit of Old Bald at 0.4 mi. Berries and wildflowers are profuse. Views of Richland Balsam, Pisgah NF, and Nantahala NF are outstanding. Backtrack.

Waterrock Knob Trail 329
mp 451.2, near US 19A and US 23 exit

Length: 1.2 mi rt (1.9 km), easy to moderate; *USGS:* Sylva North; *Trailhead:* Parking area.

Directions and Description: Park on the E side of the parking area at the entrance to paved trail. Climb partially on pavement and then on a rocky section of trail to the summit (6,400 ft) at 0.6 mi. Superb views of Smoky Mtns and Pisgah and Nantahala National Forests. (Faint trail at L of summit follows ridge for 2.5 mi to Mt. Lyn Lowery, then goes on for another 3 mi to Plott Balsam, or to the Singing Grounds on the *Ivey Trail,* 1.1 mi from Mt. Lyn Lowery. See *Mt. Lyn Lowery Trail* elsewhere for more description.) Vegetation includes balsam, yellow birch, gooseberry, moosewood, turtlehead, bush honeysuckle, love vine, mountian ash, mountain lettuce, and meadow parsnip. Views from the summit are panoramic. Return by same route.

Support Facilities: For this area the nearest Parkway campground is the Pisgah at mp 408.8., but a commercial campground is near the exit at Balsam Gap, mp 443.1, and jct with US 19A-US 23. Go under the Parkway and turn L for 2 mi on SR 1471, Dark Ridge Rd, to the Moonshine Creek Campground, P.O. Box 1, Balsam, NC 28707. Tel: 704-456-9614. Full svc, limited rec. Open April 1-November 1.

CHAPTER VII

GREAT SMOKY MOUNTAINS NATIONAL PARK

Haywood and Swain Counties in North Carolina

One of the oldest uplands on earth, the lofty Smokies cover 517,368 acres — of which 273,550 are in North Carolina. The other half of the Park comprises Blount, Cocke, and Sevier counties in Tennessee. Authorized by Congress in 1926 and dedicated in 1940 by President Franklin D. Roosevelt, the Park has become the nation's most heavily used.

Luxuriant in virgin forests, vast in scenic beauty, and diversified for outdoor recreation, the Park attracts more than 8½ million visitors annually. As a result Park officials have had to resort to rationing, requiring permits for backcountry use on the 580 miles of trails — 362.8 of which are in North Carolina.

Here is more than a network of trails, however. There are numerous areas for fishing in the 600 miles of streams, and camping and mountian climbing are provided for. In addition studies in natural sciences and research in mountain culture go on here.

The highest mountain in the Park is Clingmans Dome at 6,643 ft, accessibly by autoroad or by hiking the *Appalachian Trail*. There are also sixteen other peaks which tower over 6,000 ft. Geologists estimate that the original peaks in the Smokies were over 15,000 ft in elevation when formed 250 million years ago.

For the naturalist the Park is a paradise with more than 1,400 varieties of flowering plants, 150 species of trees, 300 mosses, and 2,000 fungi. There are more than 200 species of birds, fifty species of fur-bearing animals, 26 species of reptiles, and eighty different kinds of fish.

The Park has seven developed campgrounds, three of which are in North Carolina. (Information on these, plus two primitive campgrounds and 52 backcountry campsites, is listed in the Sierrra Club's *Hikers Guide to the Smokies* by Dick Murlless and Constance Stallings. The book is highly recommended for those who plan to hike in the Smokies. With a detailed topo map, the volume includes information on weather, roads, facilities, park regulation; it also contains descriptions of each of its 112 trails, of which 66 are in North Carolina. Also, the guidebook offers complete coverage of the Joyce Kilmer Memorial Forest, with fifteen trails.

If the guidebook is not available in local bookstores, order from Sierrra Club Books, Box 3886, Rincon Annex, San Francisco, CA 94119. Tel: 415-981-8634. (*The guidebook is currently under revision, with plans for a new edition in late 1982.*)

Because the Sierra Club guidebook has such complete details for the hiker, the following information is only a reference listing of the 66 trails in the eight sections of the Smokies in North Carolina.

Entrance to the Park on the eastern boundary is obtained at the Oconaluftee Ranger Station, near the city of Cherokee and US 19, on the Newfound Gap Road (formerly US 441). For entrance along the western boundary, travel to the city of Gatlinburg on US 441 or TN 76; the Sugarland Park Headquarters is on the Newfound Gap Road.

Big Creek Section

Entrance Directions: Take Waterville exit #451 off I-40, cross the Pigeon River, turn L, and follow road for 2.3 mi to Ranger Station. USGS quads for this section are Luftee Knob, Cove Creek, and Waterville.

Big Creek Trail — 5.8 mi (9.3 km).   **331**

Start at Big Creek Campground (1,700 ft) and end at Walnut Bottoms (3,080 ft).

Baxter Creek Trail — 6 mi (9.6 km).   **332**

Start at Big Creek Campground (1,700 ft) and end at Mt. Sterling Tower (5,842 ft).

Swallow Fork Trail — 3.8 mi (6.1 km).   **333**

Start at Walnut Bottoms (3,000 ft) and end at Pretty Hollow Gap (5,180 ft)

Low Gap Trail — 2.3 mi (3.7 km).   **334**

Start at Walnut Bottoms (3,000 ft) and end at Low Gap on *A.T.* (4,240 ft).

Gunter Fork Trail — 4.5 mi (7.2 km).   **335**

Start at Walnut Bottoms, upper end, (3,080 ft) and end at Balsam Mtn (5,520 ft).

Yellow Creek Trail — 5.2 mi (8.3 km).   **336**

Start at Walnut Bottoms (3,080 ft) and end at Camel Gap on *A.T.* (4,691 ft).

Cataloochee Section

Entrance Directions: Take Cove Creek Rd from I-40 (4 mi W of NC 209 jct) and go N for 0.5 mi to SR 1331 and Cove Creek. Turn L on SR 1331 and go 0.7 mi, turn R on SR 1395 (old NC 284), and reach Cove Creek Gap at 5.8 mi, to Park boundary. Turn L at 7.5 mi on Cataloochee Rd. (A more direct route to I-40 is being constructed.) USGS quads for this section are Dellwood, Cove Creek Gap, Bunches Bald, and Luftee Knob.

Caldwell Fork Trail
also known as **Big Poplar Trail** — 5.8 mi (9.3 km).   **337**

Start at the Cataloochee Campground (2,640 ft) and end at *Rough Fork Trail* (4,000 ft).

Booger Man Trail — 3.8 mi (6.1 km).   **338**

Start at Caldwell Fork Trail (2,700 ft.) and end at Caldwell Fork Trail (3,000 ft.)

McKee Branch Trail — 2.5 mi (4 km).   **339**

Start at *Caldwell Fork Trail* (3,090 ft) and end at *Cataloochee Divide Trail* (4,800 ft).

Double Gap Trail — 2.2 mi (3.5 km) .   **340**

Start at *Caldwell Fork Trail* (3,160 ft) and end at Double Gap on Cataloochee Divide (4,960 ft).

Cataloochee Divide Trail — 11.5 mi (18.4 km).   **341**

Start at Cove Creek Gap (4,070 ft) and end at Paul's Gap (5,130 ft).

Rough Fork Trail
also known as **Paul's or Poll's Gap Trail** — 8.0 mi (5 km).   **342**

Start at the end of the new Cataloochee Rd (2,750 ft) and end at Paul's Gap (5,130 ft).

Big Fork Ridge Trail — 2.8 mi (4.5 km).   **343**

Start at *Rough Fork Trail* (2,800 ft) and end on *Caldwell Fork Trail* at *McKee Branch Trail* (3,060 ft).

Palmer Creek Trail — 4.6 mi (7.4 km).   **344**

Start at Cataloochee Schoolhouse (2,740 ft) and end at Balsam Mtn Rd near Pin Oak Gap (4,510 ft).

Pretty Hollow Gap Trail — 4.0 mi (6.4 km).   **345**

Start at *Palmer Creek Trail* (2,990 ft) and end at Pretty Hollow Gap on Mt. Sterling Ridge (5,180 ft).

Little Cataloochee Trail — 5.0 mi (8 km).   **346**

Start at Old NC 284 (3,000 ft) and end at *Palmer Creek Trail* (2,920 ft).

Mount Sterling Ridge Trail — 7.7 mi (12.3 km).   **347**

Start at Mt. Sterling Gap on old NC 284 (3,890 ft) and end near Laurel Gap on *Balsam Mtn Trail* (5,540 ft).

Asbury Trail — 6.9 mi (11 km).   **348**

Start at Cove Creek Gap (4,070 ft) and end at Mt. Sterling Gap (3,890 ft).

Raven Fort Section

Entrance Directions: From the Blue Ridge Parkway take a spur road near mp 458. Trails begin from 5.7 mi to 13.5 mi into the Smokies. (The Sierra Club guidebook and map are essential to find them.) Another route is to approach from the Cherokee-Oconaluftee area. USGS quad maps for this section are Bunches Bald, Luftee Knob, Mt. Guyot, and Smokemont.

Flat Creek Trail — 2.6 mi (4.2 km).   **349**

Start at Heintooga Picnic Area (5,340 ft) and end at Blue Ridge Parkway spur road (4,900 ft).

Spruce Mountain Trail — 4.8 mi (7.7 km).   **350**

Start at Paul's (Poll's) Gap, Blue Ridge Parkway spur road (5,130 ft), and end at Balsam Mtn Rd (4,820 ft).

Balsam Mountain Trail — 9.9 mi (15.8 km). **351**

Start at Pin Oak Gap on Balsam Mtn Rd (4,420 ft) and end at *A.T.* at Tricorner Knob (5,960 ft).

Hyatt Ridge Trail — 9.5 mi (15.2 km). **352**

Start at Straight Fork Rd (2,935 ft) and end at Mt Yonaguska on Balsam Mtn (6,000 ft).

Enloe Creek Trail — 3.6 mi (5.8 km). **353**

Start at Low Gap on *Hyatt Ridge Trail* (4,420 ft) and end at *Hughes Ridge Trail* (4,820 ft).

Raven Fork Trail — 6.4 mi (10.2 km). **354**

Start at *Enloe Creek Trail* (3,840 ft) and end at McGee Springs on *Hyatt Ridge Trail* (5,040 ft).

Hyatt Bald Trail — 2.9 mi (4.6 km). **355**

Start at Round Bottom (3,060 ft) and end at *Hyatt Ridge Trail* (4,940 ft).

Beech Gap Trail — 3.0 mi (4.8 km). **356**

Start at Round Bottom (3,060 ft) and end at Beech Gap on Balsam Mtn (5,070 ft).

Oconaluftee Section

Entrance Directions: From Cherokee take the Newfound Gap Rd (old US 441) 3.5 mi to Oconaluftee Ranger Station; continue and at 6.7 mi reach Smokemont Campground. USGS quad maps for this section are Smokemont, Mt Guyot, and Clingmans Dome.

Bradley Fork Trail — 5.3 mi (8.5 km).   **357**

Start at the upper end of Smokemont Campground (2,220 ft) and end at Cabin Flats (3,140 ft).

Smokemont Loop Trail — 5.9 mi (9.4 km).   **358**

Start at upper end of Smokemont Campground (2,220 ft) and end at the lower end of Smokemont Campground (2,220 ft).

Chasteen Creek Trail — 4.0 mi (6.4 km).   **359**

Start at the *Bradley Fork Trail* (2,360 ft) and end at Hughes Ridge (4,660 ft).

Taywa Creek Trail — 3.6 mi (5.8 km).   **360**

Start at *Bradley Fork Trail* turnaround (2,930 ft) and end at Hughes Ridge (5,060 ft).

Richland Mountain Trail — 4.3 mi (6.9 km).   **361**

Start at *Bradley Fork Trail* (3,080 ft) and end at Dry Sluice Gap on the *A.T.* (5,380 ft).

Hughes Ridge Trail — 11.8 mi (18.9 km).   **362**

Start at Smokemont Chapel (2,220 ft) and end at Pecks Corner on the *A.T.* (5,560 ft).

Kephart Prong Trail — 2.1 mi (3.7 km).   **363**

Start at Newfound Gap Rd (2,730 ft) and end at Kephart Prong Shelter (3,560 ft).

Grassy Branch Trail — 2.3 mi (3.7 km).   **364**

Start at Kephart Prong Shelter (3,560 ft) and end at *Richland Mtn Trail* (5,300 ft).

Sweat Heifer Trail — 3.6 mi (5.8 km).   **365**

Start at Kephart Prong Shelter (3,560 ft) and end at *A.T.* 1.6 mi E of Newfound Gap (5,830 ft).

Mingus Creek Trail — 5.6 mi (9 km).   **366**

Start at the Mingus Mill on Newfound Gap Rd (2,050 ft) and end at Newton Bald (5,080 ft).

Newton Bald Trail — 4.8 mi (7.7 km).   **367**

Start at Smokemont Campground (2,200 ft) and end at *Thomas Divide Trail* (5,000 ft).

Collins Creek Trail — 4.2 mi (6.7 km).   **368**

Start at Collins Creek Picnic Area (2,500 ft) and end at *Thomas Divide Trail* (4,800 ft).

Kanati Fork Trail — 3.0 mi (4.8 km).   **369**

Start at Newfound Gap Rd (2,860 ft) and end at *Thomas Divide Trail* (4,975 ft).

Deep Creek Section

Entrance Directions: In Bryson City turn N on US 19 at the Swain County Courthouse and follow the signs for 3 mi to the Deep Creek Campground. USGS quads for this section are Smokemont, Clingmans Dome, and Bryson City.

Deep Creek Trail — 12.0 mi (19.2 km).   **370**

Start at the parking lot at the end of Deep Creek Rd (1,990 ft) and end at the overlook on Newfound Gap Rd S.

Thomas Divide Trail — 14.1 mi (22.4 km).   **371**

Start at Deep Creek Rd (1,900 ft) and end at Newfound Gap Rd S of Newfound Gap (4,650 ft).

Cooper Creek Trail — 2.3 mi (3.9 km).   **372**

Start at *Deeplow Gap Trail* and Cooper Creek Rd (2,190 ft) and end at *Mingus Creek Trail* (3,620 ft).

Deeplow Gap Trail — 3.8 mi (6.1 km).   **373**

Start at the *Indian Creek Trail* (2,440 ft) and end at the *Cooper Creek* Rd and *Trail* (2,190 ft).

Noland Divide Trail — 11.5 mi (18.4 km).   **374**

Start at Deep Creek Campground (1,780 ft) and end at Clingmans Dome Rd near Webb Overlook (5,929 ft).

Pole Road Creek Trail — 3.2 mi (5.1 km).   **375**

Start at *Deep Creek Trail* near Bryson Place (2,440 ft) and end at Upper Sassafras Gap on *Noland Divide Trail* (4,240 ft).

Sunkota Ridge Trail — 4.8 mi (7.7 km).   **376**

Start at Martins Gap on *Indian Creek Trail* (3,430 ft) and end at *Thomas Divide Trail* near Newton Bald Trail (4,780 ft).

Indian Creek Trail — 6.8 mi (10.9 km).   **377**

Start at Deep Creek Rd (1,900 ft) and end at Bryson Place on *Deep Creek Trail* (2,400 ft).

Fork Ridge Trail — 4.9 mi (7.8 km).   **379**

Start at Poke Patch primitive campsite on *Deep Creek Trail*

(3,000 ft) and end at Mt. Collins area on Clingmans Dome Rd (5,880 ft).

Noland and Forney Creeks Section

Entrance Directions: Access can be via Clingmans Dome or the North Shore Road from Bryson City (see ''Deep Gap Section'' directions). USGS quads for this section are Noland Creek, Bryson City, Clingmans Dome, and Silers Bald.

Noland Creek Trail — 9.5 mi (15.2 km).   380

Start at Noland Creek bridge and North Shore Rd (1,800 ft) and end at Upper Sassafras Gap on Noland Divide (4,240 ft).

Springhouse Branch Trail — 2.8 mi (4.5 km).   381

Start at Solola Valley on *Noland Creek Trail* (2,550 ft) and end at Board Camp Gap on Forney Ridge (3,900 ft).

Forney Creek Trail — 11.4 mi (18.2 km).   382

Start at Fontana Lake (1,710 ft) and end at Forney Ridge (5,740 ft).

Jumpup Ridge Trail — 5.8 mi (9.3 km).   383

Start at *Forney Creek Trail* (1,800 ft) and end at Welch Ridge near High Rocks (4,900 ft).

Bee Gum Branch Trail — 2.9 mi (4.6 km).   384

Start at old CCC camp on *Forney Creek Trail* (2,160 ft) and end at Forney Ridge (3,800 ft).

Jonas Creek Trail — 3.5 mi (5.6 km). **385**

Start at *Forney Creek Trail* (2,400 ft) and end on Welch Ridge (4,600 ft).

Welch Ridge Trail — 6.8 mi (10.9 km). **286**

Start at High Rocks (5,190 ft) and end on *A.T.* at Silers Bald (5,400 ft).

Forney Ridge Trail — 6.8 mi (10.9 km). **387**

Start at *Bee Gum Branch Trail* (3,800 ft) and end at Clingmans Dome Rd end (6,300 ft).

Hazel Creek Section

Entrance Directions: This section is accessible only by hiking in from an adjoining section or by boat across Fontana Lake. If by boat from Fontana Village boat dock (shuttle service is available), the distance is approximately 6 mi. USGS quads for this seciton are Tuskeegee, Thunderhead Mtn, Silers Bald, and Noland Creek.

Cold Spring Branch Trail — 3.9 mi (6.2 km). **388**

Start at *Hazel Creek Trail* (2,480 ft) and end at Welch Ridge (4,910 ft).

Sugar Fork Trail — 2.4 mi (3.8 km). **389**

Start at *Hazel Creek Trail* (2,189 ft) and end at Pickens Gap on *Jenkins Ridge Trail* (2,964 ft).

Jenkins Ridge Trail — 5.9 mi (9 km). **390**

Start at Pickens Gap (2,964 ft) and end on the *A.T.* at Spece Field (4,958 ft).

Bone Valley Trail — 1.7 mi (2.7 km).   **391**

Start at Bone Valley campsite on *Hazel Creek Trail* (2,380 ft) and end at Hall Cabin, ruins of old Kress building (2,480 ft).

Twentymile and Eagle Creeks Section

Entrance Directions: From the jct of NC 28 and US 219 (0.7 mi from Tennessee border), go 2.9 mi E to the ranger station at Twenty-mile Creek. For the Eagle Creek section, an alternate route is provided by the *A.T.*, which crosses NC 28 at Fontana Dam and ascends to the jct of trails at Shuckstack. USGS quads are Fontana Dam, Thunderhead, Tapoco, and Cades Cove (TN).

Pinnacle Creek Trail — 3.5 mi (5.6 km).   **392**

Start at Eagle Creek (1,800 ft) and end at Pickens Gap, Jenkins Ridge (2,964 ft).

Eagle Creek Trail — 9.1 mi (14.6 km).   **393**

Start at Fontana Lake and Lost Cove Creek (1,720 ft) and end at the *A.T.* Spence Field (4,890 ft).

Lost Cove Trail — 3.1 mi (5 km).   **394**

Start at Fontana Lake and Lost Cove Creek (1,720 ft) and end at Sassafras Gap on the *A.T.* (3,650 ft).

Twentymile Creek Trail
also known as **Shuckstack Trail** — 5.3 mi (8.5 km).   **395**

Start at Twentymile Ranger Station on NC 28 (1,295 ft) and end at Sassafras Gap on the *A.T.* (3,650 ft).

Long Hungry Ridge Trail — 4.4 mi (7 km).   **396**

Start at Proctor Gap at Twentymile Creek (2,350 ft) and end at Rich Gap (4,600 ft).

CHAPTER VIII

OTHER TRAILS IN THE
NATIONAL PARK SYSTEM

SECTION I
CAPE HATTERAS NATIONAL SEASHORE

Dare and Hyde Counties

Cape Hatteras, a chain of barrier islands E of Pamlico Sound, has 30,318 acres of sandy Atlantic beaches, dunes, and marshlands. It is the nation's first national seashore. Authorized as a park by Congress on August 17, 1937, the islands are havens for more than 300 species of migratory and permanent shorebirds. Major offshore fish are flounder, bluefish, marlin, dolphin, mackerel, and tuna.

Often referred to as the Outer Banks and the "Graveyard of the Atlantic," the offshore area has two ocean currents near Diamond Shoals used as shipping lanes which are hazardous for those navigating the seas. More than 600 ships have fallen victim to the shallow shoals, wind, and storms over the past 400 years.

For hikers and campers on the string of islands, the Park Service permits camping at designated campgrounds only. Facilities there are limited to cold showers, drinking water, tables, grills, and modern restrooms. The camps are (N to S) Oregon Inlet, Salvo, Cape Hatteras, Frisco, and Ocracoke; usually not open all year. Hikers using tents are requested to use stronger tents and longer stakes than usual for protection against the sand and wind. Protection against sunburn and insects is also essential. Short nature trails

175

are found near the Visitor Centers at Cape Hatteras and Cocquina Beach. Directions to the *Cape Hatteras Beach Trail* are as follows: from the jct of US 64-264 and NC 12 go to Bodie Island Visitor Center on NC 12 S for information.

Cape Hatteras Beach Trail   397

Length: 75.8 mi (120 km), easy to strenuous; *USGS:* (N to S) Roanoke Island, Oregon Inlet, Pea Island, Little Kinnakeet, Buxton, Cape Hatteras, Hatteras, Green Island, Howard Reef, Ocracoke, Portsmouth; *Trailhead:* Whalebone Junction.

Directions and Description: The trail is being designed and built now, with plans for an official opening in 1982. Inquiry should be made at the Visitor Center for information about trail development and the prospect for long-range backpacking. The trail will follow along the beach line — over dunes with sea oats and sedge; through forests of water oaks, sweet bays, and beach holly; around sound marshes; on roadways; to lighthouses — and at Hatteras Inlet will include a ferry ride to Ocracoke Island. It passes through the Pea Island Wildlife Refuge and Rodanthe, Waves, Salvo, Avon, and Frisco, ending at the Ocracoke village boundary line.

Support Facilities: In addition to campgrounds listed above, commercial camps are found in Avon, Buxton, Frisco, Hatteras, Rodanthe, Salvo, and Ocracoke. In Buxton, for example, there is the Cape Woods Camper Park, Buxton, NC 27920. Tel: 919-955-5850. Full svc excellent rec fac. Open Easter through December 15. At jct of NC 12 and SR 1232 N, go 0.5 mi S on SR 1232.

Information: For information contact the Division of Interpretation, Cape Hatteras National Seashore, Route 1, Box 675, Manteo, NC 27954. Tel: 919-473-2111, and Pea Island Wildlife Refuge, Box 1026, Manteo, NC 27954. Tel: 919-987-2394. In addition to the Seashore, the Park Service also administers Fort Raleigh National Historical Site and Wright Brothers National Memorial (see below).

Wright Brothers National Memorial

The Wright Brothers National Memorial is a 431-acre memorial museum to Wilbur and Orville Wright, who on December 17, 1903 were the first to sucessfully achieve sustained flight with a heavier-than-air machine. There are no official hiking trails on the premises.

Fort Raleigh National Historic Site

Dare County

Fort Raleigh covers 144 acres on the NW tip of Roanoke Island and is NW of the Cape Hatteras National Seashore. It was designated a National Historic Site on April 5, 1941. Parts of the 1585 and 1587 settlement sites are included. The Lindsay Warren Visitor Center displays excavated artifacts, and exhibits tell the story of Sir Walter Raleigh's "lost colony." In addition, the park includes a reconstruction of Fort Raleigh, the Waterside Theatre — which presents Paul Green's symphonic drama of the "Lost Colony" in the summer, an Elizabethan garden maintained by the Garden Club of North Carolina, Inc., and a nature trail.

To reach the park, turn off US 64-264 3 mi N of Manteo.

Thomas Hariot Trail   398

Length: 0.3 mi (0.5 km), easy; *USGS:* Manteo; *Trailhead:* Visitor Center.

Directions and Description: Hike from the Visitor Center toward the Waterside Theatre and turn L at sign. The trail has interpretive signs about the plant life which Thomas Hariot found in the area in 1585. Follow loop trail back to origin.

Support Facilities: Camping is not allowed in the park. A nearby commercial campground is Sandpiper's Trace, Ltd., P.O. Box 370, Manteo, NC 27954. Tel: 919-473-3471. Full svc, excellent rec fac. Open all year. Directions: 0.3 mi W of Manteo on US 64-264.

SECTION II

CAPE LOOKOUT NATIONAL SEASHORE

Carteret County

Cape Lookout Trails **399**

Cape Lookout National Seashore is an undeveloped and extra-ordinary primitive area. Established as a park by an act of Congress in 1966, the 58 miles of barrier islands remain uncommercialized and preserve a fragile natural resource. Campers and hikers on the islands should use care for the delicate ecological system. The islands have no signs or distance markers, and hikers will have to guess at distances. There are a number of marinas that offer access to the park; one of the nearest is at Shell Point on Harkers Island. Follow US 70 to Otway and take SR 1333 or SR 1332 to Straits. Cross the Straits Bridge to Harkers Island and board a park conces-sion ferry. Access and accommodations can be arranged at the Alger Willis Camp, P.O. Box 234, Davis, NC 28524. Tel: 919-729-2791. Hikers and campers must carry everything they need — sun protect-ing clothing, food, water, strong tent, insect repellent, and other gear. Fishing and swimming are allowed, but there are no life-guards.

Support Facilities: Coastal Riverside Campground, Rt 2, Box 683 A, Beaufort, NC, 28516. Tel: 919-728-2362. Open all year. Full svc, rec fac. Campground can be reached from Otway; at the US 70 jct with SR 1331, take the latter for 0.5 mi and then go 0.5 mi on SR 1329.

Information: Contact National Park Service, Cape Lookout Na-tional Seashore, P.O. Box 690, Beaufort, NC 28516. Tel: 919-728-2121 or 919-728-2250.

SECTION III
GUILFORD COURTHOUSE
AND
MOORES CREEK NATIONAL MILITARY PARKS

Guilford Courthouse National Military Park

Guilford County

Guilford Courthouse National Military Park was established on March 2, 1917; covering 220.44 acres, it honors the 4,300 officers and soliders of Commanding General Nathanael Greene's Continental Army in their battle against British Field Commander Charles Earl Cornwallis on March 15, 1781. Although the battle was not a total victory for either side, it was significant in that Cornwallis retreated to Wilmington, practically abandoning the Carolinas. The end of the Revolutionary War came seven months later at Yorktown, Virginia on October 19, 1781.

The park has a museum in the Visitor Center, and there are seven tour stops of historical interest. Hikers, bicycles, and vehicles are allowed on clearly designated roads and trails.

To reach the park go 0.5 mi on New Garden Road from US 220 N in Greensboro; the park is 6 mi from downtown.

Guilford Courthouse Battleground Trail   **400**

Length: 2.5 mi (4 km), easy; *USGS:* Guilford, Greensboro; *Trailhead:* Visitor Center.

Directions and Description: Follow paved trail S of parking area through mature forest of oak, hickory, walnut, and poplar, with understory of dogwood, redbud, and sourwood. The first tour stop, American first line, is at 0.4 mi. Cross railroad and reach spur trail on L to General Green monument at 0.6 mi. Continue on gravel trails through open fields of large, scattered oaks and poplars with senna, milkweed, evening primrose, lobelia, snake root, and bur

179

marigold among the wildflowers. At 1.3 mi reach tour stop five at Guilford Courthouse. Return by site six, American third line, at 1.9 mi and reach Visitor Center at 2.5 mi.

Support Facilities: Camping is not allowed in the park. A commercial campground in the area is KOA, at the jct of I-85 and NC 6, E of and near Greensboro city limits. Its address is Route 14, Box 64A, Greensboro, NC 27405. Tel: 919-274-4143.

Information: Contact Park Superintendent, Guilford Courthouse National Military Park, P.O. Box 9806, Greensboro, NC 27408. Tel: 919-288-1776.

Moores Creek National Military Park

Pender County

Moores Creek National Military Park is one of ten areas in North Carolina managed by the national Park Service of the U.S. Department of the Interior. The park was established June 2, 1926, has 86.78 acres, and is significant because it is where the North Carolina patriots won a victory on February 27, 1776 that notably advanced the American cause against the British Loyalists. On April 12, 1776, North Carolina became the first colony to have its delegation in Philadelphia vote for independence at the Continental Congress.

Entrance to the park is from the jct of US 421 and NC 210, 3 mi E of Currie and 15 mi NW of Wilmington. From Currie follow signs for 3 mi.

Moores Creek Trail   401

Length: 1 mi rt (1.6 km), easy; *USGS:* Acme; *Trailhead:* Visitor Center.

Directions and Description: Begin on the *Pathway to History Trail* W of Visitor Center and follow interpretive signs through pines and hardwoods with Spanish moss to bridge at 0.4 mi. Nature trail begins at 0.7 mi, and returns to parking lot. Facilities for handicapped on paved trail. Open daily except Christmas Day.

Support Facilities: Picnic area and shelter, but no camping allowed in the park. Outside campground is Safari Wilmington Campground, 20 mi SE on US 17, 4 mi N of 74-E. Full svc, rec fac. Open all year. Tel: 919-686-7705.

Information: Contact Park Superintendent, Moores Creek National Military Park, P.O. Box 69, Currie, NC 28435. Tel: 919-283-5591.

SECTION IV

CARL SANDBURG HOME
NATIONAL HISTORIC SITE

Henderson County

Carl Sandburg (1878-1967), poet, author, lecturer, and social philosopher, lived at "Connemara," a 240-acre farm at Flat Rock, for his last 22 years. On October 17, 1968 Congress established the farm as a historic site; it acquired the property from the Sandburg family in 1969 for commemorative purposes. The site is administered by the National Park Service.

There are seven trails on the estate. Entrance is by the Little River Rd, off US 25 at the Flat Rock Playhouse, 5 mi S of Hendersonville.

Big Glassy, Little Glassy, Memminger, Spring, Jerusalem, Loose Cow, and Front Lake Trails   402-408

Length: 3.1 mi rt cb (5 km), easy; *USGS:* Hendersonville; *Trailhead:* Parking lot.

Directions and Description: From the parking lot of the Main House, follow signs (or use brochure map) for *Memminger Trail* (0.7 mi) around *Little Glassy Trail* (0.2 mi). From the gap above the garden hike to the top of Big Glassy Mountain (1.0 mi) and back to the woodshed for the *Spring Trail* (0.3 mi). The *Jerusalem Trail* (0.3 mi), the *Loose Cow Trail* (0.1 mi), and the *Front Lake Trail* (0.5 mi) are all near the Main House and are interconnected.

Support Facilities: There is no camping on the historic site. A nearby private campground is Alpine Travel Trailer Park, Route 5, Box 417, Hendersonville, NC 28739. Tel: 704-692-6011. Go E on US 64 for 0.6 mi from jct of I-26 and US 64 (Exit 18A); turn at sign and go 0.6 mi. Open April 1-October 31. Full svc, limited rec fac.

Information: Contact Park Superintendent, Carl Sandburg Home National Historic Site P.O. Box 395, Flat Rock, NC 28731. Tel: 704-693-4178.

TRAILS IN STATE PARKS, FORESTS, AND HISTORIC SITES

NORTH CAROLINA STATE PARKS
AND RECREATION AREAS

INTRODUCTION

From the alpine ecology of Mt. Mitchell, North Carolina's oldest (1915) and highest (6,684 ft) state park, to the pocosins of Lake Waccamaw, the youngest (1976) and among the lowest (43 ft), there are many and varied settings containing ninety hiking trails totalling 219.4 miles. Trails presently exist in thirty of the state parks.

Fourteen parks with trails are in the Coastal District and have 62.9 mi of walking; nine are in the Piedmont District and have 81.4 mi of trails; and, seven are in the Mountain District, with 75.1 mi of trails. For hikers the choices are exceptionally varied — the sands of the Atlantic beaches; boardwalks over swamps and under Spanish moss; Piedmont river banks carpeted with trout lilies; up quartzite ridges to scenic views; and through rhododendron tunnels in mountain coves.

Admittance to these diverse parks is free — except for parts of the Zoological Park, where an admission fee is charged. The Piedmont and Coastal District parks are open all year, but Mt Jefferson is only open from May to November and Mt Mitchell closes when snow makes the access road dangerous. Facilities for hiking, picnicking, fishing, nature study, and camping are provided in most of the parks. Some, such as Weymouth Woods, provide only hiking and nature study. Two parks, Hanging Rock and Morrow Mtn have family vacation cabins rented by advance reservation.

Where there are swimming facilities, the areas and refreshment stands are operated daily from June 1 through Labor Day. Free passenger ferry service is provided daily during the same period for hikers and visitors to Hammocks Beach Park. Hikers who plan to fish will not need a license for saltwater fishing, but must conform to the licensing regulations of the North Carolina Wildlife Resources Commission for all freshwater fishing. Camping regulations vary; descriptions of camping and support facilities follow.

The parks are natural wildlife sanctuaries. Firearms and alcohol are prohibited, and hunting and trapping are also forbidden. Pets are

184

only allowed on a leash and are never allowed at swimming and cabin areas.

Because of noise pollution, motorcycles are restricted to paved park roads and parking lots. At each park the hiker and camper should inquire at the headquarters for additional information on the trails and for regulations on drinking water and fire restrictions.

For information on specific parks, contact them using the addresses and phone numbers listed at the conclusion of the trail descriptions. For statewide information, call or write to Parks and Recreation, North Carolina Division of Natural Resources and Community Development, P.O. Box 27687, Raleigh, NC 27611. Tel: 919-733-4181.

CHAPTER IX

COASTAL DIVISION

Carolina Beach State Park

New Hanover County

Carolina Beach State Park is located on 1,734 acres between the Cape Fear River on the W and the Atlantic Ocean on the E; it is 10 mi S of Wilmington on US 421. Tent and trailer camping, picnicking, motor boating, fishing, and hiking are activities available at the Park. It has a unique trail system running through or near salt marshes, sand hills (such as the ancient Sugarloaf), rainwater ponds, and swamp lands. Considered a naturalist's delight, the park has over fifty species of flora, including the rare Venus's fly trap and five other insectivorous plants native to the coastal environment.

Sugarloaf and Fly Trap Trails   409-410

Length: 3.4 mi (5.4 km), easy; *USGS:* Carolina Beach; *Trailhead:* Parking lot at picnic area.

Directions and Description: From 421 turn off at sign on Dow Rd and enter the park. Take L fork after the Park Office to park. Begin with the *Fly Trap Loop Trail* and connect at 0.3 mi with another loop trail on R which leads across marsh near the Marina. Take L on the *Sandhills Trail*, passing on the N side of Sugarloaf and Cypress Pond. Return to parking area at 2.6 mi. Other trails connect to the camping area. (The park trail system is under revision.)

Support Facilities: Nearby campground is Plantation Acres Campground, Route 2, Box 339-AB, Wilmington, NC 28403. Tel: 919-791-1695. Open all year. Full svc, rec fac. On US 421, 2 mi S of Carolina Beach.

Information: Contact Park Superintendent, Carolina Beach State Park, P.O. Box 475, Carolina Beach, NC 28428. Tel: 919-458-8206.

Cliffs-of-the-Neuse State Park

Wayne County

The Cliffs-of-the-Neuse State Park covers 593 acres chiefly of forests; it is on the W bank of the Neuse River. The park's most extraordinary attraction is the 90-ft cliff carved over thousands of years to show countless fossil shells, the remains of other marine species, and sedimentation at what was once the Atlantic shoreline. Spanish moss drapes the oaks and pines. Galax, a more mountainous plant, grows on the north bank of Mill Creek. Picnicking, swimming, boating, family and youth tent camping, and hiking (for a total of 1.8 mi) are provided. Entrance to the Park is on SR 1743 E 0.5 mi from NC 111, 13 mi SE of Goldsboro.

Spanish Moss, Galax, and Bird Trails   441-413

Length: 1.8 mi cb (2.9 km), easy; *USGS:* Seven Springs; *Trailhead:* Parking lot near Interpretive Center.

Directions and Description: Follow trail signs R and descend to Mill Creek. Turn L on red-blazed *Bird Trail* to loop across Still Creek and reach jct with yellow-blazed loop, *Galax Trail,* at 0.8 mi. Follow *Galax Trail* for 0.5 mi and return to parking lot. The *Spanish Moss Trail* is L of parking lot, R of Interpretive Center. Descend steeply and circle back to parking lot after 0.5 mi. (Campers have made numerous connecting trails in this area.)

Support Facilities: Camping allowed in park April 1 through November 1. Private campsite is at KOA — Lakeview, at jct of US

70A and I-85 at Selma, 20 mi W of Goldsboro. Address is Box 313A, Rt 2, Selma, NC 27576. Tel: 919-965-5923. Full svc, rec fac. Open all year.

Information: Contact Park Superintendent, Cliffs-of-the-Neuse State Park, Rt 2, Box 50, Seven Springs, NC 28578. Tel: 919-778-6234.

Dismal Swamp State Park

Camden County

Dismal Swamp Trails   **414**

The Great Dismal Swamp is a 210,000-acre wet wilderness largely in Virginia, with the Dismal Swamp National Wildlife Refuge comprising 100,000 acres in the cities of Suffolk and Chesapeake in Virginia, and in Gates, Camden, and Pasquotank counties in North Carolina. The state park, with 14,000 acres in undeveloped land, provides limited access.

More than 170 species of birds have been identified in the vast swamp; and, 28 species of mammals, including the black bear, have been listed. Among the reptiles are three poisonous snakes — the canebreak rattler, the copperhead, and the water moccasin.

Although 24.6 mi (39.4 km) of trails have been laid out on dry or semi-dry ground, they are an extreme risk to the unexperienced hiker, since they pass over covered peat moss holes and cross endless avenues of water. Permits are required for any hiking or camping in the backcountry areas.

Entrance is gained off NC 32 in Gates County near Corapeake (7 mi N of Sunbury). Contact the Superintendent of Parks, NC Department of Natural Resources and Community Development, P.O. Box 27687, Raleigh, NC 27611. Tel: 919-733-4181. Or, Refuge Manager, Dismal Swamp National Wildlife Refuge, P.O. Box 349, Suffolk, VA 23434. Tel: 804-539-7479. USGS map quads are Lake Drummond, Corapeake, and South Mills.

Fort Macon State Historic Park

Carteret County

The Fort Macon State Historic Park is best known for its 150-year-old restored fort at Beaufort Inlet. Emphasis is on its Civil War history. Facilities and services in the 285-acre park include ocean swimming (June 1 through Labor Day), fishing, picnicking, and hiking. A short loop *Nature Trail* and beach hiking provide over 2 miles of walking.

To reach the Park, which is on the eastern tip of Bogue Banks, turn S off US 70 at Morehead City, cross toll-free bridge, and turn E on NC 1190 at jct with NC 58.

Fort Macon Nature Trail   415

Length: 0.4 mi (0.6 km), easy; *USGS:* Beaufort; *Trailhead:* From parking lot go toward covertway of the Fort.

Directions and Description: Follow signs R to loop trail through shrub thicket; go to Beaufort Inlet and return. Some trees and shrubs on the trail are live oak, black locust, prickley ash, beach holly, and youpon.

Support Facilities: Camping is not allowed in the park. Commercial campground is Salter Path Family Camp Ground, P.O. Box 721, Morehead City, NC 28557. Tel: 919-726-2710. Full svc, rec fac. Open March 20-November 1.

Information: Contact Park Superintendent, Fort Macon State Park, P.O. Box 127, Atlantic Beach, NC 28512. Tel: 919-726-3775.

Goose Creek State Park

Beaufort County

Goose Creek State Park is in a coastal area; it covers 1,208 acres on the north side of the Pamlico River. Special features are the tall pines and oaks draped with ghostly gray Spanish moss and both freshwater and saltwater fishing. Primitive camping, picnicking, fishing, boating, and hiking are provided in this sandy wilderness. Bogs, sandy natural beaches, excellent freshwater fishing for bass, bluegill, and perch, and saltwater fishing for bluefish and flounder — all are features of a distinctive recreational area.

Entrance is off SR 1334, 2.4 mi from US 264 and 11.4 mi from jct with US 17 in Washington.

Goose Creek, Live Oak, Flatty Creek, and Ivey Gut Trails   417-420

Length: 6.9 mi cb (11 km), easy; *USGS:* Blounts Bay; *Trailhead:* Parking lots E or W of park boundary.

Directions and Description: Live Oak Trail is 1.2 mi rt; *Ivey Gut Trail* is 2.1 mi rt; *Flatty Creek Trail* is 0.7 mi rt; and, *Goose Creek Trail* is 2.9 mi one-way from parking lots. A combination trip on the trails beginning with *Live Oak Trail* could be as follows: Begin from the parking lot on E side of park and follow signs for a loop around the river bank. Pass the picnic area at 1.2 mi. *Goose Creek Trail* connects near the picnic area and follows W to 1.3 mi. (Side trail goes L to boardwalk and observation overlook.) At 1.4 mi there are boardwalks in the forest. At 2 mi reach jct with W parking lot, and at 2.3 mi reach jct with *Flatty Creek Trail.* Continue around the peninsula and return to W parking lot at 2.9 mi.

Flatty Creek Trail, which is a side trail of *Goose Creek Trail,* is 0.7 mi rt. A boardwalk and observation tower are at the terminus. The most northern trail is the 2.1-mi-rt *Ivey Gut Trail,* which runs from either the W parking lot or the parking lot near the trail entrance on the park road.

Plants seen in the trail areas are prickly pear, blue flag iris, bays, lizard's tail, blueberry, and marsh pennywort.

Support Facilities: Primitive camping is allowed in the park. Nearest private campground is Whechard's Water Fun Campground, P.O. Box 746, Washington, NC 27889. Tel: 919-946-1748. Turn L 1 mi S of Washington on Whechard's Beach Rd, and go 3 mi. Full svc, rec fac. Open all year.

Information: Contact Park Superintendent, Goose Creek State

Park, Route 2, Box 382, Washington, NC 27889. Tel: 919-923-2191.

Hammocks Beach State Park

Onslow County

Hammocks Beach Trails **421**

Hammocks Beach State Park, 892 acres, occupies all of Bear Island SE of Swansboro. The island is reputed to be one of the most unspoiled and beautiful beach areas on the Atlantic coast. For the hiker there are 3.8 mi of nameless trails along the beach and among the sand dunes. Some dunes are up to 30 ft high and one in the SW section of the island is 60 ft. In addition to hiking, other activities available are fishing, swimming, and bird watching.

Vegetation is sparse; there are sea oats, croton, elder, beech holly, bear grass, and, near the marsh side, some water oaks and cedars. A few deer, rabbits, and raccoons live on the island. It is also the nesting ground of the loggerhead sea turtle, an endangered species.

The Park has a bathhouse, refreshment stand, and picnic tables; a free passenger ferry operates daily (10 AM-6 PM) from Memorial Day to Labor Day. The distance to the Park is 2.5 mi (4 km) through a web of marshy islands. From NC 24, near Swansboro W, go S on SR 1511 to the Ferry Dock. (For private boat service call Shawn or George Hall at 919-326-8187.)

For information contact the Park Superintendent, Hammocks Beach State Park, Route 2, Box 295, Swansboro, NC 28584. Tel: 919-326-4881 or 919-326-2205. A nearby campground is Sound View Campsite, Swansboro, NC 28584. Tel: 919-326-8715. It is 1.3 mi W on NC 24 from US 58 jct. Full svc, rec fac. Open all year. USGS map quads are Hubert and Brown's Inlet.

Jockey's Ridge State Park

Dare County

Jockey's Ridge State Park, better known as a center for hang gliding than for hiking, covers 270 acres of "marching" sand dunes adjacent to Nags Head Woods, a maritime forest of 1,980 acres. Jockey's Ridge is named, according to one among a number of local stories, for its use as a natural grandstand for races of Banker ponies. It has a 140-ft-high dune, the largest and highest on the Atlantic coast.

A bathhouse was constructed in 1981. A hike to the top of the ridge presents an outstanding view of both the Atlantic Ocean and the Roanoke Sound. Access to the Park is from US 158 W of Nags Head. For information contact Park Superintendent, Jockey's Ridge State Park, Route 1, Box 203, Creswell, NC 27043. Tel: 919-797-4475. A nearby campground is Joe and Kay's, Box 403, Kill Devil Hills, NC 27948. Tel: 919-441-5468. Open April 1-December 1. Full svc, limited rec fac. Located 1.5 mi W of US 158 bypass on Colington Rd. USGS map quads are Manteo and Roanoke Island NE.

Jones Lake State Park

Bladen County

Jones Lake is an example of the Bay Lakes area, where shallow depressions are filled with cool, clear water. Geologically, it is thought that the oval depressions were caused by a meteorite shower. The Bay Lakes area is also known for the wide variety of bay trees and shrubs. Total length of Jones Lake trails is 2.8 mi. The park covers 2,208 acres.

Jones Lake Trails 422

Length: 2.8 mi (4.5 km), easy; *USGS:* Elizabethtown; *Trailhead:* Enter from either the campground or picnic area to make the loop around the lake.

Directions and Description: Follow signs from parking lot by water fountain 70 yd from the entrance. Follow sign into forest of juniper, pine, gum, and cypress with Spanish moss. Pass sweet bay, a shrub bog plant with large showy leaves and fragrant flowers related to the magnolia; red bay, a small evergreen with a scent of bay rum; the loblolly bay, a member of the tea family with evergreen leaves and white, fragrant blossoms; and, the bull bay tree. In hiking counterclockwise, pass a total of six lake view stations. Trail is sometimes narrow and wet. At 2.5 mi connect with nature trail and return to the parking lot at 2.8 mi. Park area has deer, raccoons, snakes, and bears.

Support Facilities: Park has camping facilities, picnicking, swimming, boating, and fishing. Open June 1 through Labor Day. Private campground nearby is Camp Clearwater. Route 3, Box 321, Elizabethtown, NC 28337. Tel: 919-862-3365. Full svc rec, fac. Opens Easter, closes Labor Day.

Information: Contact Jones Lake State Park Headquarters, Route 2, Box 215, Elizabethtown, NC 28337. Tel: 919-588-4550.

Lake Waccamaw State Park

Columbus County

The existing 273 acres of Lake Waccamaw State Park are part of a planned recreational area comprising 1,385 acres on the SE side of Lake Waccamaw, one of the clear lakes of the Carolina Bays. On a remote, gated wilderness road, the undeveloped park offers picnicking, primitive camping, and exploration. Although 8.1 mi of hiking trails are planned, no mileage has yet been constructed. Overnight campers must register with the Park Ranger.

Botanical communities of pine, cypress, running oak, gum, Caroline ipecac, pond pine in the pocosin areas, sweet bay, and fetter bush are among the many species of plant life. Wildlife is abundant — this is a natural habitat for the black bear, swamp rabbit, gray fox, deer, and mink. Among the reptiles are the alligator, cottonmouth and copperhead, and three species of rattlesnakes. There are 36 species of fish. Fowls are wood duck, wild turkey, and quail.

Access is from US 74-76 (W 3 mi from Bolton) on NC 214; near the lake turn L on paved road (vandals may have removed the signs). Take first dirt road L and continue for 4.5 mi. USGS are Bolton and Juniper Creek.

Support Facilities: Nearest private campground is 40 mi away in Elizabethtown. Address is Camp Clearwater, Route 3, Box 123, Elizabethtown, NC 28337. Tel: 919-862-3365. Open Easter through Labor Day. Full svc, rec fac. From downtown Elizabethtown go 2 mi E on Main St to get there.

Information: Contact Park Superintendent, Lake Waccamaw State Park, Route 1, Box 63, Kelly, NC 28448. Tel: 919-669-2928 or 919-646-3852.

Merchant's Mill Pond State Park

Gates County

Merchant's Mill Pond State Park is home for more than 160 species of birds in its 1,947 acres of lakes and massive gum trees and cypresses. The major fish are largemouth bass, bluegill, chain pickerel, and black crappie. Some of the native animals are deer, raccoons, turtles, beavers, snakes, and cougars. Overnight canoe trips can be arranged down Bennetts Creek to the Chowan River. A 5-mi trail is proposed through Lassiter Swamp; it would eventually join the *Dismal Swamp Trail* into Virginia. Total distance is 7.7 mi.

Merchant's Mill Pond Trail   423

Length: 7.7 mi (12.3 km), easy; *USGS:* Beckford; *Trailhead:* Parking lot at park headquarters on NC 1403, off US 158 NE of Gatesville.

Directions and Description: A short loop trail (0.3 mi) is found on a peninsula with picnic tables behind the park headquarters building. A longer 7.4-mi loop trail begins NW from the parking lot on NC 1403 and crosses the bridge. Turn R into forest of cypress, maple, oak, loblolly pine, beech, and holly. Cross boardwalk at 1 mi. Ascend to division of loop at 1.1 mi. Turn R, skirting pond, and pass Canoe Camp at 1.4 mi. Cross park road at 2.6 mi, and reach the Backpack Camp near Lassiter Swamp at 4.0 mi. (Well pump not dependable.) Turn L before well pump on return trail and pass through carpet of running cedar. Cross park road at 4.8 mi. Rejoin trail at 6.2 mi and turn R, returning to parking lot at 7.7 mi.

Support Facilities: Park has primitive camping with fresh water and pit toilets. Picnicking and canoeing. Private camp nearby is Tuscarora Shores Campground, Route 1, Box 16-BB, Winton, NC 27986. Tel: 919-358-4041. Full svc, rec fac. Open all year. On US 13 between Gatesville and Ahoskie.

Information: Contact Merchant's Mill Pond State Park Headquarters, P.O. Box 147, Gatesville, NC 27938. Tel: 919-357-1191.

Pettigrew State Park

Washington and Tyrrell Counties

Pettigrew State Park is the state's largest — 17,639 acres — with 16,000-acre Lake Phelps surrounded by 1,639 land acres. In addition to the lake — which has a reputation for being an angler's paradise for bass, channel catfish, and white perch, as well as a sanctuary for wintering Canada geese — the park has a state historic site, Somerset Place. With such a blending of nature, history, and outdoor recreation, Pettigrew is unique. The park is open all year for picnicking, fishing, boating, hiking, and camping. Entrance to the park is 6 mi S of the town of Creswell off US 64 on SR 1142, SR 1160, and SR 1168.

Carriage Drive Trail   424

Length: 6.6 mi rt (10.6 km), easy; *USGS:* Creswell; *Trailhead:* Parking lot near park office.

Directions and Description: From parking lot follow old carriage road NW on level, wide, grassy trail through virgin stands of bald cypress, sycamore, gum, and popular bordered with willows, honeysuckle, and paw paw. Views of the lake, through patches of pink wood sorrel, are found on the L at 0.4 mi, 0.6 mi, and 1.2 mi. Reach Western Canal at 2.2 mi, and the trail terminus near Moccasin Canal at 2.7 mi. Return by the same route.

For the E section, hike past the historic Collins House, a splendid nineteenth-century coastal plantation estate, at 0.4 mi. Pass the Bonerva Canal at 0.7 mi. (N trail jct is reached at 1.1 mi.) Continue R to the terminus on the Bee Tree Canal bridge at 1.4 mi. Return by same route. Some of the waterfowl in the area are osprey, great blue heron, and kingfisher. Bear, mink, deer, and bobcat are among the animal inhabitants of the forest.

Support Facilities: Park has campground open all year. Nearest private campground is Green Acres Family Camp Resort, Route 2, Box 395, Williamston, NC 27892. Tel: 919-792-3939. Open all year. Full svc, rec fac. From jct of US 64 and US 17, go 5 mi S on US 17, turn W 1 mi on Green Acres Rd.

Information: Contact Park Superintendent, Pettigrew State Park, Route 1, Box 203, Creswell, NC 27928. Tel: 919-797-4475.

Singletary Lake State Park

Bladen County

Singletary Park is headquarters for the Carolina lakes area — White, Waccamaw, Jones, Phelps, Salter's, Bay Tree Lakes, and Singletary. It has cabin and organized group camping facilities on its 1,221 acres. Total trail mileage is 1 mi.

Singletary Lake Trail   425

Length: 1 mi (1.6 km), easy; *USGS:* White Lake; *Trail head:* Park headquarters off NC 53 between Colly Creek and Cape Fear River, SE of White Lake.

Directions and Description: From the main camp road, follow lake sign at 290 yd to Singletary Lake. Turn R at edge of lake and enter forest of bayberries, cypress, gum, poplars and juniper. Area is also heavy with Spanish moss. At 0.4 mi cross service road, follow green blazes, and turn sharp R at 0.7 mi in scrub oaks. At 0.8 mi turn R off fire break into long leaf pines. Return to main camp road at 1 mi.

Support Facilities: Trail open all year, but cabin and camping facilities closed in the winter. Private campground nearby is Camp Clearwater, Route 3, Box 321, Elizabethtown, NC 28337. Tel: 919-862-3365. Full svc, rec fac. Open Easter, closes Labor Day.

Information: Contact Singletary Lake State Park Headquarters, Route 1, Box 63, Kelly, NC 28448. Tel: 919-669-2928.

Theodore Roosevelt State Park

Carteret County

The Theodore Roosevelt State Park, on the island of Bogue Banks, is a 265-acre natural area set aside to preserve a maritime forest of laurel oak, red bay, wild olive, red cedar, live oak, hollies, and pines in wet swales and marshes (freshwater, brackish, and saltwater). Unique plant life and bird sanctuaries, especially for warblers, distinguish the area. The park was given to the state by the Roosevelt family.

The Bogue Banks Marine Resources Center conducts research and houses exhibits, aquariums, and multimedia programs interpreting the coastal environment. Access to the Park is found near Salter Path, 7 mi S of Atlantic Beach on US 58.

Hoffman Trail   426

Length: 0.4 mi (0.6 km), easy; *USGS:* Beaufort; *Trailhead:* SE corner of the Marine Resources Center parking lot.

Directions and Description: Follow signs for loop trail over dunes, by swales, through the forest, and along the *East Pond Path*

— made by early fishermen. Return to parking lot.

Support Facilities: See Fort Macon State Park.

Information: Contact Marine Resource Center/Bogue Banks, Atlantic Beach, NC 28512. Tel: 919-726-0121.

Weymouth Woods State Park
Sandhills Nature Preserve

Moore County

The Weymouth Woods State Park is a 425-acre woodland tract near the city limits of Southern Pines. Studies indicate that the sandhills (or sandy ridges) were formed from sediments of clay, sand, and gravel deposited by streams in the region millions of years ago, when the area was part of an inland sea.

There are more than 600 species of plants including many kinds of wildflowers, French mulberry, longleaf pines, turkey oaks, pepperbushes, and bays. In addition to the usual wild animals there are beaver, mink, otter, and green heron. There is also a Natural History Museum, open daily. The total trail distance is 3.8 mi, including the *Pine Barrens Trail, Gum Swamp Trail,* and the *Holly Road Trail.* A self-guided trail is planned. To reach the park, turn off SR 2074 from Indiana Ave or Aberdeen Rd which connect from U.S. 1.

Pine Barrens, Gum Swamp, and Holly Road Trails   427-429

Length: 3.8 mi (6.1 km), easy; *USGS:* Southern Pines; *Trailhead:* Rear of Interpretive Center.

Directions and Description: Follow white blazes on *Pine Barrens Trail* for 1 mi through longleaf pines and turkey oaks. *Gum Swamp* is a 0.4-mi loop into a hardwood area near an abandoned beaver dam. From this trail begins the 1.9-mi *Holly Road Trail.* After crossing James Creek at 40 yd, turn L or R at 0.1 mi on yellow-blazed trail. If turn is L, a spring is at 0.5 mi. A number of bridle trails intersect the hiking trails. Return on the loop of *Pine Barrens Trail* to the parking lot for a total of 3.8 mi.

Support Facilities: The preserve is chiefly for educational purposes and does not have recreational or camping facilities. The nearest camp is the Heritage Farm Campground, 7 mi N of Southern Pines off US 1 near Vass on Carthage Rd. Full svc, rec fac. Open all year. Address is Route 3, Whispering Pines, NC 28327. Tel: 919-949-3433.

Information: Contact Park Superintendent, Weymouth Woods, P.O. Box 1386, Southern Pines, NC 28387. Tel: 919-692-2167.

State Historic Site

Johnson County

Bentonville Battleground Trail   430

As Union General W.T. Sherman's army was marching through North Carolina after burning Charlestown, Confederate General Joseph E. Johnson engaged Sherman's left wing at Bentonville on March 19-21, 1865, in an effort to prevent Goldsboro from being occupied. Following the largest battle ever fought in North Carolina, and with the loss of more than 350 men, Johnson withdrew to protect Raleigh, which fell on April 13.

The trail, mainly on all-weather roads, has 27 stations containing historic information about the battle, it is designated a State Historic Site. Entrance is 1.4 mi off US 701 on SR 1008.

Length: 13.4 mi (21.4 km), easy; *USGS:* Four Oaks; *Trailhead:* Harper House parking lot.

Directions and Description: From the Harper House, cross SR 1008 between trail markers #3 and #4 and follow public road. At 0.6 mi turn L on SR 1192. Reach jct with SR 1008, turn R, and at 2.7 mi see the UDC monument to the Confederate soldiers. Turn L on SR 1194, which later merges with SR 1009, and arrive at the Bentonville Community Building at 5.6 mi. Continue to marker #23 at 5.8 mi; here Confederate cavalry was halted by the flooded Mill Creek. Return to Community Building and take road to L, following 0.1 mi and turning R at marker #24. At 7.1 mi turn L at marker #25, pass markers #26 and #27, and turn R on a private dirt field road near a feed bin at 7.9 mi. Continue by edge of field for 0.7

mi to paved road and turn L at marker #28. Reach SR 1008 at 9.0 mi; turn R and go 0.6 mi to Ebenezer Church and jct with SR 1009. (Country store is across the road.) Turn R and go 0.5 mi to marker #20, return to SR 1008 at 10.6 mi. Follow SR 1008 to the UDC marker at SR 1194 jct at 11.6 mi. Return on SR 1008 to starting point for a total of 13.4 mi.

Information: Bentonville Battleground, P.O. Box 27, Newton Grove, NC. 28366. Tel: 919-594-0789. Also, Division of Archives and History in Raleigh. Tel: 919-733-7305.

North Carolina Marine Resources Center

New Hanover County

Operated by the Office of Marine Affairs, North Carolina Department of Administration, at Fort Fisher, the 25-acre Center houses aquariums, exhibits, conference rooms, research laboratories, and the University of North Carolina Sea Grant offices. It is one of three similar facilities in the state.

Entrance is from US 421, near Kure Beach, 0.5 mi N of Fort Fisher. Open every day except Saturday and holidays.

Marsh Trail   431

Length: 0.9 mi (1.4 km), easy; *USGS:* Kure Beach; *Trailhead:* Parking lot.

Directions and Description: From parking lot follow sign by pond, through shrub thicket of yaupon, catbrier, and wax myrtle, to marsh meadow. Pass tidal basin and cross dune and swale to Atlantic Ocean. Return on loop. Shore and marsh birds are brown pelican, willet, egret, and blackbird.

Information: Contact North Carolina Marine Research Center, General Delivery, Kure Beach, NC 28449. Tel: 919-458-8257.

CHAPTER X

MOUNTAIN DIVISION

Crowder's Mountain State Park

Gaston County

Crowder's Mountain (1,625 ft), named in honor of Ulrick Crowder, a German merchant who settled in the area in the 1780's, is part of the 1,966 acres of the Crowder's Mountain State Park. Under continuous development, park plans call for acquisition of Kings Pinnacle (1,705 ft), building an interpretive center and museum, creating a larger lake, and laying out more trails. Primitive camping is now allowed and the total connecting trail is over 15. The park has been designated a wilderness area; two rare plants — ground juniper and Brady spleenwort — and a wide variety of flora and fauna make it ideal for natural preservation in the future. In addition to hiking and camping, fishing and picnicking are permitted.

Entrance to the park is from the I-85 jct with US 74 and 29 (E toward Gastonia). Turn R at 0.6 mi on SR 1125, which is Freedom Mill Rd. After 2.5 mi turn R on Sparrow Spring Rd and reach park entrance on R after 0.6 mi.

Crowder's Trail and Rocktop Trail   432-433

Length: 5.2 mi rt (8.3 km), moderate to strenuous; *USGS:* Kings Mtn, Gastonia; *Trailhead:* Parking lot at park office.

Directions and Description: From the park office follow the signs on a well-graded and well-maintained trail N to jct with *Pinnacle Trail* at 0.4 mi. Turn R, follow yellow dot markers through mature hardwood to SR 1125 at 0.8 mi. Cross road, turn L, and skirt the ridge to jct with *Backside Trail* at 2.6 mi. Turn R. *(Backside Trail* is a connector trail with *Tower Trail,* which runs from SR 1131, Camp Rotary Rd, to Crowder's Mtn. It is 1.8 mi rt. *Tower Trail* is 4 mi rt.) At 2.9 mi climb steps and at 3 mi reach summit for impressive views from sheer 150-ft cliffs. Return SW on *Rocktop Trail,* whose jct with *Tower Trail* is at 3.4 mi; continue on rocky quartzite ridge, descend, and reach SR 1125 at 4.4 mi. Return to park office parking lot at 5.2 mi.

Pinnacle Trail and Fern Trail   436-437

Length: 3.3 mi cb (5.3 km), easy to moderate; *USGS:* See above; *Trailhead:* See above.

Directions and Description: From parking lot at park office go N on gravel trail 0.1 mi to jct of *Pinnacle Trail* and *Crowder's Trail.* Take L and follow signs through camping area. At jct with *Turnback Trail* at 0.9 mi continue, climb Kings Pinnacle (1,705 ft), and return to park boundary. Follow R at *Turnback Trail* as a connector to *Fern Trail* at 2.3 mi. Complete loops of interpretive section and lake and return to parking lot at park office at 3.3 mi. Construction project may have changed trail design and distances.

Support Facilities: Camping in the park is limited to primitive backpacking sites. A nearby commercial campground is Kings Kampers KOA, P.O. Box 418, Kings Mountain, NC 28086. Tel: 704-739-4520. From I-85, exit 8, at NC 161, York Rd, go 0.3 mi on access road. Open all year. Full svc, rec fac.

Information: Contact Park Superintendent, Crowder's Mtn State Park, Route 1, Box 278, Kings Mountain, NC 28086. Tel: 704-867-1181.

Hanging Rock State Park

Stokes County

Hanging Rock State Park, with 5,022 acres, has more than 18 mi of walking for the hiker. A labyrinth of trails to scenic heights, waterfall areas, rocky ridges and caves permits the hiker to view 300 species of flora, including the mountain camelia. Canadian and Carolina hemlock grow together here, a rarity, and a rare legume is found only in this area. The park has camping (also cabins), picnicking, swimming, fishing, and mountain climbing. Highest elevation is 2,500 ft. To reach the park, turn off NC 89 and 8, 4 mi NW of Danbury on SR 1101 W, or off NC 66 N of Gap on SR 1001 E. Trail and campground open all year.

Hanging Rock Trail   439

Length: 1.4 mi (2.4 km), moderate; *USGS:* Hanging Rock; *Trailhead:* Parking lot #1.

Directions and Description: Follow trail sign E across Indian Creek and begin ascent. (Heavy visitor traffic has caused serious erosion.) A red blaze leads to the steep 200 ft climb to the summit. Hikers have created other, bootleg trails to the summit. Return by the same route.

Hidden Falls, Window Falls, and
Upper Cascades Trails   440-442

Length: 1.6 mi rt and cb (2.6 km), easy; *USGS:* See above; *Trailhead:* See above.

Directions and Description: Follow trail signs from the picnic area at N end of parking lot. Descend 0.4 mi to shady area near

Indian Creek Falls. Continue to Window Falls at 0.6 mi. Return to the parking lot at 1.2 mi. Go W from the parking lot to Upper Cascades Fall at 0.2 mi, and return by the same route.

Torys Den Trail   443

Length: 8.2 mi rt (13.2 km), easy; *USGS:* See above; *Trailhead:* Parking lot #2.

Directions and Description: Follow the trail signs SW from the parking lot on E side of bathhouse and lake shore. Cross stream at 0.3 mi, following red blaze. Jct with *Moores Wall Trail* and *Magnolia Spring Trail* is reached 1 mi. Continue R, ascending slightly. Reach blue-blazed trail to Torys Den (and *Sauratown Trail*) at 1.5 mi. Turn L and at 2 mi reach the crest of Huckleberry Ridge near large rock formations. Descend, turn L at 2.3 mi, and reach jct with white-circle-blazed bridle trail at 2.4 mi. Turn L and continue descent on combination white-and blue-blazed trail to stream at 3.5 mi. Reach SR 2026 at 3.6 mi. Turn R and follow Charlie Young gravel road to sign on L at 4.0 mi. Turn L. (White blaze for *Sauratown Trail* continues ahead on NE side of Hall Road to Horse Parking Trail Center on Moore Spring Rd.) In descending to Torys Den, it may be difficult to determine route to cave because of extra trails made by visitors to the cave. Reach cave at 4.1 mi, and return by same route or have vehicle waiting at SR 2026 off Mickey Rd, SR 2011, reaching it from Moore Spring Rd, SR 1001, near Gap on NC 66.

Wolf Rock Trail and Moores Knob Trail   446-447

Length: 6.8 mi rt cb (10.9 km), moderate; *USGS:* See above; *Trailhead:* Parking lot #2.

Directions and Description: This combination of trails requires ascending and descending on rocky terrain.

From parking lot #2, follow the trail signs around the fence at the bathhouse. Follow S on the *Chestnut Oak Self-Guided Trail* and turn L to reach Wolf Rock at 0.8 mi. Trail to L at Wolf Rock leads to *Hanging Rock Trail.* Turn R and follow ridge to jct at 1.3 mi. Continue L to House Rock at 1.5 mi. Excellent view of Hanging

Rock and the city of Winston-Salem can be had here. At 1.9 mi reach Devil Chimney over a rocky trail for a view of Pilot Mtn. Backtrack and turn L at 2.5 mi. Descend to bridge and go through rhododendron tunnel to 2.9 mi. Turn L on red-blazed *Moores Wall Trail*. R leads 1 mi back to parking lot. At 3.5 mi turn R (L is blue-blazed trail leading to *Sauratown Trail* and Torys Den.) Continue ascending on red-blazed trail. Reach rocky area of spruce and turkey grass at 4.1 mi. Observation town with spectacular 360° view is reached at 4.8 mi. In descent, pass Balanced Rock and Indian Face on old white-blazed road; reach stream at 5.9 mi. Pass through camping area and rejoin red-blazed trail at 6.1 mi. Cross stream and return to parking lot at 6.8 mi. This combination of trails could also include Torys Den for a total of 12 mi.

Support Facilities: The park has a campground and family cabins. The campground is open all year, and the cabins are available (with reservations) from April 15 to October 15. Nearest private campground is Beaver Creek Family Campground, Route 1, Box 148, Stoneville, NC 27048. Tel: 919-427-5296. From US 220 bypass, take 135 exit near Madison, turn L, and follow signs. Open April 1 to November 1. Full svc, no rec fac.

Information: Contact Park Superintendent, Hanging Rock State Park, P.O. Box 128, Danbury, NC 27016. Tel: 919-593-8480.

Mount Jefferson/New River State Park

Ashe and Alleghany Counties

Mount Jefferson State Park covers 541 acres and includes the summit (4,900 ft) of Mt. Jefferson; it is halfway between the towns of Jefferson and West Jefferson. Panoramic views from the fire-tower reveal other mountain ranges in a threee state area — White-top Mtn in Virginia, Grandfather and Pilot mountains in NC, and the Cherokee National Forest mountains in Tennessee.

The Park has a wide variety of forest trees, shrubs, and flowers. Its chestnut oak forest is considered to be one of the most outstanding in the southeastern United States. In addition, there are maple, ash, white and red oak, black locust, and poplar. Rhododendron, mountain laurel, and flame azalea are also prominent, and so are wood lilies, galax, and dutchman's breeches. Picnicking and hiking are the major activities, and camping is not allowed.

Entrance is from US 221 between Jefferson and West Jefferson on the Mount Jefferson Road (SR 1149); go 1 mi, turning on SR 1152 for 2.1 mi to the summit.

Summit and Rhododendron Trails   449-450

Length: 1.4 mi rt cb (2.2 km), easy; *USGS:* Jefferson; *Trailhead:* Parking lot.

Directions and Description: From the parking lot climb 0.3 mi to the North Carolina Forest Service lookout tower, continue to Luther's Rock Overlook for views of the New River area, and return on the self-guided nature trail.

Support Facilities: Since camping is not allowed on Mt. Jefferson, one must go to the nearest campground, which is Greenfield Campground at the base of the park, 1 mi E of Mt. Jefferson Rd (SR 1149). Address is West Jefferson, NC 28694. Tel: 919-246-9106. Open April 1 through October 15. Full svc, excellent rec fac. Other information can be obtained from the Jefferson Chamber of Commerce. Tel: 919-246-9550.

Information: Contact Park Superintendent, Mt. Jefferson State Park, P.O. Box 48, Jefferson, NC 28640. Tel: 919-246-9653.

New River State Park Nature Trail   451

Length: 1 mi rt (1.6 km), easy; *USGS:* Jefferson; *Trailhead:* Parking lot near canoe put-in at Wagoner Rd Acess.

Directions and Description: From the jct of NC 88-16 and US 221 in Jefferson go 3.3 mi on NC 88-16 to the South Fork of the New River bridge in the community of Index. Curve R under the bridge on SR 1588 and go 2.1 mi to jct with SR 1590. Turn L, enter park gate and follow road to picnic area parking. Take the *Nature Trail* loop to the canoe take-out area across from a river island and return to the parking lot. (Canoe trail runs 26.5 mi to the Virginia state line.)

Support Facilities: Canoe-in-camping only. See above for other campground.

Information: Contact New River State Park, P.O. Box 48, Jefferson, NC 28640. Tel: 919-982-2587 or 919-246-9653.

Mount Mitchell State Park

Yancey County

Mount Mitchell State Park, extending over 1,469 acres of the ridge of the Black Mountains, is the state's highest park (6,684 ft), and Mt. Mitchell itself is the highest peak east of the Mississippi. This is also the state's oldest park, having been designated in 1915 thanks to the influence of early environmentalists such as Governor Locke Craig and President Theodore Roosevelt. The park is listed in the National Registry of Natural Landmarks.

Mt. Mitchell is named in honor of Dr. Elisha Mitchell, clergyman and University of North Carolina geology professor, who fell to his death in 1857 while on one of his many exploring trips.

Geologically the Black Mountain range is estimated to be over one billion years, erosion having worn down the summits about 200 million years ago. Fraser's fir (damaged by the wooly aphid) and red spruce give the crest an alpine look reminiscent of Canada or Maine. Some of the flowering plants are the white helebore, blue beaded Clinton's lily, and bearberry. Among the forest animals are the skunk, bobcat, deer, and bear. There is a total of 18 mi of hiking trails, including the *Commissary Road,* but not including the many connecting trails into the Pisgah National Forest. The restaurant and lounge are open May 15-October 15.

Entrance is from NC 128 off the Blue Ridge Parkway near milepost 355, 30 mi NE of Asheville.

Old Mt. Mitchell Trail   452

Length: 2 mi (3.2 km), moderate; *USGS:* Mt Mitchell; *Trailhead:* Parking lot at park office.

Directions and Description: From the parking lot at the park office ascend N on the ridge, following yellow dots to park lounge at 0.5 mi. Reach tent camping area at 1.2 mi, meet jct of *Camp Alice Trail* at 1.7 mi, and attain the summit observation tower at 2 mi. Panoramic views on a clear day are magnificent. Return by the same route or go 0.2 mi to the parking lot at the museum.

Deep Gap Trail   453
(*Part of the* **Black Mountain Crest Trail**)

Length: Park section only — 5.4 mi rt (8.6 km), strenuous; *USGS:* See above; *Trailhead:* Parking lot at the museum.

*Directions and Description:*From the parking lot at the museum and picnic area, follow the orange blaze over rough terrain to Mt. Craig (6,645 ft) at 1.1 mi; then on to Big Tom (6,593 ft), named in honor of Thomas D. Wilson (1825–1900), who found the body of Dr. Mitchell at 1.5 mi. Continue over strenuous trail to Balsam Cone (6,611 ft) at 2.1 mi, and reach Cattail Peak (6,583 ft) at 2.4 mi. Return by the same route. (Trail continues to Deep Gap Shelter, Deer Mtn, Celo Knob, and SR 1109, for a total of 12 mi one way. See *Black Mountain Crest Trail* under Toecane District of Pisgah National Forest.)

Camp Alice Trail   454

Length: 2.2 mi rt (3.5 km), strenuous; *USGS:* See above; *Trailhead:* See above.

Directions and Description: From the parking lot at the Museum, hike past the observation tower, follow the *Old Mt. Mitchell Trail,* and turn L at 0.4 mi. Descend on blue-dot trail to Camp Alice, an old logging and railroad camp, at 1.1 mi. (Regardless of the name, no camping is allowed.) Return by the same route or descend to the Commissary Road and hike R to the park office.

Balsam Trail   455

Length: 0.7 mi (1.1 km), easy; *USGS:* See above; *Trailhead:* See above.

Directions and Description: From the parking lot at the museum hike the graded trail toward the summit, turning L at 0.1 mi. Follow the self-guided loop nature trail (which is also part of the *Mt. Mitchell Trail*) back to the parking lot, turning L at each jct. The highest spring in eastern America, with an average temperature of 36° is on this trail.

Mt Mitchell Trail   456

Length: 3.2 mi rt (5.1 km), strenuous; *USGS:* See above; *Trailhead:* See above.

Directions and Description: From the parking lot at the museum hike the graded trail toward the summit, turning L at 0.1 mi. At 0.3 mi turn R on blue-blazed trail and descend over rough trail, with switchbacks beginning at 0.7 mi. Reach Commissary Road (and shelter for ten campers) at 1.6 mi. Return by the same route or continue for another 4.4 mi on switchbacks to Black Mountain Campground in the Pisgah National Forest.

Support Facilities: Camping is restricted in the park; inquiry should be made at the park office. The nearest public campground is Black Mountain Campground, 5 mi N on FSR from Deep Gap (near milepost 350) on the Blue Ridge Parkway. Limited fac. Open May 2-December 15. A private campground nearby is Clear Creek Camping Park, on NC 80. Full svc. Address is Clear Creek Camping Park, Route 5, Box 189, Burnsville, NC 28714. Tel: 704-675-4510.

Information: Contact Park Superintendent, Mt. Mitchell State Park, Route 5, Box 700, Burnsville, NC 28714. Tel: 704-675-4611.

Pilot Mountain State Park

Surry County

Pilot Mountain State Park covers 3,740 acres in two sections — on Pilot Mountain and by the Yadkin River — connected by a 6-mi, 300-ft-wide forest corridor for hikers and equestrians. In the park is the Big Pinnacle, rising 200 ft from its base, 1,400 ft above the valley floor, and 2,440 ft above sea level. Dedicated as a National Nature Landmark in 1976, geologically this summit is a quartzite monadnock. The eight trails total in the park over 16 mi (not including the corridor and the 1.3 mi of bridle trail connecting with the *Sauratown Trail* at US 52). Entrance to the park is at jct of US 52 and SR 2053, 14 mi S of Mt. Airy and 24 mi N of Winston-Salem.

Pilot Mountain Section

Ledge Springs Trail   457

Length: 1.6 mi (2.6 km), strenuous; *USGS:* Pinnacle; *Trailhead:* Parking lot on top of the mountain.

Directions and Description: Follow trail signs E to Little Pinnacle or L below base to jct with *Jomeokee Trail.* Turn R at 0.2 mi and follow yellow blazes. Descend over rocky, sometimes difficult, trail S of ledges. At 1 mi there is a spring on R, 30 yd from jct with *Mountain Bridle Trail.* Turn R, and begin steep ascent over rocky ledge area to jct with *Summit Campground Trail* at 1.3 mi. Pass R on picnic area, returning to parking lot at 1.5 mi.

Jomeokee Trail   458

Length: 0.8 mi (1.3 km), moderate; *USGS:* See above; *Trailhead:* See above.

Directions and Description: Follow trail sign E of Little Pinnacle to base of Big Pinnacle. (*Jomeokee* is an Indian word for "Great Guide" or "Pilot.") Turn R at 0.3 mi and follow rocky loop. Trail walls have caves, eroded rock formations, wildflowers, lichens, and rare nesting grounds for ravens. (Climbing or rappelling is prohibited.) Return to parking lot at 0.8 mi.

Sassafras Trail   459

Length: 0.5 mi (0.8 km), easy; *USGS:* See above; *Trailhead:* See above.

Directions and Description: Follow trail N on self-guiding loop interpretive trail among pitch pine, chestnut oak, galax, and mountain laurel.

Campground Trail   460

Length: 2.1 mi (3.4 km), moderate; *USGS:* See above; *Trailhead:* Family campground at base of N side of mountain.

Directions and Description: Ascend SW through rocky area of hardwoods, mountain laurel, and undergrowth to connect at 1.8 with *Ledge Springs Trail.* Turn L and reach the summit of the mountain parking lot at 2.1 mi.

Mountain Bridle Trail   461

Length: 2.5 mi (4.0 km), moderate; *USGS:* See above; *Trailhead:* Parking lot on top of mountain.

Directions and Description: Since this is a connecting trail with *Ledge Springs Trail,* the minimum distance for the walker is 3.1 mi without having to backtrack.

For hikers, leave the parking lot on top of the mountain, and descend W on *Ledge Springs Trail* for 0.6 mi to N terminus of *Mountain Bridle Trail.* Descend, following red blazes SE through hardwood and softwood forest for 2.5 mi to Surry County Line Rd, SR 2061, for a total of 3.1 mi. (SR 2061 begins as SR 1148, 1.5 mi E in the town of Pinnacle.)

Corridor Trail   462

Length: 6 mi (9.6 km), easy; *USGS:* See above; *Trailhead:* Surry County Line Rd, SR 2061, at horse trailer parking and exit of *Mountain Bridle Trail,* or at Yadkin River Section entrance on SR 2072.

Directions and Description: This trail can be used for horseback riding or hiking; begin at either the N or S terminus of the corridor, one in the Pilot Mountain section of the park and the other in the Yadkin River section. If using N terminus, hike S, crossing SR 2064 and SR 2048 at 3 mi. Cross SR 2070 and exit at SR 2072 in Yadkin

River section of park near entrance and N side of Horne Creek. Vehicle switching advised for hikers.

Yadkin River Section

Horne Creek Trail and Canal Trail   **463-464**

Length: 3.1 mi rt cb (5 km), easy; *USGS:* See above; *Trailhead:* SR 2072 W of park entrance, or at river parking lot near the Southern Railway.

Directions and Description: From park entrance area follow N bank of Horne Creek, cross stream, and enter picnic area. Ascend, reach sharp curve of park road, and descend to the Southern Railway at 1 mi. Connect with *Canal Trail*, between the river and the railroad, and reach terminus at 0.5 mi. Backtrack to park entrance or to the parking lot E of the trail.

Yadkin River Trail   **465**

Length: 0.7 mi (1.1 km), easy; *USGS:* See above; *Trailhead:* Picnic area on south bank of the Yadkin River.

Directions and Description: To reach this trail take NC 67 W from the town of East Bend. Turn R on SR 1546, R on SR 1541, R on SR 1538 and R on SR 1546 in Yadkin County to picnic and parking area. Follow yellow blazes to the river and return on loop through pine forest W of ranger station. (This is also an area for the bridle trail, which crosses the Yadkin River N to the *Corridor Trail* and points beyond.)

Support Facilities; Primitive campsites are provided on the 45-acre island in the Yadkin River and near the Horne Creek area. Family tent and trailer camping is provided in the Pilot Mountain section. A private campground is located W of Mt. Airy on NC 89, 1.5 mi W of I-77 on Bulah Rd. Contact Pop's and Mom's Campground, Rt. 6, Box 379, Mt. Airy, NC 27030. Tel: 919-352-4847. Full svc, no rec fac. Open all year.

Information: Contact Park Superintendent, Pilot Mountain State Park, Route 1, Box 13, Pinnacle, NC 27043. Tel: 919-325-2355.

South Mountains State Park

Burke and Cleveland Counties

South Mountains State Park is an undeveloped, remote park covering 5,779 acres of upper Piedmont ecology. Composed of numerous mountain knobs, all under 3,000 ft in elevation, the area is underlain by a mixture of mica schist and gneiss with quartzite. Mature forests of oak, poplar, spruce and pine grow here; they support an understory of three species of rhododendron, mulberry, holly, and mountain laurel. Wildflowers are abundant along the streams. The major attraction in the park is the 70-ft High Shoals Waterfall.

The Park provides 12 mi of fishable trout streams, backpack camping, picnicking, and 13 mi of old CCC roads for horseback riding and hiking. Two sites for backpack camping — High Shoals and Shinny Creek — require registration at the park office. Pit toilets are provided.

Entrance to the Park is gained from I-40 in Morganton, proceed S on NC 18 (Shelby Rd) for 10.8 mi to SR 1913 and take a sharp R at Pine Mountain sign. Go 4.2 mi, turn L on SR 1924 (old NC 18), and after 2.7 mi turn R on SR 1901. Continue for 1.3 mi, cross Jacob's Fork Creek bridge, and turn R on gravel road, SR 1904, which is the access road to the park. Proceed for 3.6 mi to the park office, crossing Jacob's Fork three times and fording it once; there is also a rocky section of road best suited for 4WD in inclement weather.

High Shoals Falls and Upper Falls Trails   623-624

Length: 4.1 mi rt cb (6.6 km), strenuous; *USGS:* Benn Knob; *Trailhead:* Parking area near park office.

Directions and Description: From the parking area opposite the park office, follow sign up the river to the picnic area. At 0.5 mi trail forks L to High Shoals and R to Upper Falls. Follow L over rocks and roots and through rosebay rhododendron to stream crossing at 0.8 mi. Use care in following yellow dots over the rocks. Climb through large spruce forest to base of falls at 0.9 mi. Waterfall

215

plunges 70 ft onto massive boulders and into a deep pool. Climb L of falls and cross over flat area at 1 mi. At 1.3 mi reach old CCC road and turn R. (Backpack campsite is L). At 1.4 mi reach jct with old CCC Headquarters Rd, and take L to *Upper Falls Trail*. Watch for sign on R off road at 1.5 mi. Reach backpack campsite 5-8 at 2.2 mi. Return to jct of old CC Headquarters at 2.9 mi and descend on L to picnic area at 3.6 mi. (Another route for return from Upper Falls could be the old CCC Shinny Creek Road.) Return to parking area at 4.1 mi.

Support Facilities: KOA-Morganton is the nearest campground. Westbound traffic turn off I-40 at Glen Alpine exit, 3 mi W from US 64 and I-40 jct. Eastbound traffic turn off I-40 at Jamestown Rd exit. Address is Morganton KOA, Rt. 2, Box 854, Morganton, NC 28655. Tel: 704-584-1733. Full svc, rec fac. Open March 15-November 1.

Information: Contact Park Superintendent, South Mountains State Park, Route 1, Box 206, Connley Springs, NC 28612. Tel: 704-433-4772.

Stone Mountain State Park

Wilkes County

Stone Mountain State Park, with 10,463 acres of forests, trout streams, waterfalls, and rugged, medium-grained biolite granite domes, borders the eastern edge of the Blue Ridge Mountains. The largest granite area is Stone Mountain, rising in grandeur 600 ft above its base and 2,305 ft above sea level. The park's wilderness environment provides habitat for deer, beaver, mink, otter, bobcat, cougar, and bear, in addition to many other mammals. Spring wildflowers are prominent. Although the park is generally undeveloped, fishing, camping, climbing, and hiking are allowed. At least 10 miles of trails are open. Camping must be at designated areas, and group campers must have advance reservations. (Climbing on the south face of Stone Mountain is permitted at present on a trial basis.) Entrance to the park is via SR 1737 NW 3 mi from the town of Traphill. (US 21 is 4.3 mi E.) Turn R at SR 1739 and follow up Roaring River for 3.8 mi to parking lot and information area. Another route from US 21 at Roaring Gap descends on a gravel road, SR 1100, to Elk Spur Church, turns R, crosses into Wilkes County, and reaches the parking lot at 7 mi.

Wolf Rock, Cedar Rock, and
Stone Mountain Falls Trails   466-468

Length: 8.2 mi rt cb (12.1 km), easy to strenuous; *USGS:* Glade Valley; *Trailhead:* Parking lot and information area.

Directions and Description: These trails are described as a continuous loop to provide for a longer hike in the park. They can also be hiked individually or in reverse of the following order. Individual trail distances are: *Wolf Rock,* 2.7 mi rt; *Cedar Rock,* 1.6 mi rt; *Stone Mtn Trail,* 3.3 mi rt; and, *Middle and Lower Falls Trail,* 1.5 mi rt. The climb from the parking lot up the W side of the dome is 0.5 mi, 1 mi rt.

Follow sign for *Wolf Rock Trail* up old road and reach summit at jct with Campsite 1-10 trail at 0.5 mi. Turn R for scenic view from Wolf Rock (2,041 ft) at 0.8 mi. Spring is uphill on L at 1 mi. Pass granite dome at Buzzard Rock at 1.2 mi, and follow old *Blackjack Trail.* Descend, turn sharp L at 1.7 mi, cross stream, climb steeply, and reach jct with *Cedar Rock Trail* at 2.3 mi. Descend, return to field S of Stone Mountain dome, and turn sharp R on the *Stone Mtn Falls Trail* at 2.5 mi. At 3 mi pass Indian Den Rock and *First Flat Trail,* which ascends to Stone Mtn ridge, on L. At 3.2 mi there is a jct, R, with *Middle Falls and Lower Falls Trail.* (Side trip to Falls is 1.5 mi rt.) Continue L to base at 3.5 mi of the spectacular 200-ft, tumbling Stone Mountain Falls (marked "Beauty Falls" on some maps).

Climb carefully the steep trail to summit of falls, which is reached at 3.7 mi. Pass stone chimney at 3.8 mi, turn L at 4 mi, and reach *First Flat Rock Trail* at 4.2 mi. Continue R and pass Hitching Rock, with magnificent views, at 4.4 mi. Begin steep incline and reach summit of Stone Mountain dome (2,305 ft) at 5 mi. Outstanding views to S and SW. Begin descent at 5.1 mi. Watch for yellow blazes painted on barren granite. Return to the parking lot at 5.6 mi. If the connecting sections of *Cedar Rock Trail, Middle and Lower*

Falls Trail, First Flat Rock Trail, and the field crossing part of the *Stone Mountain Falls Trail* are added to the 5.6 mi distance of the loop, the total distance is 8.2 mi.

Approximately 2.5 mi of *Camp Trails* exist on the W side of Wolf Rock and up Widows Creek to backpacking camp and group tent camps. Area hikers also report less-known trails extending into the forest for 6 mi or more. They cross private property to reach Doughton Park E of the Blue Ridge Parkway.

Support Facilities: Primitive camps can be found in the park. Nearest private campsite is Shady Rest Campground, Cherry Land, Roaring Gap, NC 28668. Tel: 919-363-2243. Full svc, limited rec fac. To reach it, from jct of Blue Ridge Parkway and US 21 go 2.3 mi SE on US 21, then 2.5 mi E on Mtn View Rd.

Information: Contact Park Superintendent, Stone Mountain State Park, Star Route 1, Box 17, Roaring Gap, NC 28668. Tel: 919-957-8185.

CHAPTER XI

PIEDMONT DIVISION

Boones Cave State Park

Davidson County

Boone's Cave State Park consists of 110 acres of hardwoods forest — beech, oak, elm, and ironwood. On the Yadkin River and generally undevleoped, the park currently provides picnicking, fishing, and hiking. Camping is not allowed in the park.

Daniel Boone Trail   472

Length: 0.5 mi (0.8 km), easy; *USGS:* Churchland; *Trailhead:* Parking lot.

Directions and Description: From I-85 jct with NC 150, halfway between Lexington and Salisbury, go 5 mi on NC 150 to Churchland. Turn L on Boone Cave Rd, SR 1162, to park. From parking lot descend to river bank and Boone Cave. Turn L — fishermen trail to R — and reach the cabin of Squire Boone, who moved there in 1750 when Daniel was 16. Return to road and parking lot at 0.5 mi.

Support Facilities: Nearest campground is Lazy River Family Campground, Route 4, Box 255, Lexington, NC 27292. Tel: 704-787-5785. To get there from Lexington take US 64 W 6 mi to Yadkin College Rd. Follow sign 3.5 mi NW. Open March 15-October 1. Full svc, limited rec fac.

Information: Contact Park Superintendent, P.O. Box 36, Linwood, NC 27299. Tel: 919-956-6297.

Duke Power State Park

Iredell County

Located on the northern shore of Lake Norman, the largest manmade lake in the state, is Duke Power State Recreation Area, with 1,399 acres set aside for swimming, boating, fishing, picnicking, camping, and hiking. The park is divided into two sections, consisting of two peninsulas separated by Hicks Creek. Lake Norman covers 32,510 acres and has a 520-mi shoreline.

The park harbors over 800 species of plants, with Virginia, shortleaf, and loblolly pines dominating the forest. Oaks and hickories are the most dominant hardwoods. A subcanopy of sweet gum, dogwood, and sourwood tops numerous wildflowers. Among the birds are green-winged teal, blue heron, wood duck, osprey, and sparrows. Black crappie, bass, and perch are the chief fish.

Entrance to the Park is from the town of Troutman, 6 miles S of Statesville. On US 21 and NC 115 is a jct with SR 1328. Follow to SR 1303 and then go into the Park on SR 1321.

Lakeshore Trail   473

Length: 5.4 mi rt (8.6 km), easy; *USGS:* Troutman; *Trailhead:* Picnic Area #2 parking lot.

Directions and Description: Begin at the parking lot of picnic area #2, following sign R of restrooms to white circle blazes. At jct at 0.5 mi, turn either R or L on loop. If R is taken, follow to SR 1402, crossing at gate, which is 0.7 mi on road from camping area S. At red-blazed jct, follow ahead by lakeside to end of peninsula. (Or, for short cut the red blazes can be followed for 2.5 mi loop.) Another loop trail at the peninsula runs for 0.6 mi. Continue around the lake, pass red-blazed trail, and return to parking lot.

Alder Trail   474

Length: 0.8 mi rt (1.3 km), easy; *USGS:* See above; *Trailhead:* Picnic area #1 parking lot.

Directions and Description: From nature trail sign at parking lot follow loop trail around the peninsula for a distance of 0.8 mi.

Support Facilities: Camping, including facilities for hot showers, is provided in the park, which is open April 1 through November 1. Nearest private campground is KOA-Statesville, 6 mi S on I-77 at Exit 45, Amity Hill Rd, then go N 0.5 mi. Full svc, rec. fac. Open all year. Address is Route 7, Box 388K, Statesville, NC 28677. Tel: 704-873-5560.

Information: Contact Park Superintendent, Duke Power State Park, Route 2, Box 199, Troutman, NC 28166. Tel: 704-528-6350.

Eno River State Park

Orange and Durham Counties

The Eno River State Park is a popular hiking and fishing area along 20 mi of the river between Hillsborough and Durham. Covering 1,568 acres, the park is segmented into several sections, but all areas have flood plains, rocky bluffs, and some low range white water. Hardwoods and pines, wildflowers — including profuse carpets of trout lilies, rare ginseng, and yellow orchids, wild animals — including deer, beaver, bobcat, and turkey, and excellent fishing for Roanoke bass, largemouth bass, and bream are found in the park. New trails are being planned to the E of the river near Buckquarter Creek, Cole Mill Rd, and Cabe's Mill Rd. The approach is from 3 mi NW of Durham off Pleasant Green Rd, SR 1569. See details below.

Wilderness Shelter Trail and Shaw Tract Trail   475-476

Length: 3.4 mi (5.4 km), easy; *USGS:* Hillsborough and Durham (North) Northwest; *Trailhead:* Parking lot in Section #1.

Directions and Description: From Old US 70 exit at I-85 E of Hillsborough, take Pleasant Green Rd and turn L at park sign on Cole Mill Rd Ext, opposite Cole Mill Rd. At parking lot follow sign along wood chip trail to the Eno River. Cross on swinging cable footbridge to the wilderness shelter area. Permit is required for overnight camping or staying in the shelter. The *Shaw Tract Trail* begins R and runs to a gate at 0.3 mi. Turn R and at 0.8 mi turn L near the river. Follow past Buckquarter Creek and turn L at 1 mi. Follow trail as it loops or joins with connecting trails. (Western section of trails to be eliminated for wild turkey habitat.) Return to wilderness shelter at 3.2 mi.

Cabe's Mill Trail   477

Length: 0.9 mi (1.4 km), easy; *USGS:* See above; *Trailhead:* Parking lot in Section #5.

Directions and Description: From Cole Mill Rd exit on I-85 in Durham, turn L on Sprager Rd and R on Howe St at the Orange-Durham County line. Follow service road to river, passing carpets of periwinkle, ivy, and running cedar. Reach river at 0.4 mi, and then turn L past beaver cuts and old mill foundations at 0.5 mi. Cross stream, ascend to service road, and return. (This trail is scheduled to become an interpretive trail.)

Cole Mill Access Trail and Pea Creek Trail   478-479

Length: 4.4 mi rt cb (7 km), easy; *USGS:* See above; *Trailhead:* Parking lot in Section #3.

Directions and Description: From intersection of Cole Mill Rd and Umstead Road, take dead-end park road. This area has a picnic section and easy access to the river. Follow up the river on the *Bobbit Hole Trail* for 1 mi. (Hikers and fishermen have ignored park boundary and created additonal trails up the river.) Return by the same route. For the *Pea Creek Trail,* turn L and follow down river. Pass under the Cole Mill Rd bridge at 0.3 mi. Power line cut is at 0.5 mi. Turn L at Pea Creek at 0.7 mi, and follow creek to underground cable line at 1.1 mi. Backtrack to parking lot. (Fishermen's trail extends farther down the river.)

Old Pump Station Trail   481

Length: 1.5 mi (2.4 km), easy; *USGS:* See above; *Trailhead:* Park on Rivermont Rd at Nancy Rhodes Creek, 0.6 mi E off Cole Mill Rd, in Section #6.

Directions and Description: Follow trail sign to remains of old Durham Pump Station at 0.4 mi. Turn L upstream and make a sharp L at 1 mi. Return under power line and reach Rivermont Rd at 1.3 mi. Turn L and follow road to Nancy Rhodes Creek and parking area.

Support Facilities: Primitive camping only is allowed in the park. Nearest private campground is the Daniel Boone Campground, P.O. Box 765, Hillsborough, NC 27278. Tel: 919-732-8101. Full svc, rec fac. Open April 1 - November 15.

Information: Contact Park Superintendent, Eno River State Park, Route 2, Box 436-C, Durham, NC 27705. Tel: 919-383-1686.

Kerr Lake State Park

Vance County

The Kerr Lake recreation area has eight locations, three of which have trails: Bullocksville, County Line, and Satterwhite Point. The total mileage is small, only 1.5 mi (2.4 km). Water-related recreational activities — swimming, boating, sailing, skiing, and fishing — are the primary ones in the 2,628 acres of this park. All but Townsville Landing have campgrounds.

Big Poplar Trail   482

Length: 0.4 mi (0.6 km), easy; *USGS:* Middleburg; *Trailhead:* Near washhouse S of ranger station on SR 1319 at Satterwhite Point off I-85.

Directions and Description: Since the trail is not marked, follow wide path S around the lake through hard- and softwoods to the southernmost camping area road, for a total distance of 0.4 mi.

Old Still Trail   **483**

Length: 0.5 mi (0.8 km), easy; *USGS:* See above; *Trailhead:* Opposite baseball field at ranger station at Bullocksville Park on SR 1366 from Drewry.

Directions and Description: Enter unmarked loop trail in forest of small pines, and turn sharp L at 0.3 mi to ruins of illegal liquor still. Continue in loop to point of origin at 0.5 mi.

Beaver Trail   **484**

Length: 0.6 mi (1.0 km), easy; *USGS:* See above; *Trailhead:* West of ranger station on SR 1361 from Drewry at County Line Park.

Directions and Description: Take unmarked loop trail through forest of hard-and softwoods toward lake, and return to point of origin at 0.6 mi.

Support Facilities: Kerr Lake State Park has over 1,000 family campsites. Satterwhite Point: Full svc, rec fac. Open all year. Bullocksville Park: Full svc, rec fac. Open April 1 through November 1. County Line: Full svc, rec fac. Contact ranger for open season.

Information: Contact Kerr Lake State Park, Route 3, Box 800, Henderson, NC 27536. Tel: 919-438-7791.

Medoc Mountain State Park

Halifax County

Park headquarters are on SR 1002, 4 mi E of NC 561 intersection at Hollister. The park is on the fall line of the Piedmont, and has 2,305 acres of hardwoods and pines. Winding through it is Little Fishing Creek, with bluegill, largemouth and Roanoke bass, and sunfish for the anglers. No overnight camping is allowed in the park. Total trail distance is 8.6 mi (13.9 km).

Summit Trail   **485**

Length: 3.7 mi (5.9 km), easy; *USGS:* Hollister, Aurelian Springs; *Trailhead:* Parking lot of park headquarters on SR 1002.

Directions and Description: Follow interpretive trail with yellow markers with numbered points of interest. At 125 yds turn L to begin loop trail, including the *Extension Trail* N of the summit. At 0.5 mi cross Rocky Spring Branch, and reach E bank of Little Fishing Creek at 0.7 mi. Turn R. A large granite outcropping is located at 1.4 mi. It reveals the core of the 325-ft high summit. Spring is at 1.5 mi.

To include the *Extension Trail* continue N and pass an artesian well, ruins of a dam built by the Boy Scouts of America in the early 1920's, and ruins of a another dam E. Circle back to main trail thicket of mountain laurel — rare plants for an area so far E of the mtns — and reach Medoc Mtn. Summit at 2.5 mi. Turn R off gravel road at 3.1 mi, pass old cemetery on L, and complete circle back to parking lot at 3.7 mi.

Stream Trail   **486**

Length: 2.1 mi (3.5 km), easy; *USGS:* See above; *Trailhead:* Picnic area on SR 1347, 0.4 mi off SR 1322, and 1.0 mi from SR 1002 in park.

Directions and Description: Begin from parking lot, turn L at 80 yd, and follow Little Fishing Creek on W side. At 1.2 mi is found confluence with Bear Swamp Creek. Re-enter old forest at 1.5 mi, and pass bayberry bushes, running cedar, and succession loblolly pines. Return to parking lot at 2.1 mi.

Bluff Trail   **487**

Length: 2.8 mi (4.4 km), easy; *USGS:* See above; *Trailhead:* Picnic area with trailhead for Stream Trail.

Directions and Description: From picnic area and parking lot, follow yellow blazes, and at 80 yd turn R. Turn R at bank of Little Fishing Creek. Cross bridge over dry stream beds 0.7 mi and 0.8 mi. Pass large loblolly pines. Climb steep bluff at 1.0 mi. Cross stream near natural spring at 1.1 mi. Reach highest bluff (over 60 ft) at 1.4 mi. Descend steps, cross bridge, turn R, and begin ascent. From ridge descend to stream at 2.6 mi, and return to parking lot at 2.8 mi.

Support Facilities: Only picnicking allowed in the Park; no camping night. Outside the park there is American Heritage Campground, Rt. 3, Box 184, Littleton, NC 27850. Tel: 919-586-4121. On SR 1356 near Lake Gaston. Full svc, rec fac. Open March 1 through November 30.

Information: Contact Medoc Mtn State Park Headquarters, P.O. Box 58, Hollister, NC 27844. Tel: 919-445-2280.

Morrow Mountain State Park

Stanly County

Morrow Mountain State Park is located on 4,508 acres in the heart of the lower Piedmont region and the Uwharrie range. Over 400 million years ago it was covered by a shallow sea in which volcanic islands developed; they later became the hard basalt and rhyolite deposits of this area. Established in 1935, the park is on the Pee Dee River and Lake Tillery; it offers camping, a nature museum, picnicking, boating, fishing, nature programs, hiking, and bridle trails. There are more than 15 miles for the hiker and more than 16 miles for the horseback rider. The park entrance is on SR 1798 E of jct with SR 1720, 4 mi E of the town of Albermarle, 2.7 mi N from NC 24, 27, and 73, and 3 mi S from Badin.

Laurel, Quarry, and Hattaway Mtn Trails   488-490

Length: 3.2 mi rt cb (5.1 km), easy; *USGS:* Albermarle (NE and SE); *Trailhead:* Near the Natural History Museum.

Directions and Description: Begin the *Laurel Trail* behind the Natural History Museum and circle the park cabin area through a mature forest of hardwoods, pines, and mountain laurel for a distance of 0.6 mi. For the *Quarry Trail* hike NW past the swimming pool to the picnic area. This loop trail of 0.6 mi reveals a man made gorge where volcanic slate of the Slate Belt can be studied. Return to the swimming pool, turn R on the *Hattaway Trail,* and reach jct with the bridle trail at 0.2 mi. Turn L and at 1 mi turn L toward and climb up Hattaway Mtn. From the rocky summit at 1.4 mi descend and return to the swimming pool area for walk back to the Museum.

Three Rivers Trail and Fall Mountain Trail   491-492

Length: 4.5 mi rt cb (7.2 km), easy to moderate; *USGS:* See above; *Trailhead:* Boathouse near the Pee Dee River.

Directions and Description: The *Three Rivers Trail* is a self-guiding 0.7-mi trail with ecological diversity; it runs through an open marsh to a riverbank covered by birches. From the boathouse follow the yellow blazes up the riverside to the Falls Dam and turn sharply L at 1.4 mi. Continue ascending over exceptionally rough volcanic rock outcroppings to summit at 2 mi. Descend through hardwoods, some understory plants, and wildflowers to historic Kron House at 2.5 mi. Continue E and return to boathouse parking lot.

Rocks Trail   493

Length: 4.2 mi rt cb (6.7 km), easy; *USGS:* See above; *Trailhead:* Administrative building.

Directions and Description: Beginning at the rear of the administrative building hike E on trail to family campground and follow red blazes on *Rocks Trail* (which is also a bridle trail). At 0.2 mi from the campground turn L. (Because of numerous campground trails and extra lead-in trails to the *Mountain Creek Bridle Trail,* the hiker can become confused in this area.) Pass jct of bridle trail at 0.6 mi on L; continue ahead to excellent view of the Pee Dee River. Descend over rocky area to 1.3 mi. Return from river by same trail, or, at 1.9 mi. turn R and follow the longer bridle trail past *Quarry Trail* to jct with *Hattaway Trail;* turn L and return to the Administrative Building.

Sugarloaf Mountain Trail and Mountain Loop Trail   494-495

Length: 3.7 mi rt cb (5.9 km), moderate; *USGS:* See above; *Trailhead:* Parking lot E of ranger's residence.

Directions and Description: Follow trail sign for hikers, bearing L, then crossing streams and Morrow Mountain Rd. Ascend, following ridge, and reach E end of Sugarloaf at 1.4 mi. Turn sharply R and descend steeply to base of mtn. This trail provides views of volcanic monadnocks common to the Uwharrie. Turn R, cross road at 2.2 mi, cross a stream at 2.7 mi, and enter a field near the parking lot to complete the loop. White-tailed deer and red-tailed hawks are often seen here. For the *Mountain Loop Trail* either hike the bridle trail or drive to the top of Morrow Mtn. The trailhead can be found at the picnic shelter or the overlook, it leads to a loop around the 1,278 ft peak and the park. The trail is graded, with bridges over the ravines.

Support Facilities: Campsites and vacation cabins are found in the park and are open April 1 to November 1. Nearest private campground is the Mtn. View Campground, 1.5 mi from park entrance and 0.5 mi W on SR 1798 from jct with SR 1720. Open from April 1 to October 31. Full svc, rec. fac. Tel: 704-982-0719.

Information: Contact Park Superintendent, Morrow Mountain State Park, Route 2, Box 204, Albermarle, NC 28001. Tel: 704-982-4402.

Raven Rock State Park

Harnett County

Established in 1970, Raven Rock State park is a large 5,500 acre wilderness (with only 2,723 acres presently developed). The Cape Fear River runs through its center. A major geological feature of the area is the 152-foot-high crystalline rock jutting out over the river — and accounting for the park's name. Rare rhododendrons and mountain laurels grow here, along with a long list of Piedmont and Coastal Plain plants. The area has the largest salamander population east of the Appalachians. Some of the wild animals and birds are osprey, bobcat, eagle, and deer. Prominent fish are the largemouth bass and sunfish. The total trail distance, including the back tracks, is 15.8 mi. There are also bridle (7 mi) and canoe (56 mi) trails. Access to the park is from SR 1250 off US 421, 6 mi W of Lillington. Park is open year-round.

Campbell Creek Loop Trail and Lanier Falls Trail   496-497

Length: 5.7 mi (9.1 km), easy to moderate; *USGS:* Mamers; *Trailhead:* Main parking lot.

Directions and Description: Follow trail signs from parking lot to Campbell's Creek at 0.7 mi. Cross and turn R or L. If L, at 2.3 mi is jct with *Lanier Falls Trail,* which runs a distance of 0.4 mi round trip. Return for total of 5.7 mi if Lanier Falls is included. Trails run through hard- and softwoods as well as mountain laurels to river outcropping.

Raven Rock Loop Trail   498

Length: 2.1 mi (3.4 km), easy; *USGS:* See above; *Trailhead:* See above.

Directions and Description: Follow trail signs R from parking lot to Raven Rock, a scenic area on the Cape Fear River at 0.9 mi. Stairways have been constructed for the 152-foot descent to the river and caverns. Return R on top of bluff for scenic views and reach parking lot at 2.1 mi.

Pasture Trail   499

Length: 1.4 mi (2.2 km), easy; *USGS:* See above; *Trailhead:* See above.

Directions and Description: From *Raven Rock Loop Trail* near bluffs turn R to canoe camp at 0.7 mi, and return on N side of Little Creek. A 0.5-mi trail from the canoe camp leads to a group wilderness camp. Total trail distance, including lead-in *Raven Rock Loop Trail,* is 3.5 mi.

Northington's Ferry Trail   500

Length: 4.4 mi (7.0 km), easy; *USGS:* See above; *Trailhead:* See above.

Directions and Description: From the parking lot follow W part of the *Raven Rock Loop Trail* and turn L at 0.4 mi. At the mouth of Campbell's Creek is a good fishing spot. It is the site of Northington's Ferry, which ran beginning about 1770. The return trip is another 2.2 mi, for a total of 4.4 mi round-trip.

Fish Traps Trail   501

Length: 2.2 mi (3.2 km), easy; *USGS:* See above; *Trailhead:* See above.

Directions and Description: From the parking lot follow W part of the *Raven Rock Loop Trail.* Turn L at 0.4 mi on *Northington's Ferry Trail* and follow sign R. Trail leads to rock outcropping at 1.1 mi; Indians placed trap baskets here to catch fish at the rapids. Return on the same trail, for a total of 2.2 mi.

Support Facilities: Primitive camping is allowed by permit in park. Advance inquiry is recommended. Outside the park try KOA — Fayetteville North. Take I-95 Exit 61 and go 0.2 mi on SR 1815. Address is KOA — Fayetteville, P.O. Box 67, Wade, NC 28395. Tel: 919-892-5605. Full svc, rec fac. Open year round.

Information: Contact Park Supervisor, Route 3, Box 447, Lillington, NC 27546. Tel: 919-893-4888.

Umstead State Park

Wake County

The William B. Umstead State Park covers 5,334 acres — 3,979 in the Crabtree Creek section and 1,355 in the Reedy Creek Section; it is the fourth largest state park in North Carolina. Located near the Research Triangle and the Raleigh-Durham Airport, it provides camping, fishing, summer interpretative programs, hiking, and bridle trails. The park has large stands of mature oak, tulip poplars, and loblolly pine. Beaver, wild turkey, and raccoon inhabit areas around Sycamore Creek. Abundant wildflowers and Paleozoic granite outcroppings are prominent. A number of trails are accessible only by connecting with other trails. The following descriptions cover more than 17 connecting miles of hiking. (There are also 18 miles of marked bridle trails in the park.)

232

Piedmont Division

The Crabtree Creek section entrance is off US 70, 6 mi W of the jct with US 1 and 64 at the Raleigh Expressway. The Reedy Creek section entrance is off I-40, 4 mi W of the jct with US 1 and 64 at the Raleigh Expressway.

Crabtree Creek Section

Sals Branch Trail and Nature Trail   502-503

Length: 3.6 mi cb (5.8 km), easy; *USGS:* Durham South (Southeast), Cary; *Trailhead:* Parking lot near picnic area.

Directions and Description: Follow orange blazes on trail toward the lake and through loblolly pines, running cedar, and Christmas ferns to FSR at 0.5 mi. Cross road, and pass Sals Branch beechnut grove at 0.8 mi. Turn L sharply uphill at 1.9 mi and return to parking area at 2.4 mi. The *Nature Trail,* with white blazes, is a loop trail of 1.2 mi, running by a silt filled dam and stone house foundation ruins. It circles off the picnic area for a total of 3.6 mi combined with *Sals Branch Trail* before returning to the parking lot.

Sycamore Trail and Dogwood Trail   504-505

Length: 6.5 mi rt cb (10.4 km), easy: *USGS:* See above; *Trailhead:* See above.

Directions and Description: Leave parking lot near picnic area on yellow-blazed *Sycamore Trail.* It has jcts in the forest with *Company Mill Trail* and *Dogwood Trail.* A combined hike of 6 mi round trip to Sycamore Creek is possible, or the distance is 6.2 mi if a circle with the *Dogwood Trail,* is completed. At 0.5 mi cross FSR, then again at 1.6 mi, and descend. At 1.9 mi reach jct with *Dogwood Trail.* Follow yellow blazes R, cross road at 2.3 mi, and follow *Sycamore Creek Trail* to jct with *Company Mill Trail* at 3 mi. Return on *Sycamore Creek Trail;* or, cross creek, turn L, and follow blue-blazed *Company Mill Trail* to jct with *Dogwood Trail* at 3.2 mi. Turn L and follow *Dogwood Trail* for 1.4 mi through rocks, hardwoods, and wildflowers to jct with *Sycamore Trail.* Turn R and return to parking lot.

Company Mill Trail   **506**

Length: 9.3 mi rt cb (14.9 km), easy; *USGS:* See above; *Trailhead:* See above.

Directions and Description: From parking lot follow yellow blazes of *Sycamore Trail* to green blazes of *Dogwood Trail* and then to jct with blue-blazed *Company Mill Trail* at 3.3 mi. Follow upstream on L along narrow trail on the side of a bluff for 0.2 mi. Turn L, ascend, and cross FSR at 4.3 mi. Descend and reach bank of Crabtree Creek at 5.1 mi. Follow creek bank to jct with *Beech Trail* at 5.7 mi; this is the George Linn Mill site. (At this jct the creek could be forded and exit made on the *Beech Trail* to the Reedy Creek section parking lot, which is 0.8 mi away.) Turn L, return to *Dogwood Trail* at 6.8 mi, cross Sycamore Creek, and return to the parking lot at 9.3 mi.

Reedy Creek Section

Beech Trail and Nature Trail   **507-508**

Length: 1.6 mi rt cb (2.6 km), easy; *USGS:* See above; *Trailhead:* Reedy Creek parking lot.

Directions and Description: From parking lot descend to picnic area, pass yellow-blazed nature trail entrance (self-guided loop), and at 0.4 mi pass jct with *Beech Trail,* also yellow-blazed. Descend to Crabtree Creek (where wading across the rocky stream is necessary for a connection with *Company Mill Trail*). At 0.8 mi reach the George Linn Mill site. Return by the same route to the parking lot. (The western terminus of the *Loblolly Trail* is also found at the parking lot, described under Raleigh trails.)

Support Facilities: No camping is allowed in the Reedy Creek section, but camping is provided for in the Crabtree Creek section. Nearest private campground is College Park, 4208 New Bern Ave, Raleigh, NC 27610. Tel: 919-833-7015. It is 1 mi E on US 64. Open all year. Full svc, rec fac.

Information: For Crabtree section of Umstead State Park address Park Superintendent, Route 8, Box 130, Raleigh, NC 27612. Tel: 919-787-3033. For Reedy Creek section address Park Superintendent, 1800 Harrison Ave, Cary, NC 27511. Tel: 919-467-7259.

North Carolina Zoological Park

Randolph County

Designed to be the world's largest environmentally arranged zoological, the 1,372-acre site of the North Carolina Zoological Park is part of the Uwharrie Mountains (Purgatory Mtn) in the center of the state. Since 1971, the park has been under construction, its aim to provide permanent natural habitats without bars and cages. One example of this concept is the 300 acres of "Africa" to be completed by 1983; presently natural habitats are provided for zebra, ostrich, giraffe, lion, chimpanzee, elephant, baboon, and rhinocerous. A controlled environmental aviary is also being constructed. Over 275 animals of more than sixty species are now at the Educational Center, Holding Area, and the Permanent Zoo.

Although trails are listed as part of the facilities, which include a picnic area, the trails are actually a labyrinth of gravel and paved paths totaling over two miles. In the future, trams will be provided to tempt the tired hiker. The zoo is open all year, but hours of opening and closing (usually 9-5) may vary. Camping, fires, and pets are prohibited. USGS is Asheboro.

Access to the zoo is 5.1 mi S on NC 159 from the jct of US 64 and NC 159 in Asheboro. Zoo signs are conspicuous.

Support Facilities: One of the nearest private campgrounds is Zooland Family Campground, Route 1, Box 409, Asheboro, NC 27203. Tel: 919-381-3422. Open April 1-November 1. Full svc, rec fac. From jct of US 220 Bypass and US 64, go 4 mi S on US 220, turn at Troy-Ulah exit, and go 3 mi on SR 1138 and 1114.

Information: Contact North Carolina Zoological Park, Route 4, Box 73, Asheboro, NC 27203. Tel: 919-625-1290. Also, contact the North Carolina Zoological Society, P.O. Box ZOO, Asheboro, NC 27203. Tel: 919-629-2144.

STATE FORESTS

Clemmons State Forest

Johnson County

The Clemmons State Forest has 307 acres, with over 3 mi of exceptionally educational interpretive trails. Study sites are provided for rocks, trees, animals, watersheds, and forest management. Opened in 1976, the area represents a transitional zone between the Piedmont and Coastal Plain. A Forestry Center and exhibits explain the varied facilities of the area. Picnicking and fishing are allowed, but no camping is permitted. Sections of the trails can be used by the handicapped. Entrance to the forest is off NC 1004 (old US 70) 1.5 mi N of Clayton city limits and 4.2 mi from US 70. Contact with the Forest Supervisor should be made in advance since days and hours for visitors are irregular. (Usually the forest is closed two days each week for maintenance.)

Forest Demonstration Trail   **509**

Length: 2.2 mi (3.5 km), easy; *USGS:* Clayton: *Trailhead:* Parking lot 1 mi from forest entrance.

Directions and Description: Follow signs from parking lot 100 yd to Forest Information and another 100 yd to Forestry Center and trail signboard. Turn R, and follow red blazes. At 0.2 mi cross stream near *Watershed Loop Trail.* At 0.3 mi pass shortcut trail and pass it again at 1.3 mi. (Trail is marked each 1/4 mi from trail signboard.) Return to parking lot at 2.2 mi.

Talking Tree Trail   **510**

Length: 0.8 mi (1.2 km), easy; *USGS:* See above; *Trailhead:* See above.

Directions and Description: Follow yellow blazes L from trail signboard through forest of hard- and softwood trees. There are push-button devices for recorded botanical information. Trail is exceptionally well-designed.

Support Facilities. No camping is allowed in the forest. Nearest private campground is the Lakeview KOA, on I-95 at the Selma Exit. Address is Route 2, Box 313-A, Selma, NC 27576. Tel: 919-965-5923. Full svc, rec fac. Open all year.

Information: Contact Forest Supervisor, Route 3, Box 206, Clayton, NC 27520. Tel: 919-553-5651.

Holmes State Forest

Henderson County

Holmes State Forest is named in honor of Canadian-born John S. Holmes (1868-1958), North Carolina's first State Forester, serving in that capacity from 1915 to 1945. The forest covers 231 acres, 25 of which are rich bottomland and 206 of which are steep mountainsides and rounded summits. The area has been serving forestry needs in western North Carolina for 40 years — first as a CCC camp and then as a state forest since 1972. More than 125 species of flowering plants have been identified. Only hiking, nature study, and picnicking are allowed in the forest. (Primitive camping is planned for 1983.) Entrance is from Penrose on US 64. Take SR 1528 for 2.6 mi to Little River. Turn L on Crab Creek Rd, SR 1127, and go 4.2 mi to entrance on R. Another route is a distance of 10 mi from downtown Henderson, going W on SR 1127 at jct with US 25S.

Cliffside Demonstration Trail   511

Length: 2.8 mi (4.5 km), moderate; *USGS:* Horseshoe; *Trailhead:* Parking lot.

Directions and Description: From parking lot follow sign to Forestry Center and trail system signboard at 0.1 mi. Turn L on red-blazed loop trail through hardwoods, large poplars, and some white pines, to reach summit at 1.4 mi and return to Forestry Center at 2.7 mi. The parking lot is reached at 2.8 mi.

Talking Tree Trail   **512**

Length: 0.8 mi rt (1.3 km), easy; *USGS:* See above; *Trailhead:* See above.

Directions and Description: From the trail system signboard turn R on green-blazed trail, passing a variety of trees with audio devices explaining forestry history, use, growth, and values. Cross cascades at 0.4 mi. Trail is well-graded and maintained. State Forest Trail #2.

Support Facilities: Little River Camp Resort, Route 2, Box 241, Pisgah Forest, NC 28768. Tel: 704-877-4475. From US 64 at Penrose go 6 mi S on SR 1528, following signs. Open May 15-Labor Day. Full svc, rec fac.

Information: Contact Forest Supervisor, Route 4, Box 308, Hendersonville, NC 28739. Tel: 704-692-0100.

Tuttle State Forest

Caldwell County

Tuttle State Forest honors Lelia Judson Tuttle (1878-1967), a teacher and missionary whose property was deeded to the state in 1973. The forest of 160 acres has two trails, an informative "talking tree" trail and a demonstration trail system. In addition to the interpretive trail system of the Forestry Center, there are picnic and primitive camping areas. Parts of the trail area can be used by the handicapped.

Entrance to the forest is off SR 1331, 0.8 mi from NC 18, 6 mi SW of Lenoir. On Monday and Tuesday the forest is usually closed.

Forest Demonstration Trail   **513**

Length: 1.9 mi (3 km), easy; *USGS:* Morganton (N) and Drexel; *Trailhead:* Parking lot.

Directions and Description: Follow trail signs past the Forestry Center to the signboard at 0.1 mi. Turn L on red-blazed trail through pines — white, Virginia, and shortleaf — as well as oaks, beech, and poplar. At 0.7 mi reach jct with short trail, pass Sleepy Hollow School site, and go through campsites, returning to the picnic area and parking lot at 1.9 mi. State Forest Trail #3.

Talking Tree Trail   514

Length: 0.6 mi (1 km), easy; *USGS:* See above; *Trailhead:* See above.

Directions and Description: Follow green-blazed trail from the trail signboard near the Forestry Center on a 0.6-mi loop trail with push-button devices to play recordings about forest succession and types of trees.

Support Facilities: Limited primitive camping is available in the forest. Nearest private campground (without membership restrictions) is Morganton KOA on I-40, 3 mi W of US 64 jct at Glen Alpine or Jamestown Rd exits. Address is Morganton KOA, Route 2, Box 845, Morganton, NC 28655. Tel: 704-584-1733.

Information: Contact Forest Supervisor, Tuttle State Forest, Route 6, Box 417, Lenoir, NC 28645. Tel: 704-758-5645.

TRAILS IN COUNTIES AND MUNICIPALITIES

CHAPTER XII

COUNTY PARKS
AND
OTHER AREAS

Cedarock Park

Alamance County

Cedarock Park, 414 acres, is the largest county-operated park in the state. It has old homeplaces, picnic areas, playgrounds, fishing, horseback riding, hiking, primitive tent camping, and extensive plans for the future. Hiking and bridle trails total 8.9 mi. The Park is located 6 mi S of Graham from the I-85 jct on NC 49. Turn E on Friendship-Patterson Mill Rd for 0.3 mi to entrance on L.

Cedarock Trails   515-519

Length: 8.9 mi (14.2 km), easy; *USGS:* Burlington: *Trailhead:* Parking lot near shelter #3 across from U.S. flagpole.

Directions and Description: Follow yellow blazes to Rock Creek at 0.2 mi, and reach jct with brown-blazed *Ecology Trail*. At 0.5 mi follow either blue-blazed or red-blazed trail to return to main trail. Pass old mill dam, cross creek at Elmo's Crossing, and cross meadow of wildflowers (including Star of Bethlehem) at 2.0 mi. Pass park superintendent's office, and follow road or field S to parking lot at 2.6 mi. (Fitness trail with black blazes begins at trail system sign, near yellow blaze origin, and enters forest for a loop of 1.3 mi.). The *Bridle Trail*, also used for hiking, begins at the old

Garrett Homeplace and goes S or N through hard- and softwood forests, with waterfalls, rock outcroppings, Indian relics, and a wild turkey sanctuary. It is a 5 mi circuit trail.

Support Facilities: Tent camping is allowed with permit. Nearest private campground is either the KOA in Greensboro or the Daniel Boone Campground in Hillsborough. In Hillsborough the address is P.O. Box 765, Hillsborough, NC 27278. Tel: 919-732-8101. Full svc, rec fac. Open April 1-November 15.

Information: Contact Alamance County Recreation and Parks Department, 610 N Main St, Graham, NC 27253. Tel: 919-228-0506.

San-Lee Park

Lee County

San-Lee Park is composed of 110 acres of forest, lakes, old waterworks, interpretive trails, picnic areas, campsites, and RV campgrounds. It is off SR 1510, four mi NE of Sanford, and is open all year. The city of Sanford, the county seat, has a population of 13,500. From Old US (Business) L at E Charlotte Ave, go E for 1.2 mi to Grapeviney Rd (SR 1509). At 3 mi turn R on SR 1510 and go 0.6 mi to park entrance on R. The park is maintained by Lee County Parks and Recreation Commission. There are four trails — *Muir Nature Trail, Thoreau Lake Trail, Hidden Glen Loop Trail,* and *Gatewood Loop Trail* — for a total of 3.1 mi combined. All trails are well-designed and maintained.

Muir Nature Trail   520

Length: 1.1 mi (1.7 km), easy; *USGS:* Colon, Moncure; *Trailhead:* Parking lot by Mamer's Creek.

Directions and Description: Cross bridge on Mamer's Creek, turn R, and follow signs into forest. There is a choice of upper or lower loop of the *Muir Trail*. At 0.5 mi turn L by edge of lake at steps. Follow trail through rocks, hard- and softwoods, and wild-flowers to the parking lot at 1.1 mi.

Gatewood Trail   521

Length: 1 mi (1.6 km), easy; *USGS:* See above; *Trailhead:* Parking lot near refreshments stand.

Directions and Description: Follow campground road to Colter amphitheater sign. Turn R and at 0.3 mi. reach trail junction with *Thoreau Trail.* Turn L on *Gatewood Trail.* Junction with *Hidden Glen Loop Trail* is reached at 0.5 mi. (Hidden Glen is 0.2 mi additional.) Pass Aldo Leopold Wilderness Group Campground at 0.6 mi, and return to the parking lot at 1.0 mi.

Thoreau Trail   522

Length: 0.9 mi (1.4 km), easy; *USGS:* See above; *Trailhead:* At boat lunch near bridge on Moccasin Pond, or on Gatewood Trail.

Directions and Description: Cross bridge to shoreline and follow trail L along lake's edge. Cross bridge over Crawdad Creek at 0.4 mi. Junction with *Gatewood Trail* is reached at 0.6 mi; return either L (shorter) or R for 0.9 mi.

Support Facilities: Park has campground. Outside the park is Gil Winders Campground at intersection of SU 15 and 501 and US 1. Address is Route 4, Box 1130, Sanford, NC 27330. Tel: 919-776-2229. Full svc, rec fac. Open all year.

Information: Contact Park Ranger, P.O. Box 698, Sanford, NC 27330; or, Lee County Parks and Recreation Commission at the same address.

McDowell Park

Mecklenburg County

McDowell Park is named in honor of John McDowell, a leader of Mecklenburg County's Recreation Commission. The steeply rolling land on the E side of Lake Wylie was a gift to the county by the Crescent Land and Timber Corporation, a subsidiary of Duke Power Company. Open all year and with full services, the Park provides fishing, camping, boating, picnicking, and hiking. From jct of I-77 and Carowinds Boulevard, go on the Boulevard for 2.4 mi. Turn L on NC 49 and go 4.2 mi to park entrance on R.

Chestnut, Kingfisher, and Access Trails 523-525

Length: 2.1 mi cb (3.4 km), easy; *USGS:* Lake Wylie; *Trailhead:* Campground.

Directions and Description: From campground follow *Chestnut Trail* on a numbered nature trail with 23 stations through a mature forest with cohosh and wild ginger. (Another entrance to the trail at the park office takes the numbers out of sequence.) Reach Observation Deck at Lake Wylie at 0.8 mi. (*Kingfisher Trail* leads N for 0.3 mi to playground.) Return to campground by *Access Trails* for a total of 2.1 mi. The park has more than 85 species of birds.

Information: Contact Mecklenburg County Parks and Recreation, 8711 Old Monroe Rd, Charlotte, NC 28212. Tel: 704-568-4041.

Woodland Park Trail 526
Polk County

The Polk County Community Foundation has constructed a 0.6-mi nature trail in Tryon. Entry is from Chestnut St. Turn L after crossing railroad at station on US 176. Or, reach the trail from Trade St (US 176) near the A&P store. Trail is excellent in both design and maintenance. Forest is chiefly of hardwoods. No camping. For information, contact Polk County Department of Recreation, P.O. Box 308, Columbus, NC 28722. Tel: 704-894-8199.

Dan Nicholas Park

Rowan County

Successful business executive and philanthropist Dan Nicholas donated 330 acres to Rowan County in 1968 for recreational activities. As a result the County Commissioners established a Parks and Recreational Board to develop and administer the park. Facilities include areas for fishing, picnicking, tennis, and boating, as well as four ball fields, full-service camping, a craft shop, Nature Center with plant, animal, and geological exhibits, zoo with black bears and bobcats, Environmental Education Center, and foot trails. The park is open all year.

At jct of I-85 and E Spencer take Choate Rd, SR 2125, for 1.1 mi. Turn L on McCandless Rd, which becomes Bringle Ferry Rd, SR 1002, after 0.5 mi. Continue to park entrance at 6.4 mi from I-85.

Persimmon Branch Trail   527

Length: 2.3 mi (3.7 km), easy; *USGS:* Salisbury; *Trailhead:* Concession stand.

Directions and Description: From the concession stand at the dam go to the opposite side of the lake and turn R at 0.2 mi. Begin an interpretive trail with 32 markers pointing out oak, pine, ash, elm, mosses, and ferns. Cross Persimmon Branch at 0.4 mi, turn L, and begin return loop at 1 mi.

Lake Trail   528

Length: 1 mi (1.6 km), easy; *USGS:* See above; *Trailhead:* See above.

Directions and Description: From the concession stand go to the L or opposite side of dam and circle the lake along its edge through picnic area and large campground. Lake has large variety of ducks and other waterfowl.

Information: Contact Dan Nicholas Park, Route 10, Box 832, Salisbury, NC 28144. Tel: 704-636-2089.

Bridge Creek Nature Trail   529
Scotland County

Length: 0.8 mi (1.3 km), easy; *USGS:* Laurinburg; *Trailhead:* X-Way Rd.

Directions and Description: From jct of US 15-401 Bypass in Laurinburg, go W under US 74 on X-Way Rd to nature trail sign on L. Trail, partly on boardwalks, goes through pine, birch, gum, poplar, and understory of native plants. Return by the same route. The trail was constructed by the YCC, which also assisted the Parks and Recreation Committee in opening a 60-mi canoe trail from US 15-501 N near the county line to NC 71 E of Laurinburg. This trail is in Scotland County.

Information: Contact Scotland County Parks and Recreation Commission, P.O. Box 1668, Laurinburg, NC 28352. Tel: 919-276-0412.

Cane Creek Park

Union County

Cane Creek Park is a large recreational area near the South Carolina border provided by the Union County Parks and Recreation Department. Facilities include areas for picnicking, camping (with water, electricity, and sewage hook-ups), boating, fishing, swimming, horseback riding, and hiking. Combined trails allow for nearly 10 miles of walking. A *Wilderness Trail* of 1 mi is planned near the family camping area. From Waxhaw turn on Providence Rd, SR 1111, and cross NC 200 at 5.8 mi. Turn L on Harkey Rd at 6.7 mi. Turn R into Cane Creek Park at 7.5 mi.

Blue Bird Trail   530

Length: 2.2 mi rt (3.5 km), easy; *USGS:* Waxhaw, Unity; *Trailhead:* Parking lot at Operation Center.

Directions and Description: From parking lot follow trail sign along edge of lake to open fields at 0.4 mi and 0.8 mi. Reach Cane Creek dam at 1.1 mi. Return by the same route.

Possum Trot Trail   531

Length: 2.8 mi rt cb (4.5 km), easy; *USGS:* See above; *Trailhead:* See above.

Directions and Description: From parking lot follow trail sign near the horse trail. Cross service road at 0.3 mi, cross paved park road at 0.4 mi, and pass through boat dock and picnic area at 0.7 mi. From the comfort station the hiking trails and the bridle trails crisscross a number of times, confusing both the equestrian and the hiker. Take one of the wide, well-maintained trails L through young hardwoods and pines to return at 2.8 mi.

White Oak Trail   532

Length: 3 mi rt (4.8 km), easy; *USGS:* See above; *Trailhead:* Rear of comfort station.

Directions and Description: At the rear of the comfort station in the picnic area, follow the trail nearest the lake and pass under a power line at 0.8 mi. Forest is young, with scattered wild phlox and sundrops. Reach paved road beyond gate at 1.5 mi. The loop part of this trail is heavily overgrown; therefore, return by the same route for a total of 3 mi.

Information: Contact Park Supervisor, Cane Creek Park, Route 2, Waxhaw, NC 28173. Tel: 704-843-3919.

W. Kerr Scott Dam and Reservoir

Wilkes County

The W. Kerr Scott Dam and Reservoir was constructed by the U.S. Army Corps of Engineers in 1960-62. It is named in honor of former Governor Scott (1896-1958). Two areas have been designated for public use and recreation — Bandits Roost and Warrior Creek Parks. They include swimming, boating, camping, picnicking, and hiking. The shoreline is 125 mi long. No motorcycles are allowed. A 0.3-mi *Nature Trail* is located directly behind the main reservoir office. Entrance to the parks is by NC 268, 5 mi W of Wilkesboro.

Bandits Roost Trail   533

Length: 1.6 mi rt (3.5 km), easy; *USGS:* Wilkesboro, Boomer, Moravian Falls; *Trailhead:* Parking lot.

Directions and Description: From parking lot B at Bandits Roost campground go N near the boat ramp and follow edge of Lake E to Area A campground and swimming area. Return by same route.

Warrior Creek Trail   534

Length: 8 mi rt (12.8 km), easy; *USGS:* See above; *Trailhead:* Picnic Area B.

Directions and Description: From Picnic Area B follow sign W and pass Area E campground at 1.9 mi. Continue through hardwoods, pass Picnic Area F, follow edge of lake, and complete circuit of peninsula near parking lot at 4 mi. Return by the same route or take the road through the playground.

Support Facilities: Both of the above parks have all facilities except electricity for hook-ups. Open all year.

Information: Contact W. Kerr Scott Dam and Reservoir, P.O. Box 182, Wilkesboro, NC 28697, Tel: 919-921-3390.

CHAPTER XIII

MUNICIPAL PARKS AND OTHER AREAS

Burlington

Alamance County

Town and County Nature Park

Burlington, with a population of 39,000, is a center of textile industries and biological supply plants. Alamance Battleground State Historic Site is 6 mi SW on NC 62, and the McDade Wildlife Museum is at 1333 Overbrook Rd. Lake Burlington Park and Marina is 6 mi N on Union Ridge Rd, off NC 62. Burlington Recreation and Park Department and the Burlington Woman's Club sponsor the Town and County Nature Park, with a nature trail and connecting trails for a total of 3.5 mi. Access to the park is from I-85 and NC 49N. Go on US 70 (toward Haw River), and turn L on Church St for 0.9 mi. Turn on McKinney St for 0.3 mi, R on Berkley Rd, and go 0.2 mi to Regent Park Lane. Park is at end of street.

Town and Country Nature Trail   535

Length: 1.5 mi (2.4 km), easy; *USGS:* Burlington; *Trailhead:* Near comfort station S of parking lot.

Directions and Description: Follow trail signs W on well-graded trail, with picnic areas at intervals, through oak, birch, Virginia pine, black willow, and wildflowers. Cross bridges at 0.3 mi and again at 0.7 mi. Pass S side of Haw River at 0.9 mi. Side trails go up and down the river. Cross under power line and return to origin at 1.5 mi.

Support Facilities: No camping is allowed in the park. Nearest campground is either KOA in Greensboro or the Daniel Boone Campground in Hillsborough. In Hillsborough, the address is P.O. Box 765, Hillsborough, NC 27278. Tel: 919-732-8101. Full svc, rec fac. Open April 1-November 15.

Information: Contact Burlington Parks and Recreation Dept, P.O. Box 1358, Burlington, NC 27215. Tel: 919-226-7371.

Chapel Hill

Orange County

Chapel Hill, with a population of 41,000, is the home of the University of North Carolina, the oldest state university in the U.S. The city is also known for the Morehead Planetarium, Coker Arboretum, Paul Green Theatre, and the 329-acre North Carolina Botanical Garden. The Chapel Hill Parks and Recreation Department maintains 13 park areas, three of which have nature trails: Umstead Park, Cedar Falls Park, and Westwood — for a total of 1.8 mi of hiking.

North Carolina Botanical Garden Trails　　　　　**536**

Length: 1.4 mi (2.2 km), easy; *USGS:* Chapel Hill; *Trailhead:* Parking lot near Totten Center on Laurel Hill Rd, at jct of US 15-501 Bypass, S of NC 54 jct.

Directions and Description: Follow signs for self-guided interpretive trail, and cross bridge at 0.2 mi. Guided trail turns R; another trail ascends to connect with other trails. Dogwoods form subcanopy among labeled wildflowers. Depending on trails hiked, a loop of 1.4 mi is possible. Open daily all year. (Totten Research Center is across the street.)

Support Facilities: No camping allowed in the Garden. The nearest commercial campground is the Daniel Boone Campground, 11 mi NW on NC 86 at jct of I-85. Its address is P.O. Box 765,

Hillsborough, NC 27278. Tel: 919-732-8101 or 8102. Full svc, rec fac. Open April 1-November 15.

Information: Contact North Carolina Botanical Garden, UNC-CH, Totten Center 457-A, Chapel Hill, NC 27514. Tel: 919-967-2246. Or, contact Chapel Hill Parks and Recreation Department, 200 Plant Rd, Chapel Hill, NC 27514. Tel: 919-968-4507.

Umstead Park Nature Trail   537

Length: 1.1 mi (1.7 km), easy; *USGS:* See above; *Trailhead:* Parking lot in the park.

Directions and Description: Turn off Airport Rd (NC 86) at Umstead Drive. At parking lot cross bridge, and turn L or R. If L, trail terminus is at 0.1 mi. If R, connecting trails (some from private homes) come in near the athletic facilities. Trail passes large sycamores, beside the stream.

Cedar Falls Park Trail   538

Length: 0.7 mi (1.1 km), easy; *USGS:* See above; *Trailhead:* Parking lot.

Directions and Description: Turn off NC 86 at Weaver Dairy Rd to Cedar Falls Park. From parking lot follow red-blazed trail through hardwoods around tennis court. At 0.5 mi pass ruins of old chimney. Return to parking lot. (More trails are planned. For support facilities at Umstead and Cedar Falls, see information above on North Carolina Botanical Garden.

Westwood Park has only a few yd of trail.

Durham

Durham County

Durham was founded in 1867. Since then the Dukes have established there the American Tobacco Company, changing for all time the city and making it an internationally known industrial center for tobacco products. It was a Duke, James B. Duke, who helped establish Duke University, an educational institution and medical center known worldwide. For recreation Durham has West Point on the Eno, a 40-acre city park with a historical recreation of the West Point Mill Community (1778-1942). Restored are the McCown-Mangum farmhouse, mill, blacksmith shop, pack house, and gardens. Facilities in the park allow for picnicking, fishing, rafting, canoeing, and hiking. Open daily with no camping, the park is owned by the city of Durham, maintained by the Recreation Department, and supported by Friends of West Point, Inc., P.O. Box 526, Durham, NC 27702. Tel: 919-471-1623.

West Point on the Eno Trail   539

Length: 3.4 mi rt (5.4 km), easy; *USGS:* Durham North (NW and NE); *Trailhead:* Parking area near the mill.

Directions and Description: From I-85 in Durham, take US 501 N to either Duke Blvd or Roxboro exit, and turn L into the park before crossing the Eno River bridge. From parking area follow the S bank upriver to Guess Rd at 1.7 mi. (This is the boundary of the Eno River State Park.) Return by N bank to the park for a 3.4 mi hike. Trail is unmarked and rocky in sections.

Support Facilities: Daniel Boone Campground, P.O. Box 765, Hillsborough, NC 27278. Tel: 919-732-8101. Open all year. Full svc, rec fac. At I-85 exit 164 and jct with NC 86.

Information: Contact Recreation Department, City of Durham, 101 City Hall Plaza, Durham, NC 27701. Tel: 919-683-4355.

Edenton

Chowan County

Edenton, settled in 1658, is one of the state's oldest communities. Serving as the unofficial capital of the colony for 40 years, it was the home of Joseph Hewes, a signer of the Declaration of Independence, and it has the earliest known record of political activity by women in America — the Edenton Tea Party of October 25, 1774.

Edenton National Historical Trail   **540**

Length: 1.5 mi (2.4 km), easy; *USGS:* Edenton (CE); *Trailhead:* Parking area at corner of S Broad and W Water streets.

Directions and Description: If entering Edenton on US 70, or NC 32 or 37, go to S Broad St and park at corner near W Water St. Begin walk with the Barker House across the street, following signs and using the town's map of 28 designated historic sites. Three centuries of outstanding architecture, particularly Federal, Greek revival, and Georgian, are on the trail. Water, King, Broad, Church, Granville, Eden, and Blount streets are part of the loop.

Information: Contact Edenton Chamber of Commerce, 116 E King St, Edenton, NC 27932. Tel: 919-482-3400.

Garner

Wake County

The Garner Recreational Department has two parks: Garner Recreational East and Garner Recreational South. The town has approximately 6,000 residents. It is less than 7 mi from the center of the state's capital, Raleigh. US 70 E and W is the main traffic artery. Total hiking trail mileage is 2.2 mi (3.5 km).

South Garner Park Trail   **541**

Length: 1.6 mi (2.6 km), easy; *USGS:* Garner; *Trailhead:* Parking area at Claymore Drive.

Directions and Description: Begin at park gate on Claymore Drive and circle baseball, football, soccer, and tennis fields on unblazed trail R or L. If R, cross Poole Drive at 300 yd, go L at 0.5 mi, and pass through loblolly pine forest at 0.7 mi. At 1.1 mi join additional loop trail section S between Flanders St and Claymore Drive. Return to parking area at 1.6 mi.

Support Facilities: Camping is not allowed in the park.

Length: 0.6 mi (1.0 km), easy; *USGS:* Garner; *Trailhead:* Parking lot at N end of park.

Directions and Description: Follow *Cedar Ridge Trail,* with yellow blazes to large beech nut tree. Directional markers are unclear. If you turn L, cross bridge at 0.3 mi and turn R on *Pine Ridge Trail.* Return to parking lot from E of tennis court at 0.6 mi.

Support Facilities: Camping is not allowed in the park. Commercial camping is at College Park Camp Ground, 4208 New Bern Ave, Raleigh, NC 27610. Tel: 919-833-7015. Full svc, no rec fac. Open all year.

Information: Contact Garner/Wake County Parks and Recreation Department, P.O. Box 446, Garner, NC 27529. Tel: 919-772-8765.

Greensboro

Guilford County

Greensboro is named in honor of General Nathanael Greene, who led the colonial army against Lord Cornwallis at Guilford Courthouse on March 15, 1781. The city is in the center of Guilford County and was settled by Quakers, Germans, and Scotch-Irish as early as 1749. A large city with diversified manufacturing, it is also an educational and insurance center. Among its colleges and universities are Guilford College (1837) — the only Quaker college in the South; Greensboro College (1838), the first state college for women, now coed; and, the University of North Carolina at Greensboro (1891). The city is also known for its Coliseum complex, Natural Science Center, and the Greater Greensboro Golf Tournament the first week in April.

The city's parks and recreation system is considered the most extensive in the state, with more than 20 parks and associated areas. Greensboro operates a five-lake, 137-acre Municipal Nursery at Keeley Park for production of trees, shrubs, and flowers for the other parks and city municipal buildings.

In addition to the numerous hiking paths and trails, there is a 100-mile system of asphalt bicycle trails in the City-Wide Bike System.

Bicentennial Garden Trails   543

Length: 0.5 mi (0.8 km), easy; *USGS:* Greensboro; *Trailhead:* Parking area.

Directions and Description: At the jct of Cornwallis Drive W and Hobbs Rd, turn S to parking area on R at Bicentennial Garden, 1105 Hobbs Rd. Developed by Greensboro Beautiful, Inc., the park is meticulously maintained with cultivated flowerbeds and special gardens. Follow the gravel trail to the bridge over a small stream and into a lightly wooded garden, where more than 75 plants are found in a Fragrance Garden and Herb Garden. (Labels are also in Braille.) The area is to become part of the Caldwell Memorial Park, in honor of David Caldwell (1725-1824), patriot, statesman, clergyman, physician, and founder of Caldwell Log College in 1767.

Bryan Park Complex

Bryan Park is a 600-acre recreational complex located on the S side of Lake Townsend NE of the city. Named in honor of Joseph and Kathleen Bryan, it was opened November 26, 1974. The park has two volleyball courts, a basketball court, golf course, marina, trailer and tent camping, picnicking area, nature trails, and other recreational facilities. The 22,000 sq ft Enrichment Center is totally equipped for large banquets and entertainment.

From I-85 and US 29 jct, go N on US 29 for 6.8 mi to Hicone Dr exit. From ramp cross US 29 W to Summit Ave, and go for 0.5 mi. Turn R for 2.8 mi to Center for the Deaf and turn L at 0.6 mi to park. Park in parking lot R of Enrichment Center.

Big Poplar and Lake Shore Trails   544-545

Length: 1.6 mi rt cb (2.6 km), easy; *USGS:* Lake Brandt, Browns Summit; *Trailhead:* Enrichment Center parking area.

Directions and Description: From parking lot follow signs to trails, which overlap or interconnect. Go through young hardwood forest with ground cover of running cedar, bellwort, and honeysuckle to trail jct and bear R. Pass golf course at 0.3 mi, and reach loop jct at 0.4 mi. Turn R and follow through mature hardwoods and pines W of cove and old unused *Azalea Trail* to Townsend Point at 0.6 mi. Continue on loop to jct at 1.2 mi, and return to parking area.

Information: Contact Bryan Park, Route 2, Box 266, Browns Summit, NC 27214. Tel: 919-621-3583.

Fisher Park Circle Trails   546

Length: 0.6 mi (1 km), easy; *USGS:* Greensboro; *Trailhead:* Fisher Park Circle.

Directions and Description: At the jct of the 700 block of N Elm St and Fisher Park Circle, go to NW corner of the street and park. Walkways, paths, and some paved sections connect in one of the city's oldest parks. There are large poplars, oaks, maples, weeping willows, hemlocks, elms, and pines scattered around a small stream with granite rocks. Open areas have cultivated flowerbeds.

Hagan-Stone Park

Hagan-Stone Park is one of the city's newest recreational centers. With 409 acres, it has a marina; trailer, group, and tent camping sites; picnicking; bath and restroom facilities; two unique museums — tobacco and Oakgrove School House; and, trails for nature study.

Entrance to the park is from the jct of I-85 and US 421 going SE on US 421 for 3.4 mi to NC 22 jct. Turn R and go 4.1 mi on NC 22 to SR 3411 and turn L. On SR 3411 go 0.4 mi and turn L into park entrance. Park in front of maintenance shop.

Dogwood Trail, Indian Head Trail, and Hiking Trail   547-549

Length: 5.3 mi rt cb (8.5 km), easy; *USGS:* Pleasant Grove, Climax; *Trailhead:* Parking lot.

Directions and Description: From parking lot enter forest at R corner near maintenance area and follow yellow arrow to beginning of the loop trails. *Dogwood Trail* is 0.5 mi, *Indian Head Trail* is 1.4 mi around the campground, and *Hiking Trail* is 3.4 mi around the perimeter of the park. At 0.6 mi *Indian Head Trail* turns R; continue on *Hiking Trail* to Oakgrove School House exhibit at 1.2 mi, then enter open field with pine and cedar borders. Pass picnic area at 2.4 mi on R, enter field on L at 3 mi, and return to parking area near young forest and log cottage at 3.4 mi. The trail is exceptionally well-maintained over wooded areas of leaves and along wide grassy avenues in the fields. Other trails are planned.

Hamilton Lake Trail   550

Length: 0.9 mi (1.4 km), easy; *USGS:* Gilford, Greensboro; *Trailhead:* Lake Hamilton dam area.

Directions and Description: From corner of Starmount Dr and E Keeling Rd at Lake Hamilton, hike R of Starmount Dr on pea gravel trail through an open forest of tall and magnificent hickory, oak, poplar, beech, and pine trees. A small stream is on the R. This is an excellent hike to view the beauty of autumn foliage. Reach corner of Kemp Rd and Starmount at 0.9 mi. Horses or motorized vehicles not permitted on the trail.

HESTER PARK

The Oka T. Hester Park is a new facility in SW Greensboro on Groometown Rd, E of Sedgefield Country Club. The park has a large center for community activities, a lake with paddleboats, picnic area, children's playground, tennis and volleyball courts, restrooms, and physical fitness trails. Motorized vehicles, horses, and dogs are not permitted on the trails. To get to the park, from jct of I-40 and US 29A-70A go 1.8 mi W on US 29A-70A, High Point Rd, to jct with Groometown Rd and turn L on Groometown Rd. Go 0.9 mi to Ailanthus St, turn L to Hester Park, and bear L at the gate to parking area. (Other parking areas will also provide access to the trail.)

Hester Park Trail   **551**

Length: 1.3 mi (2 km), easy; *USGS:* Greensboro; *Trailhead:* Parking area.

Directions and Description: Follow *Physcial Fitness Trail* on well-graded dirt trail through 20 stations. Instructions are listed at each station. Or, hike the trail without doing the exercises, going around the lake in a loop to return.

Lake Daniel Trail   **552**

Length: 3.5 mi (5.6 km), easy; *USGS:* Greensboro; *Trailhead:* See below.

Directions and Description: This is a 3.5 mi asphalt bike, hiking, and exercise trail near an eastward-flowing stream. Entry can be made at a number of streets between the points of origin, and there are connections between the Lake Daniel Park complex and Latham Park. To walk the distance given above, begin on Lake Drive near Battleground Ave and proceed W to N Elam Ave near Wesley Long Community Hospital. Meadows are open and grassy, with sections of ash, oak, poplar, pine, and sweet gum. Trail mileage is marked. The *Fitness Trail* section has 20 stations.

Reedy Fork Creek Trail   **553**

Length: 3.3 mi (5.3 km), easy; *USGS:* Lake Brandt; *Trailhead:* Greensboro Water Works, Lake Brandt Sta.

Directions and Description: From jct of US 220N take Lawndale Dr to Lake Brandt Rd, or take Old Battlefield Rd to Lake Brandt Rd, SR 2347, and proceed to the Greensboro Water Works and Lake Brandt spillway. Park on R of road near Dillard's (Phillips 66) store. Begin trail behind the store, following white dot markers. Pass through vegetable garden, by old barn, and across a natural gas line at 0.2 mi. Large beech trees are at 0.5 mi. Other trees are river birch, pin oak, shagbark hickory, black gum, persimmon, ironwood, maple, and poplar. Pass spur trail on R at 0.6 mi. At 1 mi turn L at fork. Reach a boggy area at 1.2 mi, and cross brook near the edge of the lake at 1.3 mi. Among the flowering plants on the trail are arum, wood betony, mountain laurel, red bud, dogwood, strawberry bush, black cohosh, filbert, and beauty bush. Pass along border of an open field at 1.7 mi. At 2.9 mi reach old woods road and bear L on slight ascent. Pass through river birch stand at 3.2 mi and exit at SR 1001 near bridge at 3.3 mi. Backtrack or use vehicle switch. The distance on SR 2324 — L after crossing the bridge from exit to SR 2347 — to return to Dillard's Store is 4.6 mi.

Support Facilities: In addition to camping in some of the city parks, a commercial campground near the city is KOA, Route 14, Box 64A, Greensboro, NC 27405. Tel: 919-274-4143. Entrance is from I-85 and NC 6 jct. Go E at exit #128.

Information: For more information on the trails described above and a number of other paths and walkways on a dozen other city parks, contact Parks and Recreation Department, Government Center, Drawer W-2, Greensboro, NC 27402. Tel: 919-372-2574. For information on the nature trail at the Natural Science Center, write to 4301 Lawndale Drive, Greensboro, NC 27408. Tel: 919-288-3769.

Henderson

Vance County

Henderson, with a population of 14,000, is the county seat of Vance County. Its Fox Pond Park is 0.2 mi off NC 39 near the US 1 Bypass. The park is owned and used by the city for year-round recreational purposes. Four trails — *Fox Pond* (#554), *Quarry* (#555), *Conoconara* (#556), and *Sutton's Island* (#557) — interconnect for 2.4 mi of hiking.

Fox Pond Trails   554-557

Length: 2.4 mi (3.8 km), easy; *USGS:* Vicksboro; *Trailhead:* Parking lot near tennis court.

Directions and Description: Begin on E side of lake. Cross bridge and boardwalks at 0.5 mi. Cross service road near cement bunker at 0.9 mi. At 1.3 mi cross over stream near dam on a swinging bridge.

End at 1.4 mi. East of parking lot is *Conoconora Trail,* which loops through gums and poplar trees around the tennis courts. Return along *Fox Pond Trail* for 0.6 mi. *Quarry* and *Sutton's Island Trails* are short loop trails of 0.2 mi each.

Support Facilities: No overnight camping is permitted in the park. Kerr Lake State Park is 6 mi N off I-85 and has campground facilities. (See Kerr Lake State Park.)

Information: Contact Chamber of Commerce, 414 S Garnett St, P.O. Box 1302, Henderson, NC 27536. Tel: 919-438-7791.

High Point

Guilford County

High Point is one of the largest industrial centers in the South, the home of more than 400 industries and the largest furniture mart in the nation. Founded in 1859, it is also the home of High Point Museum and High Point College (1924), a United Methodist institute of higher education. Among its parks are High Point City Park, Blair Park, Oak Hollow Park, and an Environmental Center. The latter is a 200-acre forest for natural science study and for hiking.

Lakeshore, Chickadee, Hillside, Fiddlehead, Dogwood, Pipsissewa, and Pine Thicket Trails   **558-564**

Length: 3.6 mi rt cb (5.7 km), easy; *USGS:* High Point (E), Guilford; *Trailhead:* Parking area.

Directions and Description: From jct of US 29A-70A and Penny Road N in Jamestown, go N for 1.1 mi and turn R at the Environmental Center; park. From Greensboro at jct of Wendover Ave and I-40 go SE on Wendover Ave for 4.5 mi to jct with Penny Road. Turn L for 2 mi to Center on L.

Follow signs from parking area to picnic shelter on *Dogwood Trail;* pass *Chickadee Trail* on R, then a textural trail (getting hikers to use the senses) on L, and come to the *Wildflower Garden Trail* at 0.1 mi. Turn L on *Wildflower Trail* and at 0.3 mi return to *Dogwood*

Trail. Pass *Fiddlehead Trail* on R, continue to *Lakeshore Trail* jct at 0.5 mi, and bear L on *Lakeshore Trail*. At 0.8 mi reach High Point City Lake viewpoint, with large oak, poplar, pine, and cedar trees. Reach Kudzu Castle at 1.2 mi, and come to jct with *Dogwood Trail* and *Hillside Trail*. Take L on *Hillside Trail* for 0.5 mi to jct with *Fiddlehead Trail*. Follow *Fiddlehead Trail* to *Pine Thicket Trail* and take R at 1.8 mi. At *Dogwood Trail* go either R or L. If L follow *Dogwood Trail* to jct with *Lakeshore,* bearing L and L again on *Fiddlehead* to complete a loop to the floating bridge at 2.8 mi. Additional jcts with *Pipsissewa Trail* and *Chickadee Trail* are at 2.9 mi and 3 mi. After loops return to parking area at 3.6 mi. Camping and horseback riding are not permitted on the trails.

Information: Contact Environmental Education, Recreation and Research Center, Route 1, Box 401, High Point, NC 27260. Tel: 919-454-4214.

Raleigh

Wake County

Raleigh, the capital city, is named for Sir Walter Raleigh and was founded in 1792; it is the seat of state government and the center for North Carolina State University, Shaw University, and six other institutions of higher learning. The State Museum of Natural History, the North Carolina Museum of History, and the North Carolina Museum of Art are also located in the city.

The Raleigh Parks and Recreation Department has a comprehensive program of more than 24 parks and recreational facilities. One is the Capital Area Greenway, with over 300 acres (and which will eventually include 100 mi of trails) in the Crabtree Creek, Walnut Creek, Neuse River, and other systems. Some of the trails are paved, allowing for bicycle and handicapped use.

Loblolly Trail 565

Length: 6 mi (9.6 km), easy; *USGS:* Raleigh (W), Durham South (Cary); *Trailhead:* Gate D at the Carter-Finley Stadium.

Directions and Description: Take Blue Ridge Rd exit on I-40, and go S for 0.4 mi to Old Trinity Rd; turn R. Park near Gate D at the Carter-Finley Stadium. Enter by gate and follow white blazes to metal gate at 0.5 mi. Cross stile at 0.6 mi, go through culvert under I-40, or cross over I-40 if water is too high. At 1.3 mi enter North Carolina State University (NCSU) forest management area with conifers and broadleaves. Pass the Preston Memorial Area at 1.4 mi, cross a weir gaging station for the School of Forest Resources of NCSU at 2.2 mi, and reach jct with the 1.1-mi *Schenck Forest Interpretive Loop Trail.* Cross Reedy Creek Park Rd near Wake County Flood Control Lake at 2.4 mi, and then cross Richland Creek at 3.2 mi. (Crossing creek may be difficult at high water.) Jct with bridle trail and park boundary is reached at 3.5 mi; pass R of lake at 3.8 mi, and cross streams at 5.1 mi. Reach parking lot immediately after crossing Camp Whispering Pines Rd at 6 mi.

Shelley Lake Trail and Ironwood Trail   567-568

Length: 3.8 mi cb (6 km), easy; *USGS:* Raleigh (W); *Trailhead:* Shelley-Sertoma parking lot.

Directions and Description: From jct of US 70 and NC 50 at Crabtree Shopping Center, take NC 50 N to Shelley Rd at 0.8 mi. Turn R on Shelley Rd, SR 1812, for 0.2 mi to jct with Leesville Rd. Follow Shelley Rd for 0.8 mi to the Shelley-Sertoma Park on L. (Another route to the park is by following Shelley Rd 1.3 mi from Six Forks Road.)

From parking area follow paved trail around the lake. (A physical fitness trail is being constructed in the area.) Cross boardwalks and go by the observation tower. Continue through forest by Lead Mine Creek, pass near residential developments, and cross North Hills Drive at 1.8 mi. Pass athletic field at 2.3 mi, parking lot and baseball field near Sanderson High School at 2.4 mi, and reach Optimist Club Park parking lot at 2.6 mi. Exit on Northclift Drive R to Six Forks Rd, or backtrack.

The *Ironwood Trail* connects with the *Shelley Lake Trail* at the dam and goes under the Shelley Rd bridge S. It winds through the forest near Lead Mine Creek Greenway for 1.2 mi; most of it is paved. It exits near North Hills Rd. Current exit is in the 5200 block of North Hills Dr. This is a National Recreation Trail. (The 2.6-mi *Buckeye Trail* N of Barksdale Dr and E of jct of Crabtree and Raleigh Expressway is chiefly for bicyclists.)

Shelley-Sertoma has facilities for picnicking and non-motorized boating.

Little Rock, Alleghany, and Dacian Valley Trails   569-571

Length: 1.9 mi rt and cb (3.0 km), easy; *USGS:* See above; *Trailhead:* See below.

Directions and Description: These three intercity trails are at the following locations: *Little Rock* is a paved bicycle and pedestrian trail (0.9 mi) in the Garner Branch Greenway from Lenoir St along Garner Branch at Chavis Park to McMakin St; *Alleghany* is a paved trail (0.5 mi) from the jct of Buncombe Dr and Allegheny Dr to Alamance Dr and Alleghany Dr 0.5 mi SE of Glenwood Ave jct with the Expressway — US 1, 64, and 70; *Dacian Valley Trail* is a foot trail (0.3 mi) in the Walnut Creek Greenway in South Raleigh near Rock Quarry Rd and construction on I-40 S.

Lake Johnson Trail   572

Length: 3.2 mi (5.1 km), easy; *USGS:* Raleigh (West); *Trailhead:* Parking lot at S side of Lake Johnson on Avent Ferry Rd and construction on I-40 A.

Directions and Description: From Expressway (US 1 and 64), take exit at Western Blvd, and turn R on Avent Ferry Rd to Lake Johnson. At parking lot enter picnic area and follow white blazes to A-frame shelter at 0.3 mi. Cross stream and pass small waterfall at 0.6 mi. Wind in and out of coves around the lake and reach the dam spillway at 1.6 mi. Follow the spillway bank or turn L at the road and enter the Walnut Creek Greenway. Turn L at 2.0 mi on paved trail. At 2.7 mi return to Avent Ferry Rd, turn L, and follow road back to the parking lot at 3.2 mi.

Support Facilities: No camping is permitted in any of the above listed trail areas. The nearest private campground is at College Park, 4208 New Bern Ave, Raleigh, NC 27610. Tel: 919-833-7015. It is 1 mi E on US 64. Open all year. Full svc, rec fac.

Information: Contact Capital Area Greenway, Raleigh Park and Recreation Department, P.O. Box 590, Raleigh, NC 27602. Tel: 919-755-6494 or 919-755-6640. Also, Chamber of Commerce, 411 Salisbury St, Raleigh, NC 27602. Tel: 919-833-3005.

Rocky Mount

Nash County

Rocky Mount, established in 1840, is an industrial area for textiles, fertilizer, furniture, chemicals, metal products, and pharmaceuticals; it is also one of the world's largest marts for bright-leaf tobacco. The city is known for its unique Children's Museum in Sunset Park, for North Carolina Wesleyan College on US 301N, and for Battle Park on Falls Road. The latter is a 54-acre recreational park, a gift from the Battle family of Rocky Mount Mills.

Battle Park Trail   573

Length: 1.6 mi rt (2.6 km), easy; *USGS:* Rocky Mount; *Trailhead:* Parking area on Falls Rd.

Directions and Description: From jct of US 64 Bypass and NC 43-48, turn on NC 43-48 (Falls Road) SE and go 0.5 mi to the parking area near the Confederate monument. After parking hike on paved walkway by site of Donaldson Tavern, a stage coach station for an overland route. (Near here Lafayette was entertained while on his southern tour in 1825). At 0.2 mi turn R to waterfalls on the Tar River. Proceed to the playground through picnic area with pine, birch, oak, gum, elm, and dogwood. Cross driveway and at 1.3 mi pass site of first Rocky Mount post office. Return to parking lot. This trail can be used by the handicapped.

Information: Contact Park Director, City Parks and Recreation Department, P.O. Box 1180, Rocky Mount, NC 27801. Tel: 919-977-2111.

Smithfield

Johnson County

Smithfield, population 6,680, is the county seat of Johnson County. Its Town Common Park borders the E side of the Neuse River on N Front St, one block from E Market St (US 70) at the bridge. The Park is maintained by Smithfield Parks and Recreation and the Year Around Garden Club. Total walking distance is 1.6 mi.

Neuse River Nature Trail   **574**

Length: 1.6 mi (2.5 km), easy; *USGS:* Selma; *Trailhead:* Either at the parking lot on N Front St or E Church St parking lot.

Directions and Description: Begin at the parking lot on N Front St, hike 0.2 mi up E bank of Neuse River to terminus, and return. Hike down the E bank of the river by the historic site of Smith's Ferry (1759-1786) and under the US 70 bridge at 0.5 mi. Continue through pristine forest of large sweet gum, oak, and green ash. Turn L at 0.7 mi and reach the tennis courts, children's playground, and parking area on E Market and S 2nd St at 1 mi. Return by the same route or go on N Front St for a distance of 1.6 mi. ORV's allowed on parts of trail. Open all year.

Support Facilities: No camping is allowed in the park. Outside the park is Polka Dot RV Resort on US 701 S at junction of I-95, 5 mi S of Smithfield. Full svc, rec fac. Open all year. Address is Route 4, Box 189, Four Oaks, NC 27524. Tel: 919-934-3181.

Information: Contact Recreation Department, P.O. Box 761, Smithfield, NC 27577. Tel: 919-934-2116.

Statesville

Iredell County

Statesville is the county seat of Iredell County and has over 110 diversified industries. It is near Lake Norman and sponsors the

Carolina Dogwood Festival, the Tar Heel Classic Horse Show, and in 1979 was host to the world's first Horseshoe Tournament. The Parks and Recreation Department maintains two parks, Lakeland Park (25 acres) and Anderson Park (36 acres). The trail system is well maintained.

Lakewood Nature Trail   **575**

Length: 1.6 mi cb (2.6 km), easy; *USGS:* Statesville (W); *Trail-head:* Parking area.

Directions and Description: From jct of I-40 and NC 115 (N Central St), go S 0.4 mi into the city and turn L on Hartness Rd. After 0.3 mi turn L on Lakewood Drive. From any of the parking areas follow the trail signs onto a paved and interconnecting trail system in a mature forest of oak, pine and poplar.

Parcourse Trail   **576**

Length: 1.1 mi (1.8 km), easy; *USGS:* See above; *Trailhead:* Parking lot.

Directions and Description: From jct of I-40 and NC 115 (N Central St), go S 0.3 mi into the city and turn R on N Race St. Continue 0.6 mi to Anderson Park near School Administration Center. From parking lot follow signs for a parcourse fitness circuit over a soft gravel trail and under an open forest of large pines and oaks. There are 17 stations.

Information: Contact Statesville Parks and Recreation Department, 432 W Bell St, Statesville, NC 28677. Tel: 704-872-2481.

Winston-Salem

Forsyth County

An industrial leader in the Carolinas, Winston-Salem is really a combination of two cities: Salem, founded in 1766 by Moravians, and Winston, an industrial center founded in 1849. R. J. Reynolds founded his tobacco company here in 1875; it has become the world's largest plant for cigarette manufacture. There are also 300 other industries in a city which is home for Wake Forest University and the North Carolina School for the Arts, as well as being the birthplace for community arts councils.

Among the parks are the Reynolds Park and Salem Lake. (See Forsyth County for other parks.) Salem Lake, a 365-acre city reservoir surrounded by 1,800 acres of land, has facilities for fishing — bass, bluegill, and catfish, picnicking, boating, horseback riding, and hiking. The gate is open all year from 6 A.M. to 11 P.M. The park is closed each Thursday. A parcourse fitness trail is being planned near the trail entrance.

Salem Lake Trail   577

Length: 6.8 mi rt (10.9 km), easy; *USGS:* Winston-Salem (E); *Trailhead:* Salem Lake Rd near entrance gate.

Directions and Description: At US 311 and NC 109 jct with I-40 at Claremont Ave, go S 0.3 mi to Stadium Drive and turn L. Go 0.4 mi and turn L for 1.9 mi on Reynolds Park Rd. Turn L for 0.4 mi on Salem Lake Rd. Trailhead is immediately beyond gate. Park near the trailhead or at the office, and follow unmarked but wide trail through poplar, Virginia pine, and sweet gum; go in and out of coves to spot near Linville Rd at 3.4 mi. (An exit could be made here.) Deer, foxes, raccoons, and copperheads are part of the wildlife in the area. (One resident near the trail reports having seen and fed bears and panthers, but city recreation personnel continue to investigate without corroborating this story.) Return by same route. Trail can be used as bridle trail. No camping in the lake area.

Winston Lake Nature Trail   578

Length: 1.2 mi (1.9 km), easy; *USGS:* Winston-Salem (E); *Trailhead:* Parking lot at swimming pool.

Directions and Description: From jct of I-40 and US 311 go N for 1.9 mi on US 311, and turn R on Winston Lake Rd. Go 0.2 mi to Waterworks Rd, turn R, and immediately turn L to Winston Lake swimming pool parking lot. From the parking area hike through the gate to vacant playground and enter mature forest of poplar, pine, and hardwoods near the river. (Trail is unmarked.) At 0.2 mi pass dam on L and begin circle around the lake to the picnic areas on the N side. No camping in the lake area.

Support Facilities: Tanglewood Park Family Campground, Clemmons, NC 27012. Tel: 919-766-6421. (For reservations call 919-766-4793.) Open all year. Entrance is from jct of I-40 (Clemmons exit) and SR 1103; go 1 mi S on SR 1103 to jct of US 158. Turn R and go 1.5 mi on US 158 to park entrance. Full svc, and exceptionally varied rec fac.

Information: Contact Parks and Recreation Department, P.O. Box 2511, Winston-Salem, NC 27102. Tel: 919-727-2063.

PRIVATE, COLLEGE, AND OTHER TRAILS

CHAPTER XIV

PRIVATE TRAILS

Henderson County

Bearwallow Mountain Trail 579

Length: 2 mi rt (3.2 km), easy; *USGS:* Bat Cave; *Trailhead:* Parking area at Bearwallow Gap.

Directions and Description: From jct of US 74 and SR 1594 in Gerton (5 mi NW on US 74 from jct of NC 9 in Bat Cave), go 2.1 mi on SR 1594, mostly a gravel road, to Bearwallow Gap. Park away from the gate, and ascend gradually on gravel road through oak, hickory, locust, and maple to the firetower on Bearwallow Mtn (4,232 feet). Scenic views from the tower are of Sugarloaf Mtn, Bat Cave area, and Little Pisgah Mtn. Flowering plants include spiderwort, bellflower, turtlehead, and phlox.

Jackson County

Blackrock Mountain Trail 580

Length: 9.6 mi rt (13.8 km), strenuous; *USGS:* Sylva (N); *Trailhead:* Driveway of Hensen property.

Directions and Description: From jct of US 19A-23 and SR 1527 at sign of Scott Creek Baptist Church (and 0.5 mi N from jct of US 19A and US 23 Business in Sylva), turn L on SR 1527 and go 0.2 mi to old US 19-23. Turn R. (It is 9.2 mi N on four-lane highway, US

19A-23, to the Blue Ridge Parkway at Balsam Gap.) Go 1.8 mi to Addie and turn L on SR 1457. Go up Buff Creek for 0.6 mi to turn on L, SR 1458. Follow up road for 0.3 mi to end of public road. Request permission from the landowner, Mrs. Ivalee Hensen, to hike on the property. (Permission may also be needed from the adjoining Brown property.)

Follow up old woods road by Henry Creek. At 0.4 mi reach fork, and bear R. A number of other logging roads on L and R may be confusing, but remain hiking in a northerly direction toward the summit at each jct. After 2.2 mi ascend on Blackrock Ridge and watch for steep footpath at 3.9 mi. Reach Blackrock Mtn (5,810 ft) at 4.3 mi. Because of lack of use the trail may have dense summer growth. Backtrack, or take logging road SE on W slope of Whiterock Ridge to Buff Creek Rd. Use of topo map is recommended. Elev gain, 3,210 feet.

Ashe County

Bluff Mountain Trail   581

The North Carolina Nature Conservancy, a private organization, owns and maintains a controlled access nature preserve on Bluff Mtn in Ashe County. It is described as a "Naturalist's dream." To hike the 2-mi loop trail, permission is needed from the Conservancy, P.O. Box 805, Chapel Hill, NC 27514. Tel: 919-967-7007.

Transylvania County

Brevard Nature Trail   582

A botanical trail system of extraordinary educational value in a 365-acre nature preserve is privately owned and maintained by Charles F. Moore, Box 8, Brevard, NC 28712. Tel: 704-884-9614. A clear mountain stream flows through a remarkable diversity of vascular flora. Hike permitted with guided tour only.

McDowell County

Bob's Creek Trail   583

Length: 8 mi (12.8 km), strenuous; *USGS:* Marion (E), Glenwood; *Trailhead:* Parking area.

Directions and Descripiton: From I-40 turn S on US 221 for 1.9 mi. At Phillips 66 svc sta turn L on SR 1153 and go 0.5 mi to SR 1786 (old US 221). Turn L for 50 yd to SR 1766 on R and go 0.5 mi to SR 1790. After 1.8 mi on SR 1790, turn sharp L and ascend gravel road for 1.4 mi. and park at the parking area near gated road.

Enter forest at trail sign and go through pine, oak, sourwood, maple, and mountain laurel. For the first 3.5 mi loop the trail ascends and descends to Hemlock Falls, Split Rock Falls, Hidden Falls, and Sentinel Rock. If the S fork of the next 5 mi loop is taken, pass Poplar Cove Spring, follow gentle contour, and descend to Big Valley. Halfway around the loop is a backpacking campsite, stream, and rock formations. A number of hemlock groves are on the trail in this 500-acre pocket wilderness.

Information: Contact Bowater Carolina Company, P.O. Box 7, Catawba, SC 29704. Tel: 803-324-1130.

Lee County

Buckhorn-King Ranch Trail   583

Length: 3.2 mi (5.1 km), moderate; *USGS:* Cokesbury; *Trailhead:* Parking area at Buckhorn Dam.

Directions and Description: From Sanford go 7 mi NE on NC 42. Turn R on Buckhorn Rd, SR 1538, and go 3.4 mi to "Dead End" sign on gravel road SR 1540 L. After 0.7 mi, and if road to the dam is impassable, park at the McNeill house, leaving message on vehicle that you are a hiker. Go 0.6 mi farther to cul de sac on S side of Buckhorn Dam on the Cape Fear River. Enter red-flagged trail R on old logging road and go downstream through sections of young and mature syca-more, oak, pine, and maple. Cross Falls Creek at 0.7 mi. Continue to ascend and descend on rocky quartz bluffs. At 1.1 mi reach old river lock and landing, with laurel and jasmine on granite bluff. Pass attractive small waterfall and pool on R at 1.4 mi, and cross Letts Landing road at 1.6 mi. At King Ranch woods road turn R (at 1.8 mi), and hike out through Har-Lee Farms to SR 1538 at 3.2 mi. Vehicle switching is necessary, or walk 1.6 mi back on SR 1538 to SR 1504 and 1.3 mi to Buckhorn Dam. Trail is maintained by Mr. and Mrs. Frank Barringer, P.O. Box 375, Sanford, NC 27330. Tel: 919-776-2417. It is also maintained by the Boy and Girl Scouts of Lee County. (See also Trails Under Construction.)

Bertie County

Cashie-Roquist-Pocosin Trail   **584**

Length: 12 mi (19.2 km), easy; *USGS:* Williamston, Windsor (S); *Trailhead:* Welcome Center.

Directions and Description: Take US 17 into downtown Windsor; at corner of Water St is Welcome Center. Leave names and number of hikers or secure reservations at the Center. Follow trail signs for 1.2 mi past historic homes and churches on Gary, Dunde, and King sts. Turn R into woods at School St, and cross Haggard Mill Creek between SR 1300 and 1301 at 2.8 mi. Cross US 13 and walk NW by the Cashie River through pine, white birch, oak, cypress, and pocosin areas. Animal life in the area is that common to eastern North Carolina, and includes black bear. Reach campsite with picnic tables at 4.5 mi, 0.2 mi before swinging bridge over the Cashie. Cross SR 1225 at 6.1 mi and NC 308 at 7.5 mi. reach SR 1114 and Hope Plantation — restored home of Governor David Stone (1808-1810) — at 8 mi. The 4-mi trail from the Plantation to Grabtown is under construction. Trail is maintained by the Wiccacon Chapter of the Boy Scouts of America, Order of the Arrow, and is open all year.

278

Information: Contact Wiccacon Chapter Advisor, P.O. Box 128, Windsor, NC 27983. Tel: 919-794-2327.

McDowell County

Catawba Falls Trail   585

Length: 2.8 mi rt (4.5 km), easy; *USGS:* Black Mountain, Marion; *Trailhead:* End of SR 1274.

Directions and Description: Turn S on Catawba St at jct with US 70 in Old Fort. Go under I-40 and turn R onto exit ramp, which is also Catawba River Rd, SR 1274. After 3 mi park near bridge. Follow private road. At 0.3 mi ford river, enter old sawmill site at 0.5 mi, and go by an old dam at 1 mi. Road ends at 1.1 mi. Cross stream, take L trail at the fork, and reach lower falls at 1.3 mi. Climb R of falls on slippery banks with rhododendron and large spruce to view upper falls plunging into pool. Return by the same route. Owner of the property is D.W. Adams. No camping.

Support Facilities: A nearby campground is Catawba Falls Campground on the Catawba Falls Rd, SR 1274, Old Fort, NC 28762. Tel: 704-668-4831.

Buncombe County

Chambers Mtn Trail   586

Length: 4.7 mi rt (7.6 km), moderate; *USGS:* Clyde; *Trailhead:* Chambers Mtn Rd, SR 1534.

Directions and Description: From US 19-23 in Clyde turn onto Charles St, and cross railroad and bridge for distance of 0.2 mi. Turn L on SR 1513 and SR 1642, and go 0.4 mi to R turn on SR 1534, Chambers Mtn Road. Proceed for 1.4 mi on paved road to where gravel road turns steeply L and NW. Parking space may be a problem; a resident's permission may be advisable. Summit can be reached by vehicle, but gate — 200 yd up the steep road — may be locked. Follow road to grassy plateau, then take switchbacks, and reach the summit at 2.35 mi. Views from the firetower of Lake Jaunluska, Pisgah Forest, and Newfound Mtn are outstanding. Backtrack.

Swain County

Cherokee Arboretum and Nature Trail   637

Length: 0.5 mi (0.8 km), easy; *USGS:* Whittier; *Trailhead:* Oconoluftee Indian Village.

Directions and Description: From jct of US 19 and US 441 in Cherokee, turn N on US 441 and go 0.6 mi to sign of Oconoluftee Indian Village; turn L. Follow road to parking area. Enter trail through stockade gate, following loop trail through forest of pines and hardwoods. More than 150 species of plants are labeled. On the trail are a restored Indian log cabin, a stream, small pool, and herb garden. A National Recreation Trail, it is maintained by the Cherokee Historical Association, Box 398, Cherokee, NC 28719. Tel: 704-497-2111. (An older trail, 4.5 mi rt, runs to Mt. Nobel, beginning at the village parking lot. Elev gain is 1,666 feet. The Village is also the home of the Cherokee outdoor drama "Unto These Hills.")

Chimney Rock Park

Rutherford County

Chimney Rock Park (2,280 feet) is a private nature preserve with commercial comforts. Two of its outstanding features are Chimney Rock, a towering remnant of igneous rock 500 million years old, and Hickory Nut Falls, which plummets 404 feet (or twice the height of Niagara) into the gorge. More than 2.5 mi of trails provide the hiker with breathtaking vistas, misty forests with fern carpets, and wildflowers. Entrance is from US 74-64 and NC 9 jct near Lake Lure. Open all year except Christmas Day. Entry fee charged.

Skyline Nature and Cliff Hiking Trails 587-588

Length: 1.5 mi rt (2.4 km), easy to moderate; *USGS:* Bat Cave, Lake Lure; *Trailhead:* Parking lot.

Directions and Description: After entry to the park, go to the parking lot and either take the tunnel to the 258-ft elevator or climb the steps up the Needle Eye. Follow signs for the *Skyline Nature Trail,* with interpretive signs at prickly pine, the hop tree, laurel, witch hazel, shooting star, and wild orchids, reach Hickory Nut Falls. Return on narrow *Cliff Hiking Trail.*

Forest and Hickory Nut Falls Trails 589-590

Length: 1.2 mi rt (1.9 km), easy; *USGS:* See above; *Trailhead:* See above.

Directions and Description: From the parking lot hike through picturesque and densely shaded forest of hemlock, oak, laurel, and pine for 0.6 mi to the misty base of Hickory Nut Falls. Return by the same route.

Support Facilities: No camping is allowed in the park. Nearby campground is Hickory Nut Falls Family Campground, P.O. Box 97, Chimney Rock, NC 28720. Tel: 704-625-4014. Open April 1-November 1. Full svc, rec fac.

Information: Contact Chimney Rock Park, Chimney Rock, NC 28720. Tel: 704-625-9611.

Haywood County

Crabtree Bald Trail 591

Length: 5 mi rt (8 km), strenuous; *USGS:* Clyde; *Trailhead:* Bald Creek Rd, SR 1505.

Directions and Description: Contact Jack Messer, Tel: 704-627-6224, for permission and informaiton on hiking this trail. An access is from jct of I-40 and NC 209 (N of Junaluska); go for 2.4 mi N to Crabtree-Ironduff School. From there take R on SR 1503, go 2 mi, and turn L on Bald Creek Rd, SR 1505, at Jones Chapel Baptist Church sign. Go 3.1 mi along Indian

Branch and follow directions by owner of the property. The panoramic views from Crabtree Bald are remarkable.

Ashe County

De Flora Nature Trail   592

Length: 0.7 mi (1.1 km), easy; *USGS:* Glendale Springs; *Trailhead:* Pine Swamp Rd.

Directions and Description: At jct of US 421 and US 221 at Deep Gap (1 mi W of the Blue Ridge Parkway and 12 mi E of Boone), go N on US 221 for 2 mi, turn R on SR 1171, Pine Swamp Rd, and go 1.1 mi to SR 1169. Turn L and go 0.7 mi to parking area on L. Trail is by marshes, ponds, streams, and through woodland with more than 150 species of flowering plants and numerous species of ferns. Some of the plants are rare. The owner maintains and conducts tours on the trail. For permission and schedule contact Dr. F. Ray Derrick, Department of Biology, Appalachian State University, Boone, NC 28608. Tel: 704-262-3025, or at home, tel: 704-264-8467.

Grandfather Mountain Trails

Avery and Watauga Counties

The private Grandfather Mtn area has 7 trails across its spectacular peaks. They are open to the public, but hikers must have permits and pay a small fee to help maintain the trails and to protect the fragile ecology. Other than back-country hiking, the mountain is famous for its hang gliding tournaments, Highland Games and Gathering of the Scottish Clans, and Singing on the Mountain. Permits may be obtained at Invershiel Texaco at jct of NC 184 and 105, 15 mi SW of Boone and 4 mi N of Linville. Permits may also be secured at the Grandfather Mtn entrance on US 221 near Linville. Camping is allowed but restricted.

Shanty Spring Trail and Calloway Trail 593-594

Length: 5 mi rt cb (8 km), strenuous; *USGS:* Grandfather Mtn, Valle Crucis, Boone; *Trailhead:* Shanty Spring parking lot across road from Invershiel Texaco.

Directions and Description: From parking area at jct of NC 184 and 105, climb a white-blazed trail L of waterfall and ascend steeply to Shanty Spring at 2 mi. (Last sure water here.) Go through spruce and hardwoods, Indian pipes and yellow orchids. From Shanty Spring climb 0.5 mi on red-blazed *Calloway Trail* to crest of ridge and jct with blue-blazed *Grandfather Trail*. A turn L for 0.6 mi leads to Calloway Peak (5,964 feet) and *Daniel Boone Scout Trail*. A R turn leads to the Swinging Bridge Visitor Center at 2.9 mi.

Grandfather Trail 595

Length: 7 mi rt (11.2 km), strenuous; *USGS:* See above; *Trailhead:* Swinging Bridge Visitor Center parking area.

Directions and Description: From parking area follow signs and blue-blazed trail up embankment. At the cliffs of MacRae Peak at 1.8 mi, ladders are necessary to climb. N terminus is at Calloway Peak and jct with *Daniel Boone Scout Trail* at 3.5 mi. Backtrack to parking area, using *Underwood Trail* if necessary to avoid MacRae Peak and ladders.

Underwood, Arch Rock, and Black Rock Cliff Cave Trails 596-598

Length: 2.9 mi rt cb (4.7 km), moderate to strenuous; *USGS:* See above; *Trailhead:* Swinging Bridge Visitor Center.

Directions and Description: From the Visitor Center parking area ascend on *Grandfather Trail* to *Underwood Trail*, 1-mi, yellow-blazed loop trail which is easiest way for hikers around the rugged MacRae Peak. Connect with the red-blazed *Arch Rock Trail* for another 1.3 mi. Scenic views from Grandview Pinnacle. Descend steeply to the yellow-blazed *Black Rock Cliff Cave Trail* (Flashlights are required to follow yellow arrows in the cave.) Return L at fork on *Arch Rock Trail* and reach road E of climb to Visitor Center.

Daniel Boone Scout Trail   599

Length: 6.4 mi rt (10.2 km), strenuous; *USGS:* See above; *Trailhead:* Boundary line of Grandfather Mtn on US 221 near former Children's Home.

Directions and Description: On US 221 between Green Mtn Creek and Boone Fork, S of Blowing Rock, enter old road and go under the Boone Fork bridge of the Blue Ridge Parkway, under construction here. (This primitive trail may be difficult to locate or to use because of undergrowth.) Ascend S from bridge to ridge. Climb ridge to Calloway Peak at 3.2 mi and reach jct with *Grandfather Trail*. Backtrack or take either the *Grandfather Trail* or the *Shanty Spring Trail*.

Jackson County

Grassy Bald Trail   600

Length: 5 mi rt (8 km), strenuous; *USGS:* Hazelwood; *Trailhead:* On SR 1701.

Directions and Description: From Waynesville go 8 mi S on US 19A-23 to Balsam Gap and go under the Blue Ridge Parkway bridge. Immediately look for the turnoff on L for Balsam. Follow Balsam Rd, SR 1701, for 0.1 mi, crossing railroad near the Balsam post office. Drive 0.3 mi to Knights Store (and Balsam Lodge and Motel sign), and turn L. Go 1.9 mi to gated road on L. Parking may be a problem because of lack of space in a developing residential area. Ascend and follow old woods road beyond the gate, turning L over stream in a cove and following switchbacks up Grassy Ridge. Bear L at 1 mi at fork and L again at the other major forks. Reach Grassy Bald (5,613 feet) at 2.5 mi. Views of Great Balsam Mountains, Judaculla Mtn and Plott Balsams are impressive. Some of the vegetation on this trail includes birch, oak, hemlock, poplar, maple, and rhododendron. Elev gain, 1,753 feet.

Franklin County

Greencroft Wilderness Trail   601

Length: 5.8 mi rt (9.3 km), easy; *USGS:* Louisburg; *Trail-head:* Greencroft Gardens parking area.

Directions and Description: From Louisburg jct of US 401 and NC 56 S, take Raleigh Rd, US 401, for 4.9 mi to Greencroft sign on L at private driveway. Park in designated space. Trail enters forest at N end of Greencroft house. For the first 0.9 mi the trail is through a Botanical Garden with more than 500 wild plants labeled, the largest private wildflower garden in eastern North Carolina. Follow signs for loop around lake and water-fall. Permission and a guide required for hiking the 2 mi of trail beyond the Garden; it goes through fern gardens, virgin forest, and flood plains, by rock outcroppings and historic sites. Open all year. Garden and trail maintained by Friends of Greencroft Botanical Gardens, Route 1, Box 192W, Louisburg, NC 27549. Tel: 919-496-4771.

Macon County

Highlands Botanical Garden Trail   602

Length: 1 mi (1.6 km), easy; *USGS:* Highlands; *Trailhead:* Highlands Botanical Station.

Directions and Description: From jct of US 64 and NC 28 in Highlands, go 0.3 mi on E Main St to 6th St and turn L. Go 0.2 mi to sign and turn R. Pass the UNC Botanical Station and park at the Garden entrance. The trail has a herb and health garden and a special garden in memory of Effie Howell Foreman. Established in 1962 and supported by state and private funds, the Botanical Garden has more than 400 labeled species, most of which are indigenous to the Highlands area, and some of which are endemic.

Self-guiding, multiple, and connecting, the trails show off ferns, azaleas, clubmosses, and bog succession with swamp pinks and lilies, insectivorous plants, lichens, and rare plants. After hiking this area, take the trail to the R around Lake Ravenel, the *W. C. Coker Rhododendron Trail*. Reach the road at 0.6 mi. At 0.8 mi turn L, cross the dam, and return to the parking area at 1 mi. A spur trail of 0.1 mi connects with Highlands Nature Center and Museum of Natural History, which could also be an entrance point from Main St. At the Museum the *Sunset Trail* begins across the road. (Biological Station tel: 704-526-2602.)

Sunset Trail   603

Length: 1.4 mi rt (2.2 km), easy; *USGS:* Highlands; *Trailhead:* Ravenel Park entrance.

Directions and Description: From jct of US 64 and NC 28 in Highlands, proceed on E Main St for 0.4 mi and park opposite the Highlands Nature Center. Follow sign and go R at 0.2 mi over rock slabs through white pine, rosebay rhododendron, hemlock, and locust. At 0.6 mi an 1879 rock engraving indicates that the park area is a memorial to Margaretta A. and S. Prioleal Ravenel. At 0.7 mi a large rock outcropping provides a magnificent sunset view of the Nantahala forests and the town of Highlands. Return by the same route.

Information: Contact Museum of Natural History, Highlands, NC 28741.

Henderson County

Hightop Mountain Trail   604

Length: 3 mi rt (4.8 km), moderate; *USGS:* Fruitland; *Trailhead:* Terry Gap.

Directions and Description: Go S of Asheville on US 25A and US 25 to the town of Fletcher (or N of Hendersonville on I-26 or US 25) and turn L on Fairview Rd, SR 1545. Proceed for

0.8 mi to SR 1551, follow it for 1.3 mi, and turn R on Hoopers Creek Rd, SR 1553. At Hoopers Creek Grocery bear L at fork on SR 1569 for 1.9 mi, and turn R on SR 1565. Ascend for 2 mi to Terry Gap; park near gated lumber road on R.

Hike up road, steeply at times, to old log barn at 0.4 mi. Continue to ascend through forests and pastures, reaching an abandoned orchard at 1.2 mi. Ascend to Hightop (3,560 feet) at 1.5 mi, here find views of Mt. Pisgah, Bearwallow Mtn, and Lake Julian. Return by same route. Vegetation is mixed hardwoods and poplar. Fields have numerous wildflowers. For permission to hike the trail contact Arnold Garren in Hendersonville, tel: 704-692-2154; or, Hazel Pressley in Asheville, tel: 704-684-6644.

Buncombe County

High Windy Trail 605

Length: 6 mi rt (9.6 km), strenuous; *USGS:* Black Mountain; *Trailhead:* Main parking lot.

Directions and Description: From jct of US 70 and NC 9 in the town of Black Mountain, go 1.3 mi W to the YMCA Blue Ridge Assembly. Park at the main parking lot below the Robert E. Lee Hall. Check in for hiking permit at the Assembly Office. Begin climb to R of hall on gravel road. Turn L at the fork, go to horseshoe curve, and leave road. Go through opening in fence on to main trail up Turkey Ridge at 0.9 mi. At next 3 jcts ascend steepest fork and reach plateau at 2 mi. Turn L on gravel road and reach High Windy (4,500 feet) firetower at 3 mi. Excellent views of the Swannanoa Valley. Return by the same route.

Support Facilities: KOA Tanglewood Lakes, Tel: 704-686-3121. From jct of I-40 (exit 64) and NC 9 go 0.5 mi N on NC 9, and 3.5 mi W on US 70.

Information: Contact Blue Ridge Assembly, Inc., Black Mountain , NC 28711. Tel: 704-669-8422.

Transylvania County

Horsepasture River Trail   **606**

Length: 2.8 mi rt (4.5 km), moderate to strenuous; *USGS:* Reid; *Trailhead:* Parking area near Horsepasture River.

Directions and Description: From jct of US 64 and NC 281 in Sapphire (10.1 mi E of Cashiers), turn on NC 281 and go S 1.8 mi to parking area on L side of highway by the Horsepasture River. Climb down any of a number of steep rocky spurs to the main trail downstream and pass Drift Falls at 0.1 mi. The ungraded trail requires considerable back and neck bending as it passes through a rugged concourse of rhododendron and rocks. Each river spur provides outstanding views of waterfalls. Cross small stream at 0.3 mi, and reach Umbrella Falls at 0.4 mi. At 0.6 mi Rainbow Falls thunders 150 feet into a deep pool, spraying a mist against the canyon walls to form a rainbow when the sun is right. On the high side of the trail wildflowers grow in profusion, fed by the sun and the mist. A creek crosses the trail at 1 mi. Ascend for 240 yd and bear sharply R, and then descend again to the riverside at Stairway Falls and a magnificent view at 1.4 mi. (An obscure and treacherous trail continues downriver.) Backtrack.

Sampson County

Laurel Lake Gardens Trail   **607**

Length: 1.1 mi (1.7 km), easy; *USGS:* Coharie; *Trailhead:* Parking lot in front of office.

Directions and Description: From downtown Salemburg follow signs off NC 242 1 mi E and turn L at Gardens sign. Follow the signs from the parking lot N and E of the lake on the *F. S. Howard Camellia Trail*. Loblolly pines, hickories, maples, and American hollies (some 20 inch in diameter) tower above a sub-canopy of the largest camellia collection in the state. Return at 0.8 mi. The *Mary Howard Azalea Trail* is E of the parking lot and winds for 0.3 mi past a stream with thousands of azaleas in a natural environment. Blooming periods for camellias range from October to April.

Support Facilities: No camping is allowed in the Gardens. Nearest campground is 4 mi S at Leisure Living Campsites on NC 24 at Roseboro, NC 28382. Tel: 919-525-5112. Open all year. Full svc, rec fac.

Information: Contact Laurel Lake Gardens and Nursery, Salemburg, NC 28385. Tel: 919-525-4257.

Jackson and Haywood Counties

Mt Lyn Lowery Trail   **608**

Length: 7.2 mi rt (11.5 km), strenuous; *USGS:* Hazelwood; *Trailhead:* Blue Ridge Parkway, mp 446.

Directions and Description: From jct of US 19-A and US 23, S of Waynesville, and the Blue Ridge Parkway at Balsam Gap, go S(SW) on the Parkway for 2.5 mi to Woodfin Valley Overlook at mp 446; park. Cross road to mp sign 446 and climb steeply up faint trail for 50 yd to steel-gated road. Follow road L to NPS boundary at 0.3 mi. (The *Ivey Trail,* blazed salmon color, connects from the valley on R near the power line.) Continue up road to second jct with *Ivey Trail* at 0.9 mi. Spring and private cottage are on R at 1.3 mi. Reach fork in the road at 1.6 mi, and to the summit of Mt Lyn Lowery (6,280 feet) at 3.6 mi.

A 50-foot lighted cross of steel faces NE toward Waynesville. It was erected by Lt. Gen. and Mrs. Sumter L. Lowery in 1964 in "loving memory of Lyn Lowery, a saint in heaven." The area, immaculately maintained, has views of Maggie Valley, Plott Balsam, the Pisgah Range, and the Waynesville area. Some of the vegetation in the area is balsam, spruce, oak, birch, American ash, wild cherry, golden rod, bluebeads, orchids, and ferns. Return by the same route. (An alternate and shorter route is to descend on the exceptionally steep *Ivey Trail,* marked as "Fire Escape," to the Oldfield Top road at 0.6

mi. Turn R, and follow *Ivey Trail* blazes to Mt Lyn Lowery Singing Ground at 1 mi. Continue on the *Ivey Trail* through the Ground, descending steeply to the road at 1.4 mi, and again reaching the road at 1.5 mi. Leave the *Ivey Trail,* remaining on the road, to return to the Parkway at 2 mi. Elev gain, 1,960 feet.

Polk County

Pearsons Falls Trail   610

The *Pearsons Falls Trail* (0.3 mi) is part of a nature preserve maintained and financed privately for the past 50 years by the Tryon Garden Club. Outstanding 90-foot cascades and botanical display. *Directions:* From Tryon go 4 mi N on US 176, and take SR 1102 on L. Follow signs. *Information:* Contact Tryon Garden Club Nature Preserve, Route 1, Box 327, Saluda, NC 28773.

Yancey County

Phillips Knob Trail   611

Length: 4.3 mi rt (6.9 km), moderate; *USGS:* Burnsville; *Trailhead:* Mitchell Branch Rd jct with Mica Springs Heights Rd.

Directions and Description: From the town square in Burnsville, go N for 0.8 mi on N Main St, which becomes Mitchell Branch Rd, SR 1373. Park near jct with Mica Springs Heights Rd. (Although the road to the R, Mica Springs Heights, leads to the summit spur, the road is narrow and rough.) It is 0.8 mi to the next jct; turn R on steep road. Reach NC Forest firetower at 2.15 mi. Views to Big Bald, Table Rock, and Black Mtn ranges are impressive. Ascent, 1,400 feet.

Madison County

Sandymush Bald Trail   612

Length: 4.4 mi rt (7 km), strenuous; *USGS:* Fines Creek, Sandymush; *Trailhead:* NC 209, 4.5 mi S of Trust.

Directions and Description: From I-40 jct with NC 209 (N of Lake Junaluska), go N on NC 209 for 8.3 mi to Ferguson's Supply Store and Jones Branch. Turn R over bridge up Cove Creek to Betsy Gap and descend to a small faded sign, "Sandymush Bald," on a gated, locked fence on the R at 13.9 mi. (If sign is passed, drive back from jct with NC 63 at Freizeland Creek for 4.5 mi.) Trail goes up Bald Branch, ascending an old rocky road for approximately 2.2 mi. For permission to hike the trail and to unlock the gate, contact Reeves Ferguson, Route 3, Box 177, Clyde, NC 28721. Tel: 704-627-6302. Or, call Denver Moore, Tel: 704-622-7219; he lives up the highway a few yards from the gate.

Panoramic views from the balds are of Harmon Den in the Pisgah to the W, the Smokies, the Cherokee National Forest in Tennessee, and the Blue Ridge Mountains near Asheville. Some of the vegetation consists of oak, birch, locust, spruce, sourwood, maple, rhododendron, thistle, yarrow, buttercup, and horsemint.

Another route for a 5-mi walk one-way to Sandymush is from NC 63 at Doggett Gap, which is 4.9 mi from NC 209 and NC 63 jct in the community of Trust. The trail, mainly an old road, follows the Madison-Buncombe county line. It traverses cattle fields, balds, forests, and tree farms. About 1 mi from the entrance reach a housing development. (A gravel road from NC 63 near Doggett Gap is under construction.) For the next 4 mi permission may be needed from the landowners.

Surry and Stokes Counties

The Sauratown Trail   **613**

The Sauratown Trail on both public and private lands, is open year-round to hikers and equestrians for a one-way total of over 19 mi (of which 6.4 mi is on paved or gravel roads). Connecting trails from Hanging Rock State Park and the Yadkin River section of Pilot Mtn State Park can provide more than 33 mi of one-way walking for hikers. The trail is significant because of its inclusion in the Mountains-to-the-Sea Trail System and for the scenic beauty of the Sauratown Mountains — a range separate from the nearby Blue

Ridge Mountains. Entrance to the trail can be at either terminus. This description will begin at the Hanging Rock State Park entrance. From Danbury go 4 mi NW on NC 89 and 8 to SR 1001, turn L, and follow the road to park entrance.

Length: 19.1 mi (32 km), easy to moderate; *USGS:* Pinnacle and Hanging Rock; *Trailhead:* Parking lot #2 in Hanging Rock State Park.

Directions and Description: From parking lot follow trail signs SW, pass L of bathhouse fence, cross feeder streams at 0.3 mi, and follow red circle blazes. Cross boardwalk to jct with *Moores Wall Trail* R and *Magnolia Spring Trail* L at 1 mi. Turn R, ascend slightly, reach blue circle blazes to Torys Den (and to *Sauratown Trail*) at 1.5 mi, and turn L. At 2 mi reach crest of Huckleberry Ridge near large rock formations. Descend, turn L at 2.3 mi, and reach jct with white circle-blazed bridle trail at 2.4 mi. Turn L. *(Torys Den Trail* goes R 1.7 mi.) Spring is at 3.5 mi, park boundary at 3.9 mi, and NC 66 at 4.2 mi. Turn L on NC 66, R on SR 1188 at 4.6 mi, and L on SR 1172 at 5.2 mi. Ascend gravel road for 3.3 mi, reaching WXII towers on summit of Sauratown Mtn (elevation, 2,700 feet) at 8.5 mi. Pass R of last WXII building and begin SW switchback descent. Trail follows ridge through chestnut oaks, blueberries, hickories, and fire pinks to saddle at 9.3 mi. Pass Crystal Mine at 9.9 mi. Begin steep descent at 10 mi. Follow rocky, irregular trail for 1.7 mi to old tobacco barn at 11.7 mi. Pass abandoned house and go through a honeysuckle grove at 11.9 mi; reach farm road at 12.1 mi. Turn R, and follow farm road to Volunteer Road, SR 1136, at 12.7 mi. Turn L for 80 yd on Volunteer Rd and turn R on private road. Reach South Fork of Yadkin River at 13.9 mi. (No bridge; river is shallow and can usually be waded.) Ascend steeply to Bowen Rd, SR 1160, at 14.2 mi. Turn R and follow gravel road to High Bridge Rd, SR 1157, at 14.8 mi. (The town of Pinnacle is 0.5 mi L.) Cross road, and pass through bed of running cedar and forests and fields of honeysuckle to Bradley Rd, SR 1155, at 16.9 mi. Cross Old US 52 at 17.6 mi, and reach railroad crossing at 17.7 mi. Turn L on paved Pilot Knob Rd, SR 1152, and at 18.3 mi turn R on SR 1151. Enter Surry County at 18.5 mi, and go under US 52 bridge at 19.0 mi. (Bridle trail turns L here into Park forest.) Reach Pilot Mtn State Park entrance at 19.1 mi.

For an additional 12.3 mi, hikers may continue on the paved entrance road to the campground for 1.2 mi, and ascend steeply on the *Summit Trail* for 2.0 mi to reach the parking area of Pilot Mtn summit. To reach the Yadkin River section, take the *Ledges Spring Trail* W at the jct of *Summit Trail* and descend 0.6 mi to the *Mt Bridle Trail* for 2.5 mi. At SR 2061, cross to the *Corridor Trail* and hike for 6 mi to the Yadkin River.

Support Facilities: Camping facilities are provided in both Hanging Rock State Park and in Pilot Mountain State Park, but there are no hook-ups. Camping schedule is April 1 to November 1. Nearest private campground is Mt. Airy Family Campground. Call 919-786-5967. Another camping area is Pop's and Mom's Campground, Route 6, Box 379, Mt Airy, NC 27030. Tel: 919-352-4847. Take exits 100 and 93 on I-77, go 1.5 mi W on NC 89 at I-77 jct, and turn on Bulah Rd, SR 1345. Full svc, no rec fac. Open all year.

Information: Contact Park Superintendent, Hanging Rock State Park, P.O. Box 128, Danbury, NC 27016. Tel: 919-593-9480. Or, Park Superintendent, Pilot Mountain State Park, Route 1, Box 13, Pinnacle, NC 27043. Tel: 919-325-2355.

The Sauratown Trail Committee is responsible for maintenance between the parks and for determining any camp locations. The Committee's address is 280 South Liberty St, Winston-Salem, NC 27101. Tel: 919-722-9346.

Haywood County

Setzer Mountain Trail   614

Length: 4.4 mi rt (7 km), easy; *USGS:* Hazelwood; *Trailhead:* Gated road at Soco Gap.

Directions and Description: From jct of US 19-276 near Waynesville, go W on US 19 10.4 mi toward the Blue Ridge Parkway, but stop 0.3 mi before Soco Gap jct with the BRP. Stop at the Texaco Sta and Blue Ridge Crafts Store because parking space is not available at the gated road on the L. From store go a few yards up the road, turn L through gate, and follow gravel road to radio towers at 1.3 mi.

Follow old Setzer Mtn road to a gap and turn L at 2 mi. (*Campbell Lick Trail* turns R for 0.5 mi to Campbell Lick Mtn.) Reach Setzer summit at 2.2 mi. Backtrack.

Buncombe County

Spivey Mtn Trail   **616**

Length: 2.6 mi rt (4.2 km), moderate; *USGS:* Enka; *Trailhead:* End of SR 1255.

Directions and Description: From jct of I-40 and US 19-23 W of Asheville, go 0.2 mi on US 19-23 N to SR 1404 (Old US 18-23 or Old Haywood Rd) and turn L between Exxon and Gulf svc stas. Travel 0.4 mi, turn L on SR 1255 (Starnes Cove Rd), and go 2.9 mi to end of paved road; park.

Hike up gravel road L of pond and barn and at 0.4 mi reach lawn of the Brodeur residence. Request permission to hike to ridge. ("Keep Off" and "Beware of Dog" signs are aimed at motor-cyclists.) At 0.8 mi reach crest of ridge, passing through young hardwood forest. Chinquapin, wild rose, spiderwort, and maculosa thistle are found in open areas. Pass under power line and climb ridge, sometimes steep, to gravel road at 1.1 mi. Turn R and reach firetower at 1.3 mi. Excellent view of Asheville and surrounding area. Return by same route.

CHAPTER XV

COLLEGE AND UNIVERSITY TRAILS

Jackson County

Biology Club Trail   617

Length: 1 mi rt (1.6 km), moderate; *USGS:* Glenville; *Trailhead:* Wolf Creek on SR 1157.

Directions and Description: From the jct of the main campus entrance at Western Carolina University on NC 107, go S on NC 107 for 1.3 mi to jct with SR 1001, Speedwell Rd. Turn R and drive 1.1 mi to SR 1157, Cullowhee Mtn Rd, at bridge over Tilley Creek. Go 3 mi, with Cullowhee Creek on R, to horseshoe curve in the road and park on large, grassy area on R beyond the curve. Hike back 50 yd to the center of the curve to Wolf Creek on R. Follow footpath up a flume with a cascading stream of pools and falls for 0.5 mi. Oak, birch, maple, hemlock, and rhododendron partially cover the damp gorge. The scenic trail has the common wildflowers and mosses, as well as a number of rare species such as walking fern and Fraser's sedge. Backtrack, or at the jct of Cherry Gap FSR, hike R to SR 1157 and go R 0.6 mi down the paved highway to the parking area.

Franklin County

College Park Trail   618

Length: 0.8 mi (1.3 km), easy; *USGS:* Louisburg; *Trailhead:* College intramural field.

Directions and Description: On Louisburg US 401 Bypass turn at Louisburg College sign and Frazier Field sign. Turn R behind college steam plant and go 0.1 mi to park entrance and sign.

Enter forest on paved, graded trail (designed to assist the handicapped); go to lake observation platform under huge beech nut trees at 0.1 mi. Footpath continues W around the lake, crossing a bridge near an old spring at 0.4 mi. Follow trail E and use spur trail to return to parking area at 0.8 mi. Open all year. Maintained by Louisburg College, the Appalachian Trail and Whitewater Club, and the Biology Department. College Box 845, Louisburg, NC 27549. Tel: 919-496-2521.

Durham and Orange Counties

Duke Forest Trails   619

The Duke University Forest, of 8,500 acres, has five divisions — Eno, between the corner of NC 86 and US 70; Blackwood, W of NC 86 and S of New Hope Creek; Hillsborough, on the US 70 Bypass; Korstian, between Mt. Sinai Rd (NC 86) and Rigsbee Rd; and Durham, on both sides of NC 751 between US 70 and US 15-501 Bypass. USGS quad maps are Durham (NW) Durham (SW), Hillsborough, and Chapel Hill.

The Forest was established in 1931. The University appointed Dr. Clarence F. Korstian as its first director; he developed the Forest into an area of research and a laboratory for forestry students. The Forest has excellent examples of plant succession. Hiking and picnicking and horseback riding are allowed, but no camping, hunting, or motorized vehicles are permitted. A wide range of trees and flowers common to the Piedmont are found in the area. More than 20.7 mi of trails are provided in the form of fire lanes, and 14.3 mi more are possible on all-weather roads.

For walking in a more formal setting, the Sarah P. Duke Memorial Gardens near the university entrance are also open to the public.

Information: For guidelines and access information to the gated trails, contact the Duke Forest Resource Manager, School of Forestry and Environmental Studies, Duke University, Durham, NC 27706. Tel: 919-684-2421 or 919-467-4332.

Moore County

Goodwin Forest Trail   **620**

Length: 4.1 mi (6.6 km), easy; *USGS:* Carthage; *Trailhead:* Forest boundary line.

Directions and Description: Although there are no developed trails in the North Carolina State University Goodwin Forest, there are 4.1 mi of single-lane access roads open to hikers. From Carthage, go W 1.3 mi on NC 22-24-27 to jct with SR 1261 on L. After 1.5 mi enter Goodwin Forest. Follow first road on L or go straight ahead. Permission for the hike is required. Contact Dr. Larry Jervis, School of Forest Resources, North Carolina State University, Box 5488, Raleigh, NC 27650.

Durham County

Hill Forest Trail   **621**

Length: 10.5 mi (16.8 km), easy to moderate; *USGS:* Rougemont, Lake Michie; *Trailhead:* Forest entrance.

Directions and Description: This network of single-lane access roads has the same restrictions as those above for the Goodwin Forest. From I-85 and US 501 in Durham, go 12.5 mi N on US 501 to Quail Roost and turn R on SR 1601, immediately turning R on SR 1614 after crossing N&W railroad. Go 1 mi to forest entrance. SR 1614 also goes through the forest to jct at 2.2 mi with SR 1613 and SR 1603 for route E to Hampton. Flat River, which has some exceptionally steep banks for the eastern Piedmont, flows S through the forest. The George K. Slocum Forestry Camp is on L of entrance and near bridge. Contact same office as above for permission to hike the trails. (North Carolina State's *Schenck Forest Interpretive Trail* is listed with *Loblolly Trail* under Umstead State Park.)

North Carolina Botanical Gardens Trail

This trail is listed under Chapel Hill city trails as part of the University of North Carolina at Chapel Hill.

Buncombe County

University Botanical Gardens Trail   **622**

Length: 0.6 mi (1 km), easy; *USGS:* Asheville; *Trailhead:* Garden entrance on W.T. Weaver Blvd.

Directions and Description: From jct of I-240 and US 19-23-70, in Asheville turn N on the latter toward Weaverville and Marshall. Go 2 mi, and turn R off the expressway to Broadway and NC 251 jct. After 0.5 mi turn L on W.T. Weaver Blvd and go 0.1 mi. Park at entrance; follow gravel and grassy trails across meadow and through the forest to a restored log cabin in honor of Hubert H. Hayes, author and playwright. Return by Reed Creek from Heath Cove through area of sycamore, white pine, and oak to curved bridge and parking area.

The 10-acre garden was set aside by the Board of Trustees of the University of North Carolina, Asheville, in 1960, but the garden has been developed and maintained by a private Board of Directors. More than 400 native species are in the garden. Open daily; free; no picnicking or camping is allowed. For information contact the University Botanical Gardens at Asheville, Inc., 24 Hampden Rd, Asheville, NC 28805.

CHAPTER XVI
TRAILS UNDER CONSTRUCTION

Clay County

Chatuge Trail   **626**

The Tennessee Valley Authority plans a trail for the Chatuge Reservoir in Clay County. *Information:* Contact Recreation Planner of Streams, Trails, and Natural Heritage Projects, Division of Land and Forest Resources, TVA, Norris, TN 37828.

Iredell County

East Statesville Park Trail   **627**

The Department of Parks and Recreation of Statesville plans short trails at Bristol Rd Community Center, Albert B. McClune Park, East Statesville Park, and Harris Park. *Information:* Contact Recreation Dept, 432 W Bell St, Statesville, NC 28677. Tel: 704-872-2481.

Forsyth County

Horizon Park Trail   **629**

A 2.5 mi hiking trail is planned for the new Horizon Park, now under construction. Entrance is from the jct of NC 8 and SR 1920 R on SR 1920, Memorial Industrial Rd; this spot is 2 mi N from jct of NC 8 and NC 66. SR 1920 reaches jct E with SR 1917, Red Bank Rd. *Information:* Contact Forsyth County Parks and Recreation Dept, Hall of Justice, Room 603, Winston-Salem, NC 27101. Tel: 919-727-2946.

Guilford County

Oak Hollow Trails   631

The city of High Point plans a hiking trail between the Oak Hollow Lake, where an equestrian trail exists, and the Environmental Center at the High Point City Lake to the E. Also planned is a segment of trail from Oak Hollow Lake to Squires Davis Rd, offering the start of a connector to the Hanging Rock-Pilot Mtn-Dan River trails complex. *Information:* Contact Parks and Recreation Dept, 221 Nathan Hunt Dr, High Point, NC 28601. Tel: 919-887-2511.

Yadkin County

Richmond Hill Nature Trail   632

A joint project of the Yadkin County Historical Society, the Yadkin County Board of County Commissioners, and the Richmond Hill Law School Commission has been to develop the Historic Richmond Hill Nature Park, with trails and picnic facilities on a 15-acre tract around the home of former Chief Justice Richmond M. Pearson. *Information:* Contact Historic Richmond Hill Nature Park, Boonville, NC 27011. Tel: 919-699-3921 or 919-463-2771.

Transylvania County, NC, and Oconee and Pickens Counties, SC

Foothills Trail   628

Duke Power Company is constructing a 43.3-mi (69.3-km) hiking trail for backpacking only from Table Rock State Park in South

Carolina to the Upper Falls near the Jackson and Transylvania County line in North Carolina. Completion is expected by 1983, and campsites will be designated later. Eight access points are planned. *Information:* Contact Supervisor, Project Recreation, Duke Power Company, P.O. Box 33189, Charlotte, NC 28242. Tel: 704-373-4011.

Durham County

ISA Nature Trail   630

A nature trail of 1 mi or more is under construction at the Instrument Society of America in the Research Triangle near Durham. It is being planned by professional landscape architects. *Information:* Tel: 919-594-8411.

Lee County

Tillman Loop Trail and Pocket Creek-Treefoil Trail   633-634

Led by Frank and Thelma Barringer, a husband and wife team in Lee County, and assisted by Boy Scout Troops #942 and #944, Girl Scouts, and hiking supporters, planning is underway for a continuous trail on the S side of Deep River. At the time of this writing the groups were building the *Pocket Creek-Treefoil Trail,* approximately 4.5 mi long and running from NC 42 W with SR 1384 NW near US 421 from Sanford. The *Tillman Loop Trail* will connect with the *Pocket Creek-Treefoil Trail* near the SR 1007 and NC 42 jct, and with SR 1318 near the "House in the Horseshoe," a state historic site. Plans eventually call for a hiking trail approximately 45 mi in length and running on private property between the "House in the Horseshoe" and Raven Rock State Park. *Information:* Contact Mr. and Mrs. Frank Barringer, P.O. Box 375, Sanford, NC 27330. Tel: 919-776-2417.

Johnson County

Wilson Park Trail   **635**

A 2-mi nature trail is planned to originate at the M. Brack Wilson Park, 0.8 mi W from US 301 in downtown Selma. *Information:* Contact Parks and Recreation Dept, P.O. Box 357, Selma, NC 27576. Tel: 919-965-3388.

Forsyth County

Walden Nature Trail   **636**

The *Walden Nature Trail* in Tanglewood Park near Winston-Salem will be completed by 1982 as a memorial to six wildlife enforcement officers who have died in the line of duty since the North Carolina Wildlife Resources Commission was formed in 1947. A number of local agencies are constructing the trail, which has interpretative displays; financial aid has been provided by the Reader's Digest Foundation. *Information:* Contact Tanglewood Park, P.O. Box 1018, Clemmons, NC 27012. Tel: 919-766-6421.

APPENDIX

Organizations and Clubs

Agencies and Other Sources of
    Information

Trail Supplies

ORGANIZATIONS AND CLUBS

North Carolina Trails Committee

The North Carolina Trails Committee was established to represent the trail interests of the citizens of North Carolina. The Committee, created in 1973 by the North Carolina Trails System Act, consists of seven members who represent different trail user groups and the three geographic regions of the state.

The Committee advises the Secretary of the Department of Natural Resources and Community Development on matters directly or indirectly pertaining to trails, their use, extent, location, and other related concerns. The Committee coordinates trail development among local governments and assists local governments in the formation of their trail plans. The Committee also advises the Department about the study of trail needs and potential.

The North Carolina Trails Committee has been involved in discussions concerning a state trails system concept since its beginning. In November 1978, the Mountains-to-the-Sea Trail was proposed as the nucleus from the Great Smoky Mountains National Park to Jockey's Ridge State Park, north of the Cape Hatteras National Seashore. A series of regional trail complexes will connect other points of interest with this statewide trail.

Citizen involvement through citizen trail task forces and other trail groups, such as the North Carolina Trails Association, will be the most significant element in creating these new trails in North Carolina.

The Committee wishes to be contacted by any citizen wishing to provide input on trail-related issues. The Committee may be contacted through the Trails Coordinator, Division of Parks and Recreation, P.O. Box 27687, Raleigh, NC 27611. Tel: 919-733-7795.

— Henry McLeod, Chairman

North Carolina Trails Association

The North Carolina Trails Association is a nonprofit association of hikers, equestrians, bicyclists, canoeists, and off-road vehicle users organized for the purposes of advocating the establishment and conservation of a system of scenic, recreation, and historic trails and related facilities in North Carolina; encouraging all persons to participate in trail activities for the mental, physical, and spiritual well-being which can be derived; and, working with federal, state, and local agencies and trail-related organizations, landowners, and individuals in planning, acquisition, development, maintenance, and proper use of trails and trail-related facilities.

The Association is the outgrowth of numerous discussions on the need for a statewide organization to coordinate the efforts of the large number of trails-oriented groups within the state. It was voted into existence at Morrow Mountain State Park on August 6, 1977, and functioned through an interim board of directors until October 13, 1979, when bylaws were adopted and a Board of Directors was elected. Membership is open to all trail users and dues are paid annually. The Association publishes a newsletter bimonthly.

Each of the five user groups has its own organization and is represented on the Board. These user groups provide a focal point for coordination of activities across the state of groups with use-specific interests.

The work of the Association embraces development of policy and guidelines on trail construction, coordination of trails construction with state and local government agencies, education of trail builders and trail users, preparation of trail guides and handbooks of useful materials, attention to land availability, encouragement of the growth of a system of hostels, and trail networks.

310

Headquarters address is P.O. Box 1033, Greensboro, NC 27402. Or, telephone Raleigh, NC: 919-828-5242.

— Larkin Kirkman, President

The following four clubs assist in maintaining the 293 miles of the Appalachian National Scenic Trail in North Carolina.

Carolina Mountain Club

On June 17, 1920, organized mountaineering began in North Carolina when a tentative southern chapter of the Appalachian Mountain Club of Boston was formed in Asheville. Dr. Chase Ambler, originator of the Weeks National Forest Land Purchase Act, was the first president. Three years later, the club withdrew from the AMC and incorporated under the name of the Carolina Mountain Club, with Dr. Gaillard Tennent its first president.

In 1930, the Carolina Appalachian Trail Club was formed, with George Stephens as its first president, but one year later the vigorous hiking club was merged into the CMC, Inc. Stephens, like Tennent, hiked actively in CMC for many years. He published extensive maps and guides, including *100 Favorite Trails,* the first comprehensive hiking guide for the Smokies and the Blue Ridge Mountains in North Carolina.

During the Appalachian Trail Conference's early years of routing, marking, logging, and maintaining in the mountains of Tennessee and North Carolina, CMC's Marcus Book was Conference Board member, succeeded in 1938 by Arch Nichols (1979 Honorary Member of ATC). In 1940 the CMC engaged the Rev. A. Rufus Morgan to work on the Nantahala A.T. section; he later started the Tennessee Eastman Hiking Club north of Spivey's Gap, and helped to establish the Piedmont Appalachian Trail Hikers, a Greensboro-based club.

Other accomplishments have been the securing of the Craggy Scenic Area; the naming of Tennent Mountain; marking Mt Craig and Big Top; naming George Masa Mountain; securing the Shining Rock Wilderness Area; establishing the Art Loeb Trail from Shining Rock to the Davidson River; and starting the Mt Pisgah-Mt Mitchell Trail System (which has been designated as part of the Mountains-to-the-Sea Trail System).

In 1968 and in 1978 CMC worked hard for the passage of the National Scenic Trail Act by the U.S. Congress, and assisted the USFS in acquiring aerial photos of the A.T. for the *Federal Register*. CMC is currently involved in a comprehensive survey of the trail environment, assisting the USFS in desirable relocations, and maintaining the A.T. from Spivey Gap to Davenport Gap, a total of 68.1 mi.

Address is Carolina Mountain Club, P.O. Box 68, Asheville, NC 28802. Tel: 704-252-6078.

— Arch Nichols

Nantahala Hiking Club

The Nantahala Hiking Club was founded in 1950 by the Rev. A. Rufus Morgan to assist in maintaining the Appalachian Trail in the Nantahala mountains area. Dr. Morgan was the NHC's first president and held that position for 18 years, during which time the membership grew to over 200 and the Club's program expanded to include "pleasure hikes" in northern Georgia, western North Carolina, and east Tennessee. As a maintaining member of the Appalachian Trail Conference, the NHC still brushes and renews blazes on 59.4 miles of the A.T. from the Nantahala River at Wesser to Bly Gap at the Georgia-North Carolina state line.

Since 1978, under an agreement with the USFS, major trail construction and maintenance has been done by the Wayah Ranger District of the Nantahala National Forest, since the A.T. is within its boundaries. The Club, in turn, brushes and blazes blue-blazed side trails, and promotes the conservation policies of the USFS.

The Club holds its monthly meetings at the Nonah Craft House in Cartoogechaye, which is a few miles west of Franklin; a monthly bulletin is published and posted in the area, including the Chamber of Commerce.

Address is Nantahala Hiking Club, Route 1, Franklin, NC 28734. Tel: 704-524-7633.

— Barbara Lull

Smoky Mountains Hiking Club

By 1924, interest in the development of National Park status for the Great Smoky Mountains had progressed and certain members of the Knoxville YMCA decided a group for adult hikers would be a useful program and it would also "stimulate further interest in the National Park movement." In October of that year, a group of interested hikers from the Knoxville area gathered on top of Mt. LeConte and formed the Smoky Mountains Hiking Club. Shortly the affiliation with the YMCA was dropped but the purpose of gaining park status for the beloved mountains was never abandoned.

The group began with three major areas of interest. The first was the construction, marking and mapping of hiking trails. Secondly, the group set up a hiking program, with hikes held at least once a month. And thirdly, the club worked to publicize the beauty and uniqueness of the Great Smokies in order to convince public officials that the area should be protected by park status.

The early goals having been reached, the club has seen itself as a watchdog for the Park and the Appalachian Trail, which it helped to construct. Currently the club is active in the campaign to have the Park included under the Wilderness Act for further protection. The club also monitors the A.T. from the Wesser Station to Davenport Gap, a distance of 95.5 miles.

With over 400 members, mostly from the Knoxville/Oak Ridge area in Tennessee, the club sponsors day hikes and overnight back-packing trips. There is a membership fee and the club publishes a monthly newsletter.

— H. Richard Bolen

TERC Hiking Club

The Tennessee Eastman Recreation Club Hiking Club is organized under the auspices of the Tennessee Eastman Recreation Club of The Tennessee Eastman Company, a Division of Eastman Kodak Company. Non-Eastman employees are welcome to attend club activities with club members.

Founded in 1946, the club now has an Eastman membership of approximately 380. It sponsors a program of both hiking and canoeing, with about fifty trips each year. While many trips are along the Appalachian Trail and in other local areas, recent years have also seen trips to Colorado and Utah, and England and Switzerland.

As a member of the Appalachian Trail Conference, the club is responsible for the maintenance of 116.2 miles of the Appalachian Trail from the Virginia-Tennessee state line near Damascus to Spivey Gap, North Carolina, a section generally following the Tennessee-North Carolina border. Trail maintenance is accomplished by a system of teams within the club under cooperative agreements with the Cherokee National Forest, the National Forests in North Carolina, and the Tennessee Valley Authority. Current special projects include relocation of parts of the trail on to federally protected land and the construction of new log shelters.

Address is TERC Hiking Club, P.O. Box 511, Kingsport, TN 37662. Tel: 615-239-9701.

— J.J. Sirola

AGENCIES AND OTHER SOURCES
OF INFORMATION

United States Government Departments

Department of Agriculture
Forest Service
P.O. Box 2417
Washington, DC 20013 (Tel: 202-447-3957 for information)

Department of Agriculture
Office of Environmental Quality
14th St and Jefferson Dr SW
Washington, DC 20250 (Tel: 202-655-4000 for information)

Department of the Interior
National Park Service
Interior Bldg
Washington, DC 20240 (Tel: 202-343-1100)

Department of the Interior
United States Fish and Wildlife Service
Washington, DC 20240 (Tel: 202-343-4717)

United States National Wildlife Refuges

Dismal Swamp National Wildlife Refuge
US Fish and Wildlife Service

Box 349
Suffolk, VA 23434 (Tel: 804-539-7479)

Mackey Island National Wildlife Refuge
Pembroke Office, Pembroke II Bldg
Suite 218
Virginia Beach, VA 23462

Cedar Island, Mattamuskeet, and Swan Quarter
National Wildlife Refuges
Route 1, Box W-2
Swanquarter, NC 27885 (Tel: 919-926-4021)

Pea Island National Wildlife Refuge
P.O. Box 150
Rodanthe, NC 27968 (Tel: 919-987-2394)

Pee Dee National Wildlife Refuge
P.O. Box 780
Wadesboro, NC 28170 (Tel: 704-694-4424)

Pungo National Wildlife Refuge
P.O. Box 267
Plymouth, NC 27962 (Tel: 919-793-2143)

National Organizations and Clubs

American Camping Association, Inc.
Bradford Woods
Martinsville, IN 46151 (Tel: 317-342-8456)

American Hiking Society
1701 18th St NW
Washington, DC 20009 (Tel: 202-234-4610)

American Society for Environmental Education
58 Main St, Box R
Durham, NH 03824 (Tel: 603-868-5700)

Appalachian Trail Conference, Inc.
P.O. Box 236
Harpers Ferry, WV 25425 (Tel: 304-536-6331)

Association of Conservation Information
458 Lowell Blvd
Denver, CO 80204

Camp Fire Club of America
230 Camp Fire Rd
Chappaqua, NY 10514 (Tel: 914-941-0199)

Center for Environmental Education, Inc.
1925 K St, Suite 206
Washington, DC 20006 (Tel: 202-466-4996)

Clean Water Action Project
1341 G St NW, Suite 200
Washington, DC 20005 (Tel: 202-638-1196)

Conservation Foundation
1717 Massachusetts Ave NW
Washington, DC 20036 (Tel: 202-797-4300)

Defenders of Wildlife
1244 19th St NW
Washington, DC 20036 (Tel: 202-659-9510)

Friends of the Earth
124 Spear St
San Francisco, CA 94105 (Tel: 415-495-4770)

John Muir Institute for Environmental Studies
743 Wilson St
Napa, CA 94558 (707-252-8333)

National Audubon Society
950 Third Ave
New York, NY 10022 (Tel: 212-832-3200)

National Campers and Hikers Association
7172 Transit Rd
Buffalo, NY 14221 (Tel: 716-634-5433)

National Geographic Society
17th and M Sts NW
Washington, DC 20036 (Tel: 202-857-7000)

National Parks and Recreation Association
1601 N Kent St
Arlington, VA 22209 (Tel: 703-525-0606)

National Wildlife Federation
1412 16th St NW
Washington, DC 20036 (Tel: 202-797-6800)

Sierra Club
530 Bush St
San Francisco, CA 94108 (Tel: 415-981-8634)

Wilderness Society
1901 Pennsylvania Ave NW
Washington, DC 20006 (Tel: 202-293-2732)

North Carolina Government Agencies

Department of Natural Resources and Community Development
Division of Parks and Recreation
P.O. Box 27687
Raleigh, NC 27611 (Tel: 919-733-4984, Parks Info)
          (Tel: 919-733-7795, Trail Info)
Division of Forest Resources (Tel: 919-733-2162)

Wildlife Resources Commission
Archdale Bldg, 512 N Salisbury St
Raleigh, NC 27611 (Tel: 919-733-3391)

Marine Resources Center
Department of Administration
116 Jones St
Raleigh, NC 27611

North Carolina Clubs and Organizations

North Carolina Trails Association
115½ W Morgan St
Raleigh, NC 27601 (Tel: 919-828-5242)

North Carolina Wildlife Federation
P.O. Box 10626
Raleigh, NC 27605 (Tel: 919-782-5418)

Carolina Bird Club, Inc.
P.O. Box 1220
Tryon, NC 28782

North Carolina Recreation and Park Society
436 N Harrington St
Raleigh, NC 27603 (Tel: 919-832-5868)

Sierra Club (Joseph LeConte Chapter)
1322 Brooks Ave
Raleigh, NC 27607

Appalachian State University Hiking and Outing Club
ASU Box 8960
Appalachian State University
Boone, NC 28608

Appalachian Trail and Whitewater Club
College Box 845
Louisburg, NC 27549 (Tel: 919-496-2521)

Berg Wanderers
Box 4071
Charlotte, NC 28207

National Campers and Hikers Association
25 Hillside Drive
Lexington, NC 27292

New Hope Audubon Society
P.O. Box 2693

Chapel Hill, NC 27514

Outdoor Club
Western Piedmont Community College
Morganton, NC 28655

Outing Club
Student Development Office
Box 5072, NC State University
Raleigh, NC 27650

Piedmont Appalachian Trail Hikers
124 Lawrence St
Greensboro, NC 27406

Raleigh Ski and Outing Club
P.O. Box 10364
Raleigh, NC 27605
Attn: Hiking/Backpacking Coordinator

Uwharrie Trail Club
1015 Powhatan Ave
Asheboro, NC 27203

Venture Program
University of North Carolina at Charlotte
Charlotte, NC 28223

TRAIL SUPPLIES

Hiking and Backpacking Supplies

The following list of stores has a complete or partial range of supplies and equipment for hiking, backpacking, and camping.

Burney's of Albemarle, Inc
Hwy 52 N
Salisbury Rd, Rt #5
Albemarle, NC 28001

Surveyor's Supply Company
Hwy 64 at Old #1
P.O. Box 808
Apex, NC 27502

Bell's Traditionals, Ltd
9 Kitchen Pl
P.O. Box 5757
Asheville, NC 28803

Carolina Enterprises
20 Stoner Rd
Asheville, NC 28803

High Energy Sports
344 Merrimon Ave
Asheville, NC 28801

Mountaineering South
791 Merrimon Ave
Asheville, NC 28804

Army-Navy of Boone
206 Blowing Rock Rd
Boone, NC 28607

Footslogger
835 Faculty St
Boone, NC 28607

New River Outfitters
206 Blowing Rock Rd
Boone, NC 28607

The Outdoorsman
623 E King St
Boone, NC 28607

Highland Books
409 N Broad St
Brevard, NC 28712

Nanthala Outdoor Center
U.S. 19
Wesser, NC
P.O. Box 68
Bryson City, NC 28713

Burlington Sporting
  Goods, Inc
1625 S Church St
Burlington, NC 27215

Coleman's Men Shop
437 S Spring St
Burlington, NC 27215

Marine Corps Exchange 5-1
Marine Corps Base
Camp Lejeune, NC 28542

Sportsman's Pro Shop
Hwy 19-23 Candler
P.O. Box 475
Candler, NC 28715

Slope and Trail
688 Western Blvd Ext
Cary, NC 27511

The Trail Shop
405 N Franklin St
Chapel Hill, NC 27514

Alanby, Inc
3040-B Eastway Dr
Charlotte, NC 28205

Austin Cushion & Canvas Co
1014 N Graham St
Charlotte, NC 28206

Base Camp Mountain
Sports, Inc
1534 East Blvd
Charlotte, NC 28203

Jesse Brown's
4369 S Tryon St
Charlotte, NC 28210

The Tennis & Ski Shop, Inc
3814 Montoe Rd
Charlotte, NC 28205

Trail Shop II
5228 E Independence Blvd
Charlotte, NC 28212

Tennis & Hike Shop
3920 Park Rd
Charlotte, NC 28209

The Hiking Post
Rt 1, Box 86D
Cherokee, NC 28719

Henderson's
Rt 2, Box 994-B
Connelly Springs, NC 28612

N.O.C. Cullowhee Outfittter
Hwy 107
P.O. Box V
Cullowhee, NC 28723

Kerr's Sport Shop
Northgate Shopping Center
Durham, NC 28201

Leisure Time Outfitters
3000 Sparger Rd
Durham, NC 27705

River Runners' Emporium
1209 W Main St
Durham, NC 27708

Carolina Outdoors Sports
140   Westwood   Shopping
  Center
Fayetteville, NC 28304

Military Surplus, Inc
Rt 15, Box 136
Fayetteville, NC 28306

Spider Web, Ltd
140 Westwood Shopping
Center
Fayetteville, NC 28304

Macon County Supply Co
19 Main St
P.O. Box 349
Franklin, NC 28734

Wagon Peddler
19 Main St
Franklin, NC 28734

The Pack Shack
2507 S New Hope Rd
Gastonia, NC 28052

New River Outfitters
Rt 1, Box 123
Green Mountain, NC 28740

Blue Ridge Mountain Sports
2805 Battleground Ave
Greensboro, NC 27403

Carolina Outdoor Sports
844 W Lee St
Greensboro, NC 27403

Memco #563
39000 High Point Rd
Greensboro, NC 27407

H.L. Hodges Co
210 E 5th St
Greenville, NC 27834

Camp Pinnacle, Inc
Rt 3, Box 327
Hendersonville, NC 28739

Berndts Army Navy Store
117 Main Ave, Pl SW
Hickory, NC 28601

Happy Hiker
"The Log Cabin"
Chestnut St
Highlands, NC 28741

Beeson Hardware
214 N Main St
High Point, NC 27261

Quality Hardware
P.O. Box 5931
2639 N Main St
High Point, NC 27262

Bill White's Sporting Goods
211-C Western Blvd
Jacksonville, NC 28540

New River Outfitters
P.O. Box 433
Jefferson, NC 28640

Neuse Sport Shop, Inc
225 New Bern Rd
Kingston, NC 28501

Smokey Mt Camping Supplies
Rt 1, Box 175
Maggie Valley, NC 28751

Russell's Sporting Goods
115 W Union St
Morganton, NC 28655

Diamond   Brand   Canvas
  Products
Hwy 25
Naples, NC 28760

Paddling Unlimited
6208 Yadkinville Rd
Pfafftown, NC 27040

Pittsboro General Store
105 Hillsboro St
P.O. Box 917
Pittsboro, NC 27312

Bob's Army Surplus
1200 S Saunders St
Raleigh, NC 27603

Carolina Outdoor Sports, Inc
Lake Boone Shopping Center
Raleigh, NC 27607

Hackneys, Inc
225 N Hills Mall
P.O. Box 17823
Raleigh, NC 27619

Sportsman's Cove
Crabtree Valley Mall
Raleigh, NC 27612

The Trail Shop
Crabtree Valley Mall
Raleigh, NC 27612

Trail Shop
3114 Hillsborough St
Raleigh, NC 27607

Wild Bills Army Navy
1210 Ridge Rd
Raleigh, NC 27607

Smith Hardware Co, Inc
S Main St
Robersonville, NC 27871

J. N. Rich, Inc
Hwy 74 E Bypass
Shelby, NC 28150

Appalachian Expeditions
Rt 1, Box 383
Swannanoa, NC 28718

Energy Alternative
32 Main St
Sylva, NC 28779

New River Outfitters
Rt 1, Box 273B
Timberlake, NC 27583

New River Outfitters
US 221 S
West Jefferson, NC 28694

East Coast Outdoor Sports
4403 Wrightsville Ave
Wilmington, NC 28403

J. W. Murchison Co, Inc
P.O. Drawer 480
75 Lullwater Dr
Wilmington, NC 28401

Appalachian Outfitters
4240 Kernersville Rd
Winston-Salem, NC 27104

Bocock-Sound Co
501 W Fourth St
Winston-Salem, NC 27102

Hills & Trails
527 S Stratford Rd
Winston-Salem, NC 27103

Page's Sports and Trophy Co.
4110 North Cherry St
Winston-Salem, NC 27106

Memco #562
7840 Silas Creek Pkw
Winston-Salem, NC 27106

Tatum Outfitters
1215 Link Rd
Winston-Salem, NC 27103

Outdoorsman
3443 Robinhood Rd
Winston-Salem, NC 27106

The Bike and Hike Shop
460-A Knollwood St
Winston-Salem, NC 27103

In addition to the above, a number of department store chains — i.e., Sears, Penny's, K-Mart, Montgomery Ward, King's and others — have supplies.

TRAIL INDEX

ABOUT THE AMC

The Appalachian Mountain Club is a non-profit volunteer organization of over 25,000 members. Centered in the northeastern United States with headquarters in Boston, its membership is worldwide. The AMC was founded in 1876, making it the oldest and largest organization of its kind in America. Its existence has been committed to conserving, developing, and managing dispersed outdoor recreational opportunities for the public in the Northeast and its efforts in the past have endowed it with a significant public trust and its volunteers and staff today maintain that tradition.

Ten regional chapters from Maine to Pennsylvania, some sixty committees, and hundreds of volunteers supported by a dedicated professional staff join in administering the Club's wide-ranging programs. Besides volunteer organized and led expeditions, these include research, backcountry management, trail and shelter construction and maintenance, conservation, and outdoor education. The Club operates a unique system of eight alpine huts in the White Mountains, a base camp and public information center at Pinkham Notch, New Hampshire, a new public service facility in the Catskill Mountains of New York, five full service camps, four self-service camps, and nine campgrounds, all open to the public. Its Boston headquarters houses not only a public information center but also the largest mountaineering library and research facility in the U.S. The Club also conducts leadership workshops, mountain search and rescue, and a youth opportunity program for disadvantaged urban young people. The AMC publishes guidebooks, maps, and America's oldest mountaineering journal *Appalachia*.

We invite you to join and share in the benefits of membership. Membership brings a subscription to the monthly bulletin *Appalachia;* discounts on publications and at the huts and camps managed by the Club; notices of trips and programs; and, association with chapters and their meetings and activities. Most important, membership offers the opportunity to support and share in the major public service efforts of the Club.

Membership is open to the general public upon completion of an application form and payment of an initiation fee and annual dues. Information on membership as well as the names and addresses of the secretaries of local chapters may be obtained by writing to: The Appalachian Mountain Club, 5 Joy Street, Boston Massachusetts 02108, or calling during business hours 617-523-0636.

NOTES

NOTES